2000 Days in China

China 1998–2009
A Western Experience

by John Hemmingsen
with Cherie Hemmingsen

"2000 Days in China," by John Hemmingsen. ISBN 978-1-60264-538-7.

Published 2010 by Virtualbookworm.com Publishing Inc., P.O. Box 9949, College Station, TX 77842, US. ©2010, John Hemmingsen. All rights reserved. No part of this publication may be reproduced, stored in a retrieval system, or transmitted in any form or by any means, electronic, mechanical, recording or otherwise, without the prior written permission of John Hemmingsen.

Manufactured in the United States of America.

"The world is a book and those who do not travel read only a page."
St. Augustine

Bureaucrat – An official who works by fixed routine without exercising intelligent judgment.
(Webster's Encyclopedia Dictionary – 1989)

Map of the People's Republic of China

Table of Contents

~ !! ~

Cast of Characters

I know how frustrating it can be when there are many characters in a book, especially ones with foreign-sounding names! I've interacted with so many people in my years in China – far too many folks to do justice to in this account. The main characters that you will meet in reading this story are listed below for your reference; I've also mentioned their status as of late 2008.

A few notes about Chinese names and the way they are used in this book: in China the family name is always used first, followed by a person's given name (what we call a "first name" in the West). However, I tend to use a person's English name when I cannot pronounce the Chinese name (which is often). And in our day-to-day business at Esco we often refer to a worker simply as "equipment Li," "molding Li," "maintenance Chen," etc.

Wang, Guochen/**Simon**: the little boy I first encountered when he was seven years old. He is now a tall, bright 17-year-old.

Han, Ting Ting/**Jane**: a girl I first met when she was nine; she is now in her final year of high school.

Li, Xin/**Gaylene**: a friend of Jane's; they were always together and at the same level at school.

Wang, **Zi Wei**: a fabulous singer who Cherie met while teaching at a Chinese middle school. She is now at university studying Chinese folk music.

Wei, Yu: a plant manager and woman extraordinaire; petite, Iron Lady, beautiful, and brilliant! Her husband is Mark.

Liu, Min: a man who was most helpful, particularly in the initial stages of the business. Liu Min went to a university in China and studied in English. His wife is Annie and his son is Chin Chin.

He has another son (by his first wife) who lives with Liu Min's parents in another province.

Liu, Yu Feng/**Francis**: a brilliant and competent technical director; SCW's first "local" hire; he is bright and understands the nuances of English, even jokes. His wife is Min Min, a computer science teacher. They have a darling baby daughter.

Liu, Li: a beautiful, wonderful piano player. John went to her wedding. She had a baby in 2007.

Phoa (Angpueh,): our first contact and tour guide. He is from Singapore, and now works for Esco as Asian Sales Manager.

Bai, Ling Mei/Stella: an English teacher at a Chinese college when she was hired by SCW. She now has a good job selecting factories in China for exporting goods to big-box stores like Sam's Club and Costco.

Esco employees: all of the below are intermittent players; they are also friends and associates who very much helped the business and helped relieve the long days of living in China as an expat:

- Bill Blakely
- Joe Burdett
- Randy Green
- Larry Huget
- Mark Mallory
- Fred McBane
- Chris Oldfather
- Steve Pratt
- Dean Richards
- Dave Singfield

- Jim Songer
- Ray Sykes
- Percy Chang
- Ray Verlinich
- Archie Vos
- Dan Burdett

And so many others … Sorry if we forgot to list you!

Glossary:

ESCO   ESCO Corporation a global Steel technology company

SOE   a state owned enterprise

JV   a joint venture

PRC   Peoples Republic of China

SCW   Shanxi Chengfeng Wearparts Ltd. a JV company between ESCO and Taiyuan Heavy Machinery Co. Ltd.

TZ   Taiyuan Heavy Metals Co. Ltd.

GM   General Manager

DGM   Deputy General Manager

MBA   a university degree, Master of Business Administration

Temperature   **to convert from Celsius to Fahrenheit**

$^\circ C = 1.8 \times {^\circ}F + 32$

Example $30^\circ C + (1.8)\ 30 + 32 = 86^\circ F$

Measurement   **English versus Metric** Measurement

1 Km = ~0.6 Mile

10 mm = ~2.54 inches

1m = 39.937 inches

30 centimeters = ~12"

1 kilo gram = ~ 2.2 pounds

1 metric ton = ~1.1 tons

Electric Arc Furnace
Efficient method for melting steel scrap to make high quality steel products. It is a batch process in SCW's case each batch is about 13 metric tons.

A.O.D.
Argon Oxygen Decarbonization – secondary steel making process to produce steel with superior physical properties.

Ferro Alloys
Addition agents to molten steel bath to attain chemical specifications for different alloy steels. There are some 400+ ferro alloy compositions available around the world.

Pattern
Model of part or item to be produced made of wood or composite material.

Molding
Process where sand with binders is placed around a pattern and, after the sand sets up, the pattern is removed. This leaves a cavity of the desired shape to be filled with molten steel. At SCW, the size of product could range from 100 kg to 30,000 kg.

Heat Treatment
High temperature process wherein the steel attains the desired physical properties.

Figure 1 Making steel in Electric Arc Furnace

List of Photographs

Since I have spent the past 12 years working in and traveling around China – and shared the stories of my exploits here with friends and relatives – many of them suggested I write a book chronicling my experiences and impressions of this fascinating country and its people. I resisted at first – after all, I am a businessman, not a writer! But after a great deal of pressure from the aforementioned, I finally endeavored to write about my China experience, as I believe that others may appreciate the glimpse into this Asian nation that my time there has afforded me. I wanted to capture some of the significant events and experiences I have been privileged to witness during some 2,000 days in China – a time of remarkable change in this country, as well as for me and for the joint venture (JV) I helped establish here for Esco Corporation.

So on a cold, dry winter day in Taiyuan, the capital city of Shanxi Province, I sat in the lobby of my Chinese four-star hotel and began recording my story. I dedicate this endeavor to my loving wife Cherie, who – although she has accompanied me on several trips to China over the years, totaling perhaps 200 days – has borne the brunt of being left alone "back home" in the United States (and later Canada) for long periods of time.

Why am I in China? Esco Corporation, a Portland, Oregon-based world leader in steel foundry technology, was approached early in 1994 by a large state-owned enterprise (SOE) in China seeking to form a joint venture (JV) with a world-class foreign company. China was emerging from a deep isolation – there had been very little foreign investment for decades – but was looking to modernize rapidly. As Vice President of Manufacturing for Esco Corporation at that time, I was selected to visit the SOE later that year to determine the feasibility of such a venture. Thus began my long, instructive connection to this country. Despite the many obstacles (both bureaucratic and cultural) in the ensuing years, with persistence we have been able to build not only a viable business in China, but a successful one.

Most of the story is narrated from my perspective, with occasional interludes from Cherie. Her experiences here have been unique from mine, so I asked her to add her insights about Chinese family life and education to this account. Many people from Esco Corporation, as well as the many Chinese and expats I have met over the years, are included in the story. The people and events are true as I remember them. Various Esco Corporation personnel have had a significant and supportive effect on my dealings within China. I only hope I have represented them fairly.

I have told this story in three parts, followed by an epilogue. In "Part I: Building the Business," I relate how I personally became involved in China and what challenges I faced while attempting to build a business from scratch. In "Part II: Establishing Personal Relationships," I offer profiles of some remarkable people I've befriended during my tenure in China. Finally, "Part III: Exploring China – History, Future, and Impressions," explores in detail the Chinese people and culture, the significant changes I have witnessed in a rapidly developing China, and some of the problems that plague this nation on its march towards becoming a dominant industrial power.

My experience here has been an educational and rewarding one, both personally and professionally. In China, I have had to develop patience and an understanding of a totally different culture. I have also learned to be an educator and trainer. Merging Chinese culture and tradition with Western modernization and technology has been somewhat of a challenge, which I detail herein. Although I may be regarded as something of an "old hand" due to my long tenure in and around China, I do not profess to be an expert regarding the Chinese mystique! I am still peeling back one small layer of the onion each time I visit.

Note: I have exercised some caution in what I've chosen to include in this account. During our numerous stays in China, both Cherie and I have been told about personal experiences of human rights abuse and exposure to corruption here. In one case a friend of Cherie's wrote a letter consisting of several pages of onion skin paper detailing the maltreatment of her father, ultimately resulting in his death. Therefore, I have been careful not to include details or names of individuals who have divulged such information to us.

PART I: BUILDING THE BUSINESS

Chapter I: First Visit to China, 1994 (Initial Impressions)

As our rickety Dragon Air L1011 plane made its landing approach into Beijing in October 1994, there was a loud explosion. One of the starboard engines outside our window had blown up! Both my wife Cherie and I had not only heard the explosion but also saw the flames coming out of the engine so when the pilot announced that the plane had blown a tire on touchdown we both looked at one another and mouthed "Bull". Thankfully we landed safely despite this seeming disaster. Our plane was directed to the extreme end of the runway and instructed to wait for emergency vehicles to come to our assistance. Also, thankfully, Cherie, and I were fortunate to be sitting in first class, where there was less unsecured luggage to be tossed about in the chaotic landing – contrary to what happened in the economy section where loose luggage was scattered everywhere. Apparently no body on the flight suffered injury. Our surprise was that the safety rules in China were a far cry from what we were accustomed to.

From what we could see out the airplane windows as we waited, the Beijing airport was similar in size, structure and facilities to a '50s-era airport in the U.S. The emergency vehicles arrived about a half hour later. Imagine our surprise that they were horse-drawn. (The police arrived on bicycles.) The pilot who happened to be British kept the passengers continually informed regarding progress and difficulties explaining to the Chinese officials what had happened and advising all to remain calm as the situation was now not dangerous as the emergency was over. After about two hours of delays sitting in the darkened plane the pilot was ordered to taxi to the terminal, where we were allowed to deplane. After exiting through Chinese Customs and Immigration, which was much quicker than I would have thought, my wife and I proceeded by taxi to our hotel, located in the northeast corner of Beijing. What an entry into China!

Our hotel was the Holiday Inn LiDo, which was the first Western-style hotel in Beijing, established in the early '80s. Here we met up with two of my colleagues, Mark Mallory, who like me, was also based in Portland, Oregon, and Phoa from our Singapore operations, who was to be our translator. I was in China to investigate the prospects of a joint venture between a large state-owned enterprise (SOE) in Shanxi Province and my employer, Esco Corporation, which specializes in the design, manufacture, and global distribution of metal products for the mining, construction, and mineral processing industries. Earlier that year, the SOE, Taiyuan Heavy Machinery Company Ltd. (TZ), with some 20,000 employees, had expressed its desire to form a joint venture with Esco Corporation. As Esco's Vice President of Manufacturing globally, I was nominated to visit the TZ facilities in the city of Taiyuan to determine if such a deal was in the interest of Esco Corporation. Thinking this might be a once in a lifetime experience, I had asked Cherie to accompany me.

China, in 1994, still had many travel restrictions, especially to areas and cities remote from Beijing and Shanghai. Since we already had our official invitation letters in hand, we were set to embark from Beijing to Taiyuan. Taiyuan, the capital of Shanxi Province, is an ancient city (more than 2,500 years old) located some 325 miles (510 KM) southwest of Beijing. The city is situated on a high plateau (some 1,200 meters, or about 4,000 feet) and surrounded by mountains. In 1994, there was neither a highway connecting the two cities, nor any airline flying between them. Accordingly, we purchased tickets for passage on the National Railway System. Fortunately, we were able to get "soft" class tickets, which were deemed luxury class travel.

The next morning after elbowing our way through throngs of people at the Beijing station, we were able to find the correct train and our compartment. The soft-class train compartment was about six feet square and was entered from the main passageway through a sliding door that confoundingly refused to stay closed. The compartment had four sets of bunk beds and was supposed to accommodate 8–12 people. We were quite fortunate in this case that there were only the four of us (Mark Mallory, Phoa, Cherie, and me) in occupancy. However, the carpet on the floor of our compartment was filthy with cigarette burns and disgusting, unidentified stains resembling slug trails. The linen on the bunks looked like it may have been changed three months prior – or maybe not. We all decided to keep our shoes on for the entire 13-hour trip!

The unisex toilet room was adjacent to our compartment. It was also approximately six feet square with a sliding door opening from the main passageway. This door, at least, seemed to work both ways – open and close. Immediately opposite the door against the back wall was a hole in the steel floor and two handles on the wall next to it. While it initially seemed convenient to be located near a toilet, as our trip progressed, the stench emanating from this area became overpowering. A cigar smoker, I was able to somewhat modify the reek through continuous puffing on my stogies – one of the few times Cherie was not on my case for smoking. Cherie's weapon of choice was perfume. What a combination.

I luckily did not find it necessary to use the facility during the trip. However, poor Cherie found herself making frequent trips to the toilet. It was a major endeavor for her to keep things dry – walking across urine puddles on the floor, hiking up her long skirt, pulling her pants down, squatting, doing her duty – all while holding her breath. On one of her several trips to the toilet, she noticed a small sign in Chinese between the two handles. She asked a Chinese passenger who spoke some English what the sign read. He replied, "We men don't know, we don't go in, only stand at the door and let go."

During the long trip, we were provided with thermoses of boiled water, so we had something safe to drink. Fortuitously, Cherie had brought numerous packages of instant coffee and tea bags. We also were able to use the hot water to cook some dried noodles we had purchased so we had something to eat on the way.

Unfortunately, the windows of the compartment were so dirty that it was impossible to see outside. After some effort we were able to open the double windows a small amount and view some of the passing countryside. We were surprised to see massive amounts of coal being moved by both rail cars and extremely overloaded hand-packed trucks for the coming winter season.

We each sat upright on the cleanest parts of our chamber for the duration of the journey. About three hours into the trip, my two colleagues and I decided to pass the time by playing some friendly small-change poker. Unaware of the Chinese laws against gambling, we blissfully went ahead with our game. At different times many Chinese, including police, soldiers, and civilians, would park themselves in our open doorway and watch with great interest. We were playing penny ante with the Chinese currency (small change for us), but big sums for the natives. Fortunately, no charges were laid and no arrests occurred! This was likely because we were foreigners and more of a curiosity to the natives and probably would have caused many problems had the police charged us. Phoa, our translator, was a native of Singapore and therefore also a foreigner.

We finally arrived at the Taiyuan rail station around 7 p.m., disembarking into the dark autumn evening. The outside temperature was pleasant – about 18°C (64°F). As we passed through the station, Phoa darted ahead, instructing us, "Follow me!" To which Cherie replied, "Yes sure, you and 1.3 billion other black-haired Chinese!" We did manage to keep him in sight and get a taxi to our nearby hotel on the main street of the city. We noticed the absence of traffic partly because there were few streetlights, partly due to the Chinese custom of driving without headlights, but mostly because there were just so few cars.

We had wanted to stay at the four-star Shanxi Grand, but it was closed for extensive renovations after only four years of operation. (In retrospect, this should not have been a big surprise, given the condition of the train.) We were obliged to stay at a hotel that was rated only two stars; the gap in quality from four to two stars in China can be quite large, as we learned. Our hotel was dirty with smelly toilets, albeit it was cheap at about 100 Yuan per night ($12.50 USD). As it was late, and we were exhausted from the uncomfortable train ride and the culture shock, we all retired to our small rooms without complaint. Unluckily for us, we were in Room 905 – the power went out at least three times during our short stay, and of course the elevator was out. At least we got our exercise when we had to come and go, and the stairway was double-wide and quite elegant. We were not too inconvenienced though – Cherie had thoughtfully brought flashlights in her luggage.

The restaurant in the hotel was massive, and the staff was comprised of very beautiful young women who wore elegant silk "Susie Wong" dresses with slits, which were comedic because they exposed not skin, but the hideous, thick tights favored by Chinese women at the time. This was our first exposure to a real Chinese restaurant. The number of staff was enormous, perhaps 10 times what we would experience in the west. Our first meal in China was good: we had *congee* (a rice porridge) and eggs. To cut an egg with chopsticks is somewhat of a poking trick. A well-cooked fried egg is required!

I would probably never have gone to China if it weren't for my career in the steel industry. In 1963, after graduating with a bachelor of applied science in metallurgical engineering from the University of British Columbia, I started out as a graduate trainee in a major integrated steel plant, progressed through various supervisory positions, and ultimately earned a senior executive position in manufacturing. I spent 13 years in the basic steel industry, and for the past 30+ years, have been working in the steel foundry industry.

This journey to China had actually been a decade in the offing – TZ had first approached Esco regarding a licensing agreement in the early 1980s. At the time, Esco Corporation had manufacturing facilities in Canada, the United States, and Europe, with licensees in South Africa, Chile, Brazil, Argentina, Spain, Australia, and Japan.

The early 1980s were a "coming out" period for China. Under the direction of Chairman Deng Xiaoping, the nation was recovering from the disastrous effects of the Cultural Revolution and was beginning a massive modernization program. To this end, legislation was passed allowing some opening up of the country's industries to Western and European technical and manufacturing expertise and advances. Yet formidable hurdles remained: at this time, the condition of the travel and communication systems in China was primitive to say the least, and there were tough travel restrictions for both citizens and foreigners. For example, for a Chinese citizen to travel from his city of residence to another part of China, he/she needed to obtain permission from the government to do so. To travel outside the country, many more levels of permission were required. For a foreign business person to visit China, an official invitation letter from the government or receiving industry needed to be obtained. When the businessperson arrived, he/she was monitored constantly by Communist party officials.

Due in part to some of these obstacles, it took two years after the initial communication with TZ to complete (supposedly) the licensee agreement. This was a typical licensee agreement wherein Esco Corporation would supply technical and manufacturing training and support to allow the manufacture and sale of its products by TZ in China. In return, Esco Corporation would receive royalties from the sales.

Shortly after signing the agreement in 1984, arrangements were made to send the first contingent of TZ personnel to the U.S. and Canada for orientation and training. This group of 12 people included senior management personnel, political counterparts, and government watchdogs. In 1984, I was VP of Manufacturing for Esco Ltd. in Canada, a wholly owned subsidiary of Esco Corporation in the United States, so I met the Chinese contingent when they were escorted to Canada to visit our facilities there. I noticed how the group was constantly under the scrutiny of Communist party officials while they traveled.

During this time, my wife Cherie, our teenaged son, Brock, and I were living in a fairly large house (~3,000 square feet) in Whitby, just east of Toronto. One evening we hosted a gala dinner for the group, along with senior managers and supervisors from our plant in Ontario. This made a dinner party of about 25 guests. The main floor of our house included a large living room, a dining room, a den lined with books, a kitchen with a large sun-garden eating area, a bathroom, and a family room. In addition, the main entrance opened up into a large foyer complete with a parlor grand piano with, that night, a hired professional playing a selection of classical and popular tunes. After eating, small groups of Chinese broke off to explore the house further. With the guests dispersed in various parts of the house, the Communist party controllers found it extremely difficult to monitor their charges. In the absence of the controllers, we found that at least two of our visitors spoke some English. This appeared to distress the controllers, but it was very amusing for us to observe their frustration while running from room to room to see if anything was amiss. We assumed the controllers could not understand any English.

This was an awesome experience for all the Chinese visitors – even though they were very senior people at TZ, their living quarters in China were typically only about 400 square feet per family. Another discrepancy of scale also awed them: the main highway running through Toronto consists of 12 lanes of heavy traffic – something these people had never witnessed back then, even when passing through Beijing on their way to the airport. What a memorable experience for my family and colleagues in Ontario, as well, to witness our visitors' reactions: it was fun to hear our foreign guests "oohing" and "aahing" about the fish and other food we served. At our house's front entrance there was an old brass Chinese sign that apparently meant "wishes for wealth" and they translated it to mean "BIG BUCKS." Shortly after this visit of senior managers and officials, another group of professionals and supervisors (again overseen by a communist party official) came to North America for orientation and training. After working with this group in Canada for one week, I felt that this would probably be my last experience with the Chinese since the License Agreement was run by the USA part of Esco.

But over the ensuing years (1984–1991), difficulties in communications and travel arrangements – both for Chinese leaving the country and foreigners coming into China – and fallout from the disastrous Tiananmen Square protests of 1989 caused the demise of the agreement. In 1991, Esco Corporation wrote off the agreement as a failure. I, too, figured the curious dinner party at my house would be the extent of my involvement with China.

But China was not through with us. In 1993, a few years after Esco had abandoned the initial licensee agreement with TZ, China recognized the need for more meaningful and rapid modernization and productivity improvements of its SOEs. Accordingly, the government (now under the direction of Chairman Jiang Zemin) expanded the decade-old legislation allowing SOEs to seek and form joint ventures with appropriate companies from the developed world, leading to TZ's renewed interest in Esco and my mission here now, in the autumn of 1994.

———————

In Taiyuan, the next morning after breakfast, Mark, Phoa, and I met in the hotel lobby and were picked up by the TZ company car and driven to the company's campus. Cherie hired a driver and guide of her own to help her tour the region for the day.

The drive from our hotel to the TZ facility took about 25 minutes, with the majority of the drive along Yingze St., the main street of Taiyuan. Yingze was three lanes wide each way with a median barrier separating the traffic (except for major intersections). In the daylight I could see that the city was quite dirty, with much garbage lying around on the street. The day was also thick with air pollution. We were informed that the city was surrounded by mountains, although due to the dense pollution, we could see no sign of them around us. I noticed that there were few private cars, bicycle riders everywhere, few businesses, and, indeed, very few streetlights. The side streets were narrow and cluttered with vendors selling everything; vegetables, fruits, meats, fish, cigarettes, and clothing on racks. I figured this must be the real China and coupled with the hotel accommodations the night before, I wondered if I would ever be able to entice other Esco employees to spend appreciable amounts of time here if a JV ever came to be.

When we entered the main gate of TZ, there were red banners welcoming the foreigners – us – to China and to the facility. TZ is a huge SOE – the campus covers about one square mile in area – and as I mentioned earlier, the company then employed over 20,000 people. But there was much more to it: as a SOE, the company was responsible for providing K–12 and technical college schooling, hospital services, hotel facilities, and housing for all employees and their families, as well as retirees. All these facilities were located within the campus. In short, SOEs were accountable for all workers and their families, including retirees, from cradle to grave. (Retirement age was mandated as 55 years for males and 50 years for females.) This is where the term "Iron Rice Bowl" (cradle to grave) applies.

After passing through the main gate, it was a short distance to the main office. Here we were escorted to a great hall carpeted in red, with sofas lining the walls and a very large conference table surrounded by 30 chairs. After we three Esco representatives were seated, the president of TZ, his main lieutenants, and Communist party officials came into the room. Following introductions and card exchanges, tea was served. Once the pleasantries were exchanged, a two-hour discussion was held to determine the intent of each party. Subsequently, I was allowed to inspect the proposed facility for the joint venture.

The site under consideration for the JV consisted of a plant and equipment covering some 73,000 square meters in area (~20 acres); less than 5 percent of the whole area of TZ's campus. Included in the equipment were three electric melting furnaces, an AOD furnace, numerous molding facilities, heat-treating furnaces, numerous overhead cranes, and other auxiliary equipment necessary for the production of steel castings. The foundry and equipment was all Russian-designed and built during the early 1960s. All the buildings were brick and all beams and columns inside were concrete. At the time, this part of the TZ campus employed between 600–800 workers, who were mostly just standing around. Production and productivity were very low. It appeared to me that not only the technology but also the manufacturing techniques here had not improved since the 1960s. However after further inspection, I believed that with Esco Corporation's experience and expertise, we would likely be able to get the steel-castings operation to world standards within three to four years. Based on this conclusion, we agreed to recommend pursuing the JV further to the Esco Corporation executive committee.

That evening, Mark Mallory, Cherie, Phoa, and I were the honorees at a mandatory state gala. Attending on the Chinese side were the top managers and party officials from TZ, as well as the mayor of Taiyuan and the vice governor of Shanxi Province. This banquet was a standard Chinese custom with massive amounts of food, numerous toasts with Chinese "white liquor" (clear distilled spirits) – called *Mao-tai* or *fenjou* – and much noisy talking. It should be noted that Chinese white liquor has alcohol contents up to 70 percent. This strong alcohol, much food, and noisy talking are supposed to develop and cement relationships. It certainly left an impression on us as first-time visitors! We thought the whole "custom" was carried to excess and was a complete waste of our time. Cherie's (and others') solution, was to put the very small *fenjou* glass upside down on the table, to signal an emphatic "NO THANK YOU!" However both Mark and I as senior Esco Corporation executives were expected to keep up with the many toasts. Keep up we did!

Following the banquet, we went back to our hotel for the night and next morning re-boarded our train for the long return trip to Beijing. Nothing extraordinary occurred on the return trip (our expectations were low), except that this time we *had* to sit upright, as our compartment now had the full complement of eight people.

Back at the LiDo, we had some time to organize our next junket, which was to visit an Esco customer in Inner Mongolia. The customer was a mine called An Tai Bao (ATB) – one of the largest coal mines in China. For years ATB had been controlled by Occidental Petroleum and was operated on Western principles using foreign manufactured equipment. As a result there were many expats from companies such as Caterpillar, Cummins, P&H, etc., in residence there. For the past two years, Phoa our Asian Sales Manager, had been servicing the mine, selling Esco Corporation products for use on the foreign-supplied equipment. During his visits he had established good relationships with both the operating and purchasing personnel and he thought it time to introduce an Esco Corporation executive to the mine: me.

As with Taiyuan, in 1994, there were no regular plane flights or modern highways to connect Beijing to the city in Inner Mongolia where the mine was located. However, ATB had a small private plane: a Dash 7 that seated 18 people and was used primarily for shuttling executives, other personnel, and small supplies to the mine from Beijing.

Mark, Phoa, and I were booked on the next day's flight to ATB. Cherie would stay in Beijing for the two days we would be away, and Phoa arranged for a driver to show her the sights. Early the next morning, we arrived at the Beijing Airport to catch our flight. We found that the place to board was not from the main terminal gates, but outside and through a chain link gate which led to the waiting aircraft. No security or any other check was in evidence. On boarding we got the last seats and I noticed that every available space was full and there was no room for any carryon baggage in the cabin. The plane was small, with limited in-plane stowage – all luggage and mine supplies had to be squeezed in the two small storage compartments, one in the nose and one aft of the plane. Phoa and Mark were carrying laptops and were forced to have these stashed in the nose cavity. Mark stated "I'm not overly happy to have my computer stored." Phoa echoed back "neither am I, but the pilot told me that's where they go and that's the end of it."

The two-and-a-half hour flight was routine, although today we had great views of the mountains and portions of the Great Wall, since it was sunny and clear. When we landed and the overfull nose cavity was unloaded, Mark's laptop fell onto the tarmac. I was amused at the stunned look on his face. It was incredible! Later we learned that this was the plane's first flight with a newly built engine. I was glad it worked OK! We were then driven to the expat compound, assigned rooms where we could drop off our luggage, and then taken to the mine site.

The three of us visited the key personnel that Phoa had contacts with and then had a short introductory meeting with a senior manager. Liu Min, the general foreman for shovels, was out on vacation so his lieutenant escorted us to the mine where equipment using our product was working. Liu Min was one of Esco's critical contacts at this mine so it was a disappointment for me not to meet him then. After the mine tour, we toured an immense warehouse which contained many millions of dollars worth of various steel and other supplies necessary to operate a large mine. Outside this warehouse, a footprint was being developed for an even larger warehouse. We were astonished to see that although there was a large Komatsu excavator nearby, all the labor was done by picks and shovels and an immense workforce of both men and women. Despite rapid modernization China still was a backward country.

Late in the afternoon, we returned to the expat compound and then visited a local restaurant for dinner (no state banquet this time), where we were very careful to select only well-cooked and hot items to eat since cold or raw items would be suspect because of the water they were washed in. In the morning after breakfast with several expats, we packed and went to the Dash 7 for the return to Beijing.

After returning to the LiDo from the visit to the mine, we met up with Dave Singfield, another Esco Corporation employee who was in China to supervise the installation of an Esco lip into a 15 cubic meter dipper bucket for another mine customer in the south of China. We were also reunited with Cherie, who gave us a detailed description of her two days in Beijing on her own.

Cherie's impressions of Beijing:

I signed up for a citywide tour going to the Great Wall and a cloisonné place – basically, all the usual tourist places. I had a seatmate, a gentleman from Sulawesi. He was in Beijing for an Asia-wide concrete symposium. "Mr. S." spoke limited English and wanted to practice.

I had long gray hair at the time and people seemed curious and fascinated. At the Great Wall all sorts of people wanted to have their picture taken with the "strange looking grey-haired foreigner"; at that time the women, coming out of the Mao era, all had short, straight hair. They mostly wore Mao-style outfits, (especially not stylish shorts with tights like I was wearing at the time). I was likely the first foreigner many of them had ever seen. Mr. S. bought me a certificate that said I had climbed the Great Wall.

Toilet users had to pay a stipend to use the huge, open cubicle, a very smelly and nausea-producing facility. I did not have any of the necessary small coins. Again my traveling companion was looking out for me; he had the necessary stipend and paid for me to use the facilities. Thank you kind sir!

I would expect that by now, if my tour seatmate had supplied much of the concrete to China during China's incredible boom, he is a very wealthy man. At the time, he desperately wanted to meet John and to sell him minerals and supplies for the steel foundry. Possibly that is why he was so nice to me. But, I prefer to think he was just a nice man who liked to talk and wanted to practice his English. Later, he even came to the hotel and brought me a beautiful silver brooch. John was too busy to talk to Mr. S, or more likely did not want to get involved.

In 1994, shopping was done primarily at the friendship store, a state-run shop that sold Chinese as well as Western goods exclusively to tourists, foreigners, diplomats, and government officials; indeed at one time Chinese citizens were not allowed to shop there. It was really the only place that foreigners could shop. Department stores as we know them did not exist. I went into a small Chinese store once to try to buy a cashmere sweater and that created a fuss. After a few minutes a person came from the back and said "no sell go away" – I did!

Beijing back then had few cars – most were taxis or government vehicles – and there were bicycles everywhere. The ring road system, concentric roads servicing the ever-sprawling city of Beijing, was still in its infancy. I saw much and enjoyed much and felt that John missed a good deal by having to work. Sometimes there are advantages to being a spoiled, somewhat indulged wife!

It didn't bother me much that John and I were often incommunicado for days at a time in this foreign country. I did not find it particularly daunting to return to my room by myself in China; I felt relatively safe. That was in opposition to Indonesia, where we had previously traveled, and where again I had been left alone (in Jakarta) for several days while John toured huge mines. Indonesia is considered a "soft" Muslim country – yet women were treated with suspicion when travelling unescorted, and I did not feel safe.

It is still fascinating to fly into Beijing at night and see the low glow of lights, spaced far apart (except for the restaurant areas, where they are brighter and tighter). To fly into Vancouver or Portland or any major Western city there are bright lights and many lights. I find China sepia-colored during the day and dimly light at night.

Next, we were off to visit a copper operation located in Dexing, Jiangxi Province, located in south China; Cherie was included in this trip. To get there we would have to fly from Beijing to Nanchang (about two hours away), then have a van with a driver and interpreter (controller) motor us over local roads another six hours to Dexing. We left Beijing around 11 a.m., arriving in Nanchang as scheduled, around 1 p.m. We were met by the driver and controller and were informed that it was too late in the day to drive to Dexing – they feared that in the darkness there might be bandits on the road. We were therefore advised that we would have to overnight in Nanchang and leave early the next morning for Dexing.

The hotel was located in the middle of the city, was Russian-built in the 1960s, and had seen better days. It was almost acceptable as far as cleanliness but was sparsely furnished. As it was early afternoon and the weather was pleasant at 25°C, we decided to walk and see the sites of the city. Nanchang did not experience visits by many foreigners so we were curios – especially Cherie with her long grey hair which was unusual in China. Some people on bicycles actually fell off while continuing to look back at her after passing us. After about an hour of this we decided it was better to go back to our hotel and not create any more accidents.

Next morning after an early breakfast we set out on the colorful six-hour drive to Dexing. The van we were driving in had seating for eight but no seat belts. There were seven of us in the van (Mark Mallory, Dave Singfield, Phoa, Cherie, me, the driver, and the controller). The driver was an older man perhaps in his early fifties who spoke no English, while the controller, a man in his late twenties, was very fluent. During the trip, he constantly extolled the virtues of Communist China and was extremely proud of the "one child" policy. Several times he told Cherie how awful it was for older people like the driver to have had more than one child. This communist official was obviously well indoctrinated in the party line. Everything is done by the government was for the betterment of the country and the people. Even though we saw very few private cars on the way, this individual informed the group China had more cars on the road than America.

The road between Nanchang and Dexing was essentially two semi-paved lanes that passed through farming country and many villages. Conveyances of various types utilized this road, and much of the way the road was crowded to six "lanes" spilling onto the shoulder – sometimes with traffic coming at us on the wrong side of the road. The traffic consisted of only a handful of private cars but many extremely overloaded trucks and tractors (single cylinder engines) pulling trailers with precarious loads of rocks or bricks. In addition there were many crammed-full buses, numerous bicycles, horse- and donkey-drawn carts, flocks of sheep, and even a flock of ducks being herded on the road. It was also the habit of the farmers to spread their rice on the road so that the rice hulls could be separated by the traffic running over them. I assume that the gravel bits in the rice could harm teeth? While driving through the various villages, people would stare intently at we foreigners passing through. We also noticed at each village the numerous hookers dressed in sleazy tight fitting short dresses and extreme high heel shoes attempting to get our attention.

After about three hours of knuckle-biting and nerve-racking driving, we stopped at a small restaurant in a village on the roadside for lunch. The restaurant doors were open. Inside were about five round tables and a sawdust-covered dirt floor. The Chinese habit of the day was to throw bones and scraps on the floors during mealtime and then sweep them up sometime later. We ordered hot cooked dishes and cold beer – but alas, there was no such thing as air-conditioning or cold beer. We settled for warm beer.

After lunch, we proceeded on our hazardous journey. At one point we crossed the Yangtze River on a beautiful carved marble bridge that was under repair. The surface was being restored along with the rebar. The rebar was being taken out and straightened for reuse using manual labor and hand tools. By now I was beginning to get an appreciation of the state of the art of construction in China in 1994. We finally arrived at Dexing by mid-afternoon. Dexing is a mining town of about 500,000 people and the copper mine is located on a mountain right in the city. We checked into the Dexing Company hotel, where Cherie and I were given the bridal suite, which had a large sign in English over the entrance reading "Love Nest." It was fairly large compared to some of our other hotel rooms in China, with a big bedroom, sitting room and bathroom with tub. However the bathroom floor was completely wet from the faulty pipes and toilet leaks. Some love nest!

After stowing our luggage, we went downstairs to meet our colleagues in the lobby, adjacent to the main dining room, to discuss our plans. We had just settled down on the sectional sofas when Dave noticed an enormous black rat scurry across the floor and disappear under one of the sections. Mark pulled the piece away from the wall and we discovered a large parabolic hole in the wall. The hole was dark and oily from years of rat entry and exit. Smart rat: located right next to dining room. The rat was well fed as it was easy for him to eat right off the dining room floor; the Chinese custom of using the floor for bones and scraps, which we'd observed at lunch, provided him with ample food.

We were treated to a gala state dinner, much like the one we'd enjoyed in Taiyuan. The dinner was hosted by the president of the mine. Other invitees included his management team, the controller and we five for a total of 14. Conspicuously absent was our driver, who was left to fend for himself. We were seated at a round table with a lazy Susan, customary at Chinese meals, with the host on my right and Cherie on my left. The rest of the foreigners were dispersed among the mine's management team. As is also the custom, numerous dishes were presented, both hot and cold. Many toasts were made and drinks downed. Most of us foreigners avoided drinking too heavily. We had judiciously nominated Mark as our head "toaster and replier," and he bore the brunt of the alcohol intake. As the senior person from Esco Corporation, I was served both my food and drinks by the mine president, who kept putting slices of river eel on my plate. River eel is considered a delicacy in this region but I found it mushy and tasted like mud. However, most of the other dishes were delicious. Whenever the president looked away or was in discussion with others I would quickly place the eel slices on my wife's plate who somehow found ways to dispose of it, perhaps to the resident rat? The host must have thought that I relished river eel because he continued to replenish my supply. After the two-hour gala, a red-faced Mark and the balance of our party bid good night and we retired to our rooms.

After breakfast the next morning, the Dexing company van picked up Mark, Dave, Phoa, and me, and after a short drive we arrived at the mine site. Cherie was assigned a driver who was to take her for the day to visit a famous pottery city some two hours away. At the mine, we met with the general foreman of mining (a woman which would have been extremely unusual in North America) to discuss the technical details of replacing the worn lip of a dipper bucket with a newly arrived Esco lip. The dipper is the working piece at the end of a large digging machine. This dipper bucket was about 10 cubic meters in size and the lip section of about 4 metric tons was worn out and would be cut out by oxy-acetylene torch and a new one welded in place. Dave and Phoa were set to remain at the mine site for three to four days during the lip installation. We were finished with the mine site just before noon and Mark and I were driven the short distance back to the hotel while Dave and Phoa remained at the site for the balance of the day.

Back at the hotel Mark and I had lunch. As it was another warm day, we decided to explore Dexing city. The open markets displayed many fruits and vegetables, some we had never seen before. We were pleasantly surprised with the appearance and high quality of the produce. But there were shocks: 1. Meat and fish hanging out in the open heat with flies buzzing around. 2. There were many dog carcasses hanging in the marketplace.

After Mark and I returned to the hotel, we found a "sports" room with a pool table. Although the table had a full set of balls, the felt was torn and the cues had no tips. We ended up playing modified pool; it worked well enough to pass the time.

Just before dinner, Dave and Phoa returned from the mine, and Cherie returned from her trip. She then told us about her day.

Cherie's day-trip to the pottery city:

The Dexing copper mine provided me with a driver who did not speak English and a translator who spoke minimal English – not an auspicious start. However, I was determined to see the pottery city of Jingdezhen, which has been producing quality porcelain pieces for over a thousand years, so we set off on our drive in a "Shanghai Mercedes." It looked much like a standard Mercedes from the outside, but the similarity ended there. The seats were covered with bamboo matting that was very slippery. With every corner I hung onto anything I could so that I would not slide from side to side. I prayed the door would not open and flip me onto the road. We went through seemingly endless small villages – each village had a massive sow and her little piglets trailing along on the main street. There were markets and factories, and peasants threshing grain with a pedal thresher. Grain was spread on about half the roadway to dry. I vowed thenceforth to wash my rice when the label said "wash before using"! We saw scrawny peasants attached to ploughs. I did not see one mechanized farm vehicle. It was very fascinating and different from anything I had ever experienced before. It was like being transported straight into a Pearl S. Buck book. One of my most vivid memories was seeing a young boy dragging on a cigarette, sucking in like an elderly man. He looked so drawn, so thin, so dirty, so old, so hungry. We made eye contact: me the rich American in the car, eating a Power Bar that I did not need; him hungry. His eyes haunted me.

When we finally got to the pottery city there were streets lined with stunning ceramics – vividly beautiful blue pottery, all sorts of dishes, dainty paper-thin rice bowls and vases, and huge quantities of pink piggy banks. I now know where piggy banks are made! I did buy some dishes for our son and his family and some of the amazingly thin pottery to give as gifts. China is famous for its fine porcelain. The pottery is almost see-through and is packaged in boxes, some of the boxes almost as nice as the pottery.

On the return trip back to Dexing city we stopped for a lunch at a restaurant with a dirt floor. I was very careful about what I ate but my fellow travelers enjoyed immensely the dishes they ordered. They were particularly proficient at spitting the bones and chunks of grit onto the floor. Little children came to the window and grinned with curiosity at "the foreigner" inside. I grinned back. They stuck their runny noses to the windows; all of them left their marks

As is usually my habit, after lunch I needed to find some facilities. The bathroom I found was a hole in the ground, completely surrounded by beautiful white grubs – maggots. I had to stand on the maggots, and they were very slippery, and oh what a stench! Making my task more challenging was the biggest pig I had ever encountered tethered in close proximity, who snorted and reeked the whole time. So much for privacy!

The most interesting part of the trip was the conversation with my translator – the one who spoke very little English. We persevered, though, all day! I learned that he was 27 and was engaged to be married but had only met the young woman once. He was planning to go to either India or Pakistan to work for several years, but was not sure whether he would marry her before or after he went away. Either way, she would not be going with him; if he married her she would live with his mother. He was very emphatic that he was going to be a good Chinese and not have a child. The translator came from a family of four children. The driver came from a family of seven siblings. As the translator translated back to me there was revulsion in his tone towards the driver for being one of seven and for having four siblings himself. I was stunned at the vehemence, the programming, that the way to be a good Chinese was to not have more than one child! I believe this individual was another indoctrinated idealistic communist functionary. Tired after the long day, I was glad to get back to Dexing, to John, and to our little hotel "love nest."

The next morning, ready for the ordeal of driving back to Nanchang, our young controller could not be found. After two hours of fruitless phone calls trying to track him down, we decided to return to Nanchang without him. Since Phoa (our Chinese interpreter) would remain with Dave at the copper mine, the group traveling was Mark, Cherie, and me (all non-Chinese speakers) with our faithful driver who spoke no English. This could be a dangerous situation since this action was not sanctioned by the Communist party. Mark joked "Phoa are you trying to get rid of us?" Phoa more seriously said "it may not be a wise decision to go without the official." I looked at Mark and Cherie and stated "let's get on with it" and the decision was made.

We had little choice. Our return flight from Nanchang back to Beijing was scheduled to leave at 3:40 p.m., and it was now 9:45 a.m. The schedule was extremely tight, given our experience of reaching Dexing two days prior. Phoa informed the driver of the critical time frame and off we went at racing speed, passing all other conveyances with abandon. About two hours into the trip, we passed through a village where a small girl wearing a fancy red dress was somehow pushed into the path of our speeding car. The driver swerved just in time to avoid hitting her. This was an extremely close near miss! We foreigners were shaken out of our reveries and the driver immediately broke out into a heavy sweat, sped the car up even more and rapidly fled the scene. Around 5 km down the road, he spotted (smelled) a roadside toilet, pulled the car over, and ran in to relieve himself. It seemed to do the trick – as he was a little more relaxed afterwards. Cherie, Mark, and I discussed the situation and wondered why the girl may have been pushed into our path. Perhaps answers would come later?

The balance of the drive was uneventful and, amazingly, we did make our flight. Later we inquired of knowledgeable people, what would have happened if the driver had hit and injured or killed the little girl. We were told that most likely the villagers would have taken him away and killed him, leaving us abandoned in the middle of nowhere and perhaps paying a large fine. What an end that would have been to our first experience in China! Instead, we all stayed one more uneventful night at the LiDo in Beijing, reflecting on the array of sights, sounds, and smells we'd encountered in our amazing two-week visit to this very foreign nation. I suspected that this was just the beginning of a relationship with China for me, since Esco would likely be moving forward with the joint venture – but little did I know that I would be spending many years living and working there.

Upon returning home to Portland, Mark Mallory and I put our collective thoughts into a presentation recommending that Esco proceed to the next stage with the joint venture, including beginning negotiations with TZ and the various government agencies in China. Esco decided to move forward, and a core group was formed to hammer out the conditions of the JV so that it could be presented to the Esco Corporation board of directors at the earliest possible date. Esco Corporation's goal included majority ownership, majority management control, and last but not least, control of the workforce.

The core group initially consisted of Mark Mallory as leader; Phoa, who had served as our translator in China; and Liu Min, the general foreman for shovels whom I had missed meeting in Inner Mongolia, but whom we had recently hired away from ATB mine. Liu Min was a great catch: he was a graduate engineer from Beijing University and had taken most of his classes in English, a level of education that was unusual. When he graduated, in the mid '80s, there were only 30,000 students attending universities in China – a lingering repercussion of the disastrous Cultural Revolution. After graduation, Liu Min had been hired by ATB and furthered his English and technical skills through contact with the expats at the mine site.

At the time, the laws and regulations for the JV system in China were new and still being developed. The group began initial talks with TZ and the Chinese officials in early 1995. These talks were held mostly in Taiyuan, but occasionally in Beijing. During the next six months Mark traveled to China numerous times to convene with the core group. In the meantime, while in close contact with the group's activities, I was back at my regular duties and also involved with the search for a location and building of a new foundry in Europe. This added activity necessitated much travel between the U.S. and Europe for me.

Within nine months, Mark reported that negotiations were progressing on the China JV front, but very slowly. Mark received an application for employment from a Chinese woman who possessed several advanced degrees, and spoke excellent Mandarin and English. She also had a green card and her husband was an associate professor at a Portland, Oregon–based university. Yan Chou was in her mid-forties and greatly impressed Mark during the initial interview. Mark called me and extolled her virtues, but said that her salary requirement was higher than what Mark himself was paid. I recommended he hire her regardless, which subsequently he did. Yan was to be the general manager of the operation in China, if and when it came into being. We were off to a good start, it seemed. Yan Chou became a valuable part of the team, especially with the negotiations with the Chinese.

However, after a further three months of negotiations, things came to an impasse, as the Chinese would not agree to transfer the control of employees to the joint venture. Control of people would entail allowing the joint venture to pick the optimum number of employees (about 160) from the 600–800 currently in the steel foundry operation. If the JV only took 160 people, TZ would have to somehow accommodate or absorb the excess people into its other endeavors.

Negotiations stalled; however, we had seen enough in China to grasp the value of having a presence there: we saw the economy expanding at an incredible rate and were more determined than ever to have a presence in the country. We added another member to our team, Fred McBane, a retired employee of some 45 years with Esco Corporation. During his career, Fred had been involved worldwide with all aspects of foundry operations. The small but growing team now consisted of Mark Mallory, Phoa, Liu Min, Yan, and Fred, and was charged with finding new suitable targets for a joint venture in China. The search was on, and many trips to China to visit different parts of the country ensued as various operations were put to consideration. After about a year of searching to no avail, we were surprised to be contacted again by TZ. They wished to resume negotiations because they had decided transfer of the control of employees was now a possibility. What a surprise! Over the ensuing months, negotiations were finally completed.

Esco Corporation had achieved its main goals – majority ownership, majority management, and control of personnel. The JV was on.

The JV agreement between TZ and Esco Corporation resulted in the creation of a private company, with Esco Corporation ownership at 55 percent. The Chinese contribution consisted of a transfer of land, buildings, and equipment to the JV on a 20-year lease agreement. (Note: at the time, land and other assets were all owned by the state in China.) Esco Corporation's contribution to the JV was cash and technical expertise. The company, christened Shanxi Chengfeng Wearparts Ltd. (SCW), was to come into official existence in June 1998.

Though the JV was finally set to begin operations in June 1998, it had already lost one of its first employees: Yan Chou, our designated GM, unfortunately had contracted cancer some nine months before and was unable to take up her duties. Despite drastic treatment, she subsequently succumbed to the disease. Phoa took over as interim GM. The rest of the Esco Corporation management team consisted of Fred as technical expert, Percy Chang as sales manager, Miensheng as financial officer, and Liu Min as plant engineer. Percy, originally from Taiwan, had worked five years for Esco Corporation in Portland. This small group all transferred to the JV in Taiyuan in June 1998. As part of the agreement, TZ nominated the foundry manager, Mr. Zhang Yi, and the human resource manager, Mr. Wang. The SCW board of directors included Jim Songer, a vice president of Esco Corporation; Mark Mallory; myself; Mr. Gao, the CEO of TZ; and Mr. Chen of TZ.

As VP of manufacturing globally for Esco Corporation, I would be accountable for the manufacturing, technical, and quality aspects of the JV. Accordingly, I arranged to meet Fred and the rest of the team in Taiyuan in early June of that year, to inspect the facilities and to supervise the handover of the assets to the JV.

I arrived in Beijing on June 8 to an extremely hot and dry summer afternoon. The weather was not the only difference I noted since my last trip to China in 1994. There now was a daily flight from Beijing to Taiyuan (what a difference four years makes). After waiting for 6 hours at the Beijing airport for the 55-minute flight to Taiyuan I boarded the plane. The plane was a Russian built Yak of unknown age and many of the seat backs did not lock in place. I was again surprised by the lack of safety procedures in China. The plane landed in Taiyuan late in the evening and I took a taxi to the Shanxi Grand hotel, which had reopened with a four-star status and was rated as a "Western" style hotel. Almost all foreigners stayed here while in Taiyuan.

In the lobby bar, I was greeted by Fred McBane, who welcomed me with an invitation to drink some scotch whiskey in the adjacent bar. We spent about an hour discussing the current status of the JV and planned for my inspection tour the next morning.

Breakfast (included with the cost of the room) at the Shanxi Grand was a pleasant surprise: the buffet featured a hodgepodge of traditional Western and Chinese foods. After breakfast, Liu Min picked Fred and me up in his brand-new VW Santana, which cost at that time $34,000 USD, an astronomical amount to the average Chinese worker. (This was before China became a member of WTO). It was an extremely hot, clear day at 38°C – instead of clouds, a heavy pall of pollution hung over the city.

Soon we arrived at the main gate of the TZ campus and after 10 minutes of being checked over by the guards, we were allowed to proceed to our new operation. Liu Min parked his car in the courtyard outside what was supposed to be our office building. About 200 feet opposite the office facility was one of the main production buildings. Its edifice was brick, and every window was either broken or missing. It had a large entranceway with two swinging doors hanging askew; only one of four hinges was holding them up. The entry was one of the main portals into the large foundry complex we were about to inspect. We proceeded to the doorway, but there were no lights inside, so it was pitch black. Luckily we'd had the foresight to bring numerous Chinese flashlights with us, when we decided to proceed inside. This building was some 600 feet long by 60 feet wide by 35 feet high. Immediately, we were overpowered by the smell of urine, made stronger by the heat. We realized that the employees had been using the brick walls as a urinal. We subsequently found out that none of the toilet facilities in the whole complex were functional; all the sewer lines were plugged up. In addition to the urine, we observed many piles of feces in all areas of the complex.

The complex we were inheriting was huge – with many more buildings of similar size and structure to inspect. In addition, all the production and auxiliary equipment had to be inspected. As we walked around inside the complex guided by our flashlights and what little light shone through the broken windows high above us, we noticed numerous open, unguarded holes and pits, and mounds of dirt and garbage throughout. In one small electrical control room we inspected with our flashlights, we observed a piece of graphite electrode jammed between a high voltage knife switch and the power supply. That was some reckless danger! The outside areas were in even worse condition, with some crane runways piled with debris halfway up the columns. This debris consisted of spent sand, cement discards, scrap castings, scrap assets, wood, paper and plastic. The site was in shambles compared to what we'd observed in 1994. It appeared as if the whole operation had come to a standstill and been abandoned sometime in the years since then.

After four days of inspection, we concluded that most of the equipment would need re-commissioning and that the inside and outside areas would require the removal of an estimated 20,000–25,000 tons of debris. This would all have to be accomplished before Esco Corporation could formally accept the TZ portion of the JV. I asked Fred what he thought it would take. He gruffly replied, "Give me three months." We agreed that we would delay the official beginning of the JV until September.

During this three-month period, the Esco group selected the JV's supervisors and team leaders. Their knowledge of the various workers helped with selection of the best-qualified 150 people from the 600–700 on the current roster. The chosen employees then completed a rigorous orientation and training process, in preparation for the new company's culture and expectations. Although joining a private company was exciting, it was also a shock to them knowing that they would have to do real work and could be fired for lack of performance – a stark contrast to working for an SOE where, as I mentioned earlier, employment was essentially for life. At the same time, the financial and general managers were engaged in dealing with the various government agencies, banks, and other necessary institutions to assure a successful startup for the new JV.

With Fred's constant pushing, the debris situation was handled by TZ (in total some 800 carloads of junk were removed to parts unknown). While this was going on, the new workers were commissioned to unclog the sewers, scrub the toilet areas and, in general, clean the whole place up. Once the sewers were working, new toilet facilities were installed, much to the surprise of the workers. Fred then issued a plant-wide notice stating anybody caught relieving themselves anywhere other than in the toilet facilities would face termination. And you know what? We never did have to terminate anyone because of noncompliance. Critical equipment was inspected, upgraded to operating standards, and put into service. As there were very few lights or fixtures to replace, an immediate upgrading of the lighting systems was begun.

True to his words, Fred and the team were miraculously able to clean the complex up, get the critical equipment in operational shape, have working sewers, and install enough lighting for safe operations all in time for the official signing of the JV agreement on September 8, 1998. Accordingly, Steve Pratt, CEO of Esco Corporation, traveled to Taiyuan, and in the presence of the management team and many Chinese dignitaries, signed the JV agreement creating the private company SCW (Shanxi Chengfeng Wearparts Ltd.). The first production heat was poured that day and a great celebration ensued that evening.

Now the real work began to transform SCW from a '50s-era dinosaur into a modern, world-class operation. I arrived back in Taiyuan some two days later, full of plans of how to do so. During my career, my greatest asset was my ability to work with people in all aspects of operations. I felt that in China, this skill would greatly help us in our endeavors.

Unfortunately, I soon realized that language and culture would be major hurdles to overcome. I was not making much headway with Chinese; it is a totally tonal language, and I am tone-deaf. In the SCW operation, the Chinese/English speakers were few: they included Phoa, Percy, Liu Min, and Miensheng. None of the employees supplied by TZ spoke any English. Nevertheless, we brought the supervisors and team leaders together for training sessions in basic operations. Since Percy, Phoa, and Miensheng were busy with other aspects of the business, Liu Min with his engineering background served as the communication vehicle between Fred and I with the various employee groups.

Although China had shown significant improvements since my first visit in 1994, there were still massive hurdles to clear in order to achieve world-class operations. China did not have a market economy, quality standards, or a sense of time management. Business in China was generally conducted on the basis of relationships, gifts, banquets with plentiful food and drink, and even bribes or under-the-table money. It's not about what one knows and accomplishes, but who one knows and can influence that counts. In general, the SOE's main goal was to employ people (remember the iron rice bowl?) and if it made money in the process, so much the better. Raw materials and supplies were also purchased based on relationships – and as such were usually of inferior quality and unreliable delivery. When a product *was* finally manufactured it frequently did not meet quality standards and delivery was late, but nonetheless it was usually found acceptable by the buyer since he could not get the product any better elsewhere. In our situation, this was totally unacceptable, as at least half of our products would be exported where the world's quality standards prevailed. It was going to be a long road to achieving our goals!

Indeed, one of our first experiences with corruption in China occurred that fall when Fred went to one of the Taiyuan customs houses to pick up a sophisticated gauging tool ordered from our Portland operations. All the requisite paperwork was in order and the proper duties paid but the official in charge demanded Fred pay him a substantial amount for his services. After a heated exchange of words, Fred finally yelled, "Keep the expletive, expletive thing," and walked. Realizing that Fred was not about to deal, the official finally agreed to release the gage with no payment. So that was one way to deal with corruption.

To break into the Chinese domestic market (given the way business was traditionally conducted) we had to start from scratch. Most of the larger mines and construction companies in China knew Esco Corporation by reputation but were not prepared to pay premium prices for quality products, reliable service, and on-time deliveries. We decided to let Percy and the sales team start working on some of the more progressive prospective customers to attain a foothold. We knew this shift in mindset would take some time. Meanwhile, we decided to concentrate our internal efforts on improving quality, productivity, and delivery reliability to service the export markets. This was deemed the most expedient way to get some business for the new venture. In short we were relying on Esco Corporation's global reputation to attract attention in the export markets.

After two weeks, I returned to Portland and although I was in daily touch, I generally left the SCW team to do its work. I returned during the third week in October of that year. There was some progress in regard to the improvement parameters we had set out – although we were far behind our (Western-based) implementation schedule.

One gratifying situation was that the new toilet facilities were all still working and the cleaned-up complex was being properly maintained. Poor Fred had this work against him once. The week before I arrived, Fred, Percy, Phoa, and Liu Min all fell ill after eating a bad dinner (they attributed it to spoiled turtle). The next day, while in the plant, Fred suffered an instant urge to relieve his bowels. Unfortunately he did not make it to the newly clean and operating toilets in time. When he finally reached the bathroom he needed a total change of clothes. Luckily he had his cell phone and called Phoa to get him some clean garments from the hotel. This process took 40 minutes and the poor man had to wait in the toilet while many employees came and went. Fred probably would have preferred to make use of the old 'go anywhere' rule that time; but at least he didn't have to be fired for noncompliance!

The JV employees were indeed grateful for the clean, odor-free toilet facilities. They were even more surprised each month when they received their pay in full – *and* that it was 20 percent higher than what they would have received as full pay for equivalent jobs at TZ. (During this time period TZ was only able to pay their employees about 60 percent of wages due).

Progress without product, however, was slow. The plant was now making about three tons of casting per day (T/D) for export. But we had many employees standing around or hiding in the wings, as we were staffed for an expected output of 40 tons per day. The quality of the end products met world standards, but only after significant reworking. After spending 28 days with the team that fall and meeting with the various supervisors and team leaders, we revised our goals and time lines. Tonnage for the balance of 1998 was to average four T/D – almost all slated for export.

During this trip and my stay at the Shanxi Grand, I was approached one day in the lobby by a young boy who assertively stated, "Hello! My name is Simon. Will you speak English with me?" I was captured! As the Shanxi Grand was the only "Western style" hotel in Taiyuan and was known to have foreigners staying there, Simon's father had begun dropping him off at the hotel lobby on weekends to ferret out any English speakers to practice with. Simon, even then at age seven, was determined to learn; he was also attending a private English Language school on Saturdays. This introduction was to develop into a long-term relationship with Simon (whose Chinese name is Wang, Guochen), his family, and many of his friends and their families.

Figure 2 Simon at age 7 and John, the author

I returned home to Portland in late November. During discussions at Esco that fall with Mark, Jim Songer, and Larry Huget (our boss), we realized that the "Chinese operation" was going to absorb a significant amount of my time in order to achieve the goals we had set out. So much for a once in a lifetime experience; I had already been there three times and spent 50 days total in the country – and was looking at many more visits in the future. I was going to get to know this nation much, much better.

Early in 1999, it became evident that Fred could not single-handedly achieve the goals we had; there was just too much production and ancillary equipment to recommission, too many procedures to be developed, and too many people to be trained. Accordingly, I recruited some of our technical people from Esco's other plants to come to SCW for extended periods of time to set up procedures and training in the areas of their expertise.

I was one of these people, and as a result, I traveled to China six times during that year, spending a total of 160 days there. Joe Burdett from our Port Coquitlam, British Columbia, operation also spent many days setting up procedures and training in SCW's molding department. With the old Beijing airport greatly overcrowded, smoke-filled, dirty, and confusing (there were very few English announcements, and even those could rarely be heard over the all-encompassing noise), it was the custom of SCW to have English-speaking people meet incoming foreigners at the airport to ensure that they could navigate to the correct domestic flight to Taiyuan.

On Joe's first trip in early 1999, he was met at the immigration exit by two Chinese greeters bearing a sign with his name upside down. When he identified himself, they shouted in unison, "Welcome to China!" They then grabbed his luggage and led him by his arm to one of the filthy airport restaurants to wait the five hours for his domestic flight departure. Joe kept nervously asking them if the flight was on time, with their answer being a casual, "no problem." After about four hours of this Joe decided to check out the situation himself, and found out the flight had already been boarded.

He approached the gate agent, who's English was limited. "What should I do?" he asked.

"Run!" she replied.

"Where?!" exclaimed Joe.

"This way to the plane," she indicated. "Run!"

Joe ran to the gate, lugging his two bags, and boarded the plane. His luggage was placed on the seat beside him. He arrived in Taiyuan on time. Another exhilarating welcome to China!

Joe also quickly became initiated into the vastly different Chinese work culture, in which there was little initiative to work without direct orders. One day, Joe noticed three workers were making a large mold while several others were standing around. He asked the supervisor to get the idle workers to help. Three men were ordered into action, but the three who had been working on the mold then promptly left the scene. Clearly it was going to take time for the Western work ethic to catch on. Joe made many trips to Taiyuan throughout 1999 and into 2000. With his 40+ years of service in the field, he was respected by the supervisors and employees in SCW's molding area. Consequently, this area made slow but deliberate progress in terms of quality and productivity. Unfortunately, it was often "three steps forward and two back" – Joe found that between his trips, the progress would slide somewhat.

Liu Min and Fred continued to work in the meantime with each department, inspecting and refurbishing critical equipment. In many cases this involved removal and scrapping of useless assets, moving walls, etc., which was an antithesis to the state-controlled assets policy wherein *nothing* got scrapped. Zhang Yi, the TZ-nominated foundry manager, although a good person, could not bring himself to make the changes necessary to achieve our goals. Fred and I accordingly took the accountability and swung the wrecking hammers. Mr. Wang, the human resource manager nominated by TZ was another matter; he was primarily interested in his political future and not in contributing to the success of the JV.

Similarly, early in the year, we found that our financial officer was more interested in the politics of the job rather than the nuts and bolts work we needed done, so we parted ways. In his place we hired a brilliant young lady named Annie Chen who had attained one of the highest marks ever achieved on the UFE (Uniform Evaluation Exam for Chartered Accountants, purported to be the toughest exam of all). She came from Beijing and became a valued member of our team. However, the entire Esco

Corporation team continued to be composed of expats or English-speaking Chinese from other parts of China. Taiyuan, with its recognized pollution problem, was not a desirable place to live, so we had trouble recruiting talented people from outside Shanxi Province. In addition, at this point in time Taiyuan universities were graduating very few English-speaking people with technical skills.

As we delved into our second calendar year running the JV, we Westerners were grasping some of the deeper cultural differences that would affect our ability to grow the business. For example, we found that the Chinese are intelligent and willing learners, but the culture often inhibited their ability to work, communicate, and achieve in a foreign company environment. The Chinese are traditionally reticent to admit or address problems "head on"; they are reluctant to make decisions, in case they may be wrong and perhaps disciplined for it; they have trouble thinking subjectively or "outside the box," partly due to the education system which encourages them only to repeat what the teacher has taught; the Chinese tend to communicate to foreigners only what they believe the foreigner wants to hear; workers often do not plan and execute well, primarily because the communist culture was driven from the top down – no one makes a move unless so ordered from the top; and finally China is just now emerging from a time and culture in which time was meaningless into the modern world, where time is everything.

Given the above, we saw that we had enormous work ahead in transforming SCW into a world-class foundry. In addition to allotting my time to providing resources for other parts of the manufacturing operations, my focus during most of 1999 was establishing procedures and operating practices for the melting and pouring of the new alloys we were introducing. At each introduction of a new procedure, there was much discussion (with Liu Min as my translator) with supervisors, team leaders, and workers. Although I was respected because of my age (59 years at the time) coupled with my 38+ years of experience in modern steelmaking, my Chinese counterparts had not seen many of the practices and methods I intended to incorporate. Trying something new was strange to them. Again, we made slow progress, and I, like Joe, experienced backsliding in my absences.

The journeys themselves were exhausting. My plane from Vancouver, B.C., (there was no flight to Beijing from Portland at the time; the trip from Portland to Vancouver added an extra six hours of transit time) would typically arrive in Beijing around 2 p.m. after a 12-hour flight. The only regular flight from Beijing to Taiyuan was scheduled to depart at 8:15 p.m. and was invariably late – which resulted in a typical door-to-door time for me of 26 hours. The Beijing airport was still the same small, overcrowded, noisy, dirty, and smoky place, so I loathed the long layover there. On my third trip, in June, I decided to try to shorten the journey by a couple of hours. In early 1999, a new two- and three-lane expressway connecting Beijing to Taiyuan had opened. The distance between the two cities by road was 325 miles, which was almost exactly the distance between Portland, Oregon, and Vancouver, B.C. I had driven that I-5 route numerous times and it usually took between five and five-and-a-half hours, including the border stop. I accordingly made arrangements with Percy (now the permanent GM of SCW) to arrange for a car to meet my flight in Beijing and drive me back to Taiyuan – which should have gotten me there around three hours earlier than the flight.

I arrived in Beijing on time, passed quickly through Immigration, and walked through the exit doors in search of my driver. Among the many signs in English greeting foreigners, I saw my name (upside down, of course) borne by my driver and his companion. By 1999, China had changed the policy of having a party controller assigned to each foreigner for most areas in China, so the driver's companion was just that: someone to help him find and drive me to my destination. It was early summer and the temperature was hovering around a stifling 39°C. The parking lot was located directly across the road outside the main exit. I was led by my driver to the car, except ... it took almost 15 minutes for the driver and his companion to locate where they had left the car. These two had never been out of Taiyuan, let alone visited Beijing. I began to suspect we were in trouble when we turned the wrong way on a one-way exit from the parking lot. After about an hour of attempting to navigate out of the parking lot, a uniformed attendant moved some barriers and directed us to the correct exit. It was hot and uncomfortable, as the car had no air conditioning. After finally exiting the parking lot (it was now 3:30 p.m. and rush hour in Beijing) ... we got lost in the middle of Beijing. As the license plate on the car was not from Beijing the car was conspicuous – and we were stopped by a policeman who asked the driver for identification. The driver immediately broke out into a sweat. Fortunately for him an accident occurred in the next traffic lane from us and diverted the policeman's attention. We escaped! However, it took another two hours to find our way to the expressway entrance. Once we got to the entrance, the two Chinese pulled over and stopped for numerous cigarettes.

Once on the expressway, we sped along the three-lane divided highway though Hebei Province. The first three hours were through flat country gradually rising towards the mountains surrounding Shanxi Province. Once we reached Shanxi Province, we passed through a long tunnel under a mountain and began the long climb towards Taiyuan. Passing through a valley in the mountains, I observed a large coal-powered power plant spewing pollution all over the valley, which severely limited visibility on the roadway. Between Beijing and Taiyuan we had to stop at about 10 tollbooths (with the total costs being about $12.50 USD, which was quite expensive in Chinese terms). We eventually arrived in Taiyuan around 11 p.m. – later than if I had taken the flight. Foiled again!

Later that June, a journalist from *Fortune* magazine, accompanied by his wife and a photographer, checked into the Shanxi Grand. They were accompanied by a large group of Chinese officials and photographers and were ushered into the lobby like royalty by the hotel's top management. The special guest turned out to be Roy Rowen, who for many years prior to World War II worked as a correspondent for *Life* magazine, mainly in China. As it so happened, his last days in China prior to this trip were spent in Taiyuan City in 1949, where Chang Kai Chek's troops were being shelled by Mao's forces. This had been a time of great uncertainty in China, just before the Communists' final victory, and Roy and his people had subsequently been evacuated. He and his crew had returned to China 50 years later to do a feature on U.S. business ventures in China for *Fortune*. As Taiyuan was the last city he had been to in China, he thought it was the appropriate place to begin his dispatch.

As a regular resident of the hotel and an expat, I was introduced to Roy, his wife, Helen, and *Fortune*'s photographer Fritz Hoffman. Roy decided he would begin with interviewing Fred and I, followed by a visit to our plant the next day. The next morning a large tour bus showed up at our plant. A big group of Chinese officials accompanied by photographers disembarked followed by Roy, his wife, and the photographer, with flashes going off everywhere to capture the auspicious event. Once the event was recorded on film, all the officials climbed back on the bus and departed for parts unknown, leaving Roy and his team to their own devices.

After many hours of touring; interviews in situ with Mark, Fred, Joe, Liu Min, and I; and many photos, Roy, his wife, and photographer departed to tour the city that they had not seen for 50 years. That evening, Roy requested that we allow Fritz to spend the next two days with us doing a more in-depth study of our operation. The next day was Friday so we said that would be OK, but we noted that on Saturday we would not be working. In fact, that Saturday evening we expats were to attend a special gala dinner hosted by our Chinese partners at the most expensive restaurant in the city. Roy asked if Fritz could instead attend with us and take pictures of a real Chinese celebration. We agreed.

Saturday, on this rare occasion, was a non-workday so we expats decided to have a relaxing day; we met in the lobby at noon and decided to walk around outside for an hour before lunch, as it was a pleasant day. After a good walk, Joe, Fred, and I dropped into a pub called the Silk Bar that Fred had found on one of his frequent forays around the city. We ordered lunch and cold (this time) beers. After a couple of hours at the bar and much discussion of all the toasts and Chinese liquor that would be consumed at the dinner, Fred noticed a very large (4 liter) and dusty bottle of Courvoisier on the top shelf of the bar. Fred said "I wonder how long that bottle has been sitting gathering dust". We decided then and there to modify the dinner party. No Chinese white liquor for us tonight! We would introduce our hosts to Western-style alcohol. Fred called the bar manager over to our table and asked "how much for the bottle?" In her limited English she replied "I will have to ask the owner." She came back shortly and said "1,800 Yuan" ($250 USD). I replied "too much." She again called the owner and when she returned to the table she said "1600 Yuan." I replied, "still too high." We left shortly thereafter, however our evil plan remained in our minds. On the way to the hotel, we discovered a liquor store, went inside, and Fred purchased three 1.5 liter bottles of Remy Martin for 525 Yuan each; almost the same price as the bar wanted, but more volume!

SCW attendees at the dinner included Mark, Liu Min, Fred, Joe, and I, with Fritz in tow to document the occasion. Our hosts included SCW directors Gao Zhijun and Mr. Chen, accompanied by three of their top-ranked lieutenants. After an animated discussion, it was agreed that for this party, the foreign devils (*lao weis*) could supply the liquor. An excellent dinner ensued along with the many mandatory toasts. One of the toasts I proposed was to director Chen. We had full snifters of Remy, locked our arms together, and simultaneously drained our glasses all the time swearing loyalty to the cause. During the dinner and toasts Fritz was busy snapping pictures.

On Sunday, Roy and his entourage departed to continue their assignment in other parts of China. We had spent a lot of time together, between the interviews and photographs of the operation, and had developed an excellent rapport with Roy and his party. I particularly enjoyed Roy, who was in his mid-70s at the time, and was active, gregarious, charming, and interesting. His wife, Helen, was equally appealing. Roy Rowan has authored several books, one of which I have read, titled *Chasing the Dragon*. In this book Rowan included an anecdote regarding an English Lord (Sir John Keswick), a lifelong resident of China, who wrote and published a book on the country titled *What I Know about China*. His book was 100 blank pages depicting his knowledge of China as an "old China hand."

When the October 1999 issue of *Fortune* magazine hit the newsstands, numerous colleagues and I were pleasantly surprised that our JV operation in Taiyuan was featured in some detail with many quotes from Fred and Mark. My young friend Simon, who met Roy in the hotel lobby, was also mentioned in the feature. However, despite all the shots Fritz had taken, no pictures of our operations were included except for a very prominent picture of me entwined in the toast with director Chen. The picture showed our full glasses, my prominent Citizen wristwatch, and my ever-present cigar in hand. Needless to say, even though the article was positive, I received much ribbing regarding all the "hard work" I do in China.

By August 1999, the Esco Corporation team felt that the two TZ nominees – the foundry manager Mr. Zhang Yi, and the human resource manager, Mr. Wong – were impeding progress towards world-class status for the SCW operation. Accordingly, we asked our business partner to replace them with two more progressive candidates. It was now mid-September and one of Fred's last acts in China was to help me interview the two candidates. We were satisfied with Zhang Ying Tao, the nominee for foundry manager who was in his early fifties and professed an eagerness to promote change. The HR nominee, Mr. Luo, was a younger man who, although a youth Communist party member, professed that he valued the opportunity to join the JV. We agreed to accept both candidates for the designated positions.

This was Fred's swan song. After 15 consecutive months of living in Taiyuan, he had successfully completed the mission assigned to him. Before his departure, we decided to honor him with a picnic/BBQ for all SCW employees and their families. This was a tradition at almost all Esco Corporation global facilities, but would be a totally new experience for our Chinese employees. However, when we checked with our JV partners, we was found out that the rules prohibited family functions – so we were forced to downsize to an employee-only event.

Joe was in town on one of his frequent visits, so that made three of us who were familiar with organizing and cooking at BBQs. This was to be a real Western-style cookout and we wanted our first effort to be spectacular! We had to get Liu Min and Percy to translate to our maintenance people how to construct BBQs out of oil drums. We would need at least eight of them to cook enough food to serve the whole crowd. We then organized the purchase of the food and drinks. As steak was not then available in Taiyuan, most of the meat to be cooked would be chicken legs and lamb skewers. We obtained potatoes for baking, as well as many traditional Chinese foods including vegetables and fruit. Fuel for the BBQs would be coke, which was readily available at the plant. For beverages, we decided to provide Coca-Cola and Sprite, which were popular in China. In keeping with the Western theme, we arranged for beer kegs to be delivered to the BBQ. We decided not to supply any Chinese white liquors, as they have a potent alcohol level. There really was no problem with drinking on-site, as the employees lived on campus and would arrive either by bicycle or on foot.

The night before the BBQ, we were invited to the apartment of one of our inside sales women to prepare the meat for the next night. She provided an assortment of fruit, soft drinks, and some beer to tide us over while we marinated the large chicken legs. The apartment being Chinese size (small!), it was somewhat crowded with Percy, Joe, Liu Min, Fred, and I. However we crowded together, had a good time, and accomplished our mission.

Everything was going according to plan. We had advised Liu Min and the maintenance department that the BBQs would need to be lit by 5:30 p.m. the day of the BBQ to be hot enough to begin cooking by 7 p.m. In the meantime, Percy had coordinated with the appropriate people to buy and deliver the rest of the food and refreshments on time for the festivities. The supervisors were organized to set up all the facilities and tables in the courtyard. Unbeknownst to us Westerners, the Chinese were big fans of karaoke. Percy was aware of this and ordered the required equipment to be delivered to the site.

Saturday dawned a rare clear day – little pollution – with the temperature forecast at BBQ time to be 22°C. We Westerners arrived at the site by 6:30 p.m. – and were dismayed to see that the BBQs had not been fired up! We put a "hurry-up offense" on and got them going. We began cooking the large chicken legs one hour later and it was slow going. In the meantime the beer was flowing and people were getting hungry. In many instances employees began taking undercooked legs from the BBQ. I figured we were going to have numerous no-shows for work the next day. As the evening wore on, Liu Min and I visited the various tables of employees, who seemed to be seated by departments. Even though we had not provided Chinese white liquor, many employees had brought their own supply and were toasting boisterously. At about 8:30 p.m., the karaoke started up. It was amazing how many excellent singers stepped up to the microphone. Around 10 p.m. the party wound up and everyone departed for home in a happy mood, despite the delays. I guess we did OK after all!

But as far as business matters, that was another story. As 1999 came to a close, we still had not developed any significant domestic business. Consequently, as with 1998, we only averaged about four tons per day production for export business. Still, a lot of progress had been made: quality was improved, productivity was slowly improving, education and training of the workforce was ongoing, and housekeeping, thank goodness, was maintained. With changes in Esco Corporation management, came shifts on the SCW board: Mark Mallory assumed the chair, and I – with the addition of Ray Verlinich, our corporate controller – completed the Esco complement. The Esco Corporation management team at the JV now consisted of Percy Chang as GM, Annie Chen as finance manager, and Fang Ho from Singapore as sales manager – all imports. Liu Min remained as plant engineer and my technical interpreter. We were still limited to very few English-speaking employees in the SCW organization, with the notable exception of some recent university graduates (mostly young ladies) in our inside sales department. Things were at least stable. But Y2K was just around the corner; we were wondering what would happen, and how our systems would respond.

After watching the New Year progress from Australia to Japan to China, through Europe, and eventually to the west coast of North America (where I was) without any major computer glitches, I calmly left for China on the first day of the new millennium. I arrived in Taiyuan on the evening of January 2. This is typically the coldest month in Taiyuan, with temperatures as low as -20°C. (In the summer Taiyuan is very hot and dry, and in winter its cold and dry – unlike the Pacific Northwest, where I hail from, Taiyuan has an annual precipitation of less than 18 inches.) That year the cold weather had started in December and was continuing throughout January. As a result many of the plant's water and air lines had frozen up, causing disruptions in production on many days. As operations were so slow, I flew home after only 20 days, planning to return to SCW in mid-February for a prolonged 65-day stay.

We were now operating at about 8 T/D, but it was still mostly export business. Since we were recommissioning another molding line using different sand and binders, I asked Randy Green from our Port Hope, Ontario, foundry to come to SCW. Randy's hands-on experience not only in the molding area but also in melting, heat treatment, and welding would be valuable for this stage of development at SCW. Randy arrived in Taiyuan during the last week of February. The weather had moderated enough to operate the plant, but was still cold with daytime temperatures hovering around -10°C.

Randy's knowledge and enthusiasm impressed the supervisors and workers and soon the recommissioned process was in operation. This success allowed Randy to move on into the other areas of his expertise, where he also achieved positive results with training employees. Randy's first trip lasted until March 18.

While Randy was in Taiyuan, I spent as much time with him as possible. He, in turn, spent time with me while I was developing and instituting new practices in the melting and pouring area; in this way we cross-trained each other. Liu Min, still our only English technical translator, was however harried and split among his duties as plant engineer and translator for the rest of us.

There were other challenges. When it came to actually making the steel for a new alloy for SCW, it was decided to begin the heat (i.e., start melting) at 2 p.m. There were many difficulties with making this first time heat, and it was almost 10 p.m. when the final calculations for the alloy compositions were necessary. Although I had spent many hours of discussion with the crew, they remained skeptical of the calculations – so I did it for them. Randy was present and exclaimed, "Boss, I never knew you could do heat calculations!" I merely smiled. (It should be noted that a normal electric arc furnace alloy heating process takes about two hours. With this heat, it took eight hours.)

After another hour, the molten steel was ready for pouring and moved to the area to be poured into the molds Randy and his crew had prepared from the newly recommissioned molding line. The weather was still cold, which had a negative effect on the strength of the sand in the molds. As a consequence, we had numerous run-outs, a condition where the liquid steel runs out through the sand. Finally after completing the pour, we wrapped up and returned to the hotel around midnight. A typical day at the plant was about 12 hours. This had been a long day of 18 hours.

In another instance while introducing another alloy composition, we began the heat again at 2 p.m. By midnight, with various problems along the way, we had come to the point where it was almost impossible to balance the elements necessary to meet the specifications. I advised the crew they had two opportunities to deal with the situation. The first was to "pig" the heat, i.e., scrap it, or, secondly, to dilute the heat by adding good clean steel scrap. Since we had already spent 20 hours in the plant and the second option would require a further two to three hours, I advised the crew to take the first option, and then everyone could go home. I then left, but on my return at 6 a.m. I was surprised they had chosen option two – and so saved the heat. Even this early in the game in China, I had some pleasant surprises.

Since mid 1998, I and all Esco Corporation visitors stayed at the Shanxi Grand hotel. Over the years many other expats working on different projects in China would also use the hotel as their base of operations. Mark Nolan of Boeing was a long-term resident and we had developed a close friendship. One Friday we had arranged with Randy, Mark, and a couple of other expats to meet in the hotel lobby at 6:30 p.m., have a few beers and then go out for dinner. I was in the lobby waiting at 5:45 when Percy called and told me he had an important customer who wanted to meet me. I told Percy that I had made previous commitments but he said I would be back at the hotel in time to meet my friends. Percy (who was in the parking lot) picked me up shortly after the call. I again informed him that my time was limited; but he insisted, "I'll have you back in time." While driving around the city streets for 40 minutes, I was becoming more and more concerned that I would not be back at the hotel in time to meet my friends. Precisely at 6:30, Percy announced, "We are here!" We had arrived at a large restaurant – and to my surprise and embarrassment, when we entered and were directed to a large private room, I was greeted with a loud chorus of "Happy Birthday!" I turned to Percy and retorted, "You idiot!" Percy had assembled not only my friends from the hotel, but also many others I had established friendships with in China. Included in the party were the SCW management team and directors Gao and Chen from TZ. Needless to say the party was a blowout. There was an excellent variety of Chinese cuisine, including dog and donkey – both of which were prepared like pastrami. We finished the party with a huge cake. This was March 13, two days before my 60th birthday, which due to all the activities at SCW I had completely forgotten.

Apparently the 60th birthday in China is a very auspicious one. For my 60th birthday, my young friend Simon and his family also insisted on a Chinese birthday party for me. I was feted at a nice restaurant owned by Simon's aunt, along with his family, some relatives, and friends. Although Simon and one other kid were the only English-speaking Chinese at the party, we had a jolly time: good food, some beer, a cake, and fireworks. All during the celebration, pictures were constantly being taken, particularly of me wearing a ridiculous hat similar to those used in birthday celebrations in the west.

I had Randy return in early June to continue with the work he had begun during his first trip earlier that year. Both Randy and Percy were avid golfers and I enjoyed an occasional flogging around the course with them. Golf was just becoming popular in China. Taiyuan, being somewhat remote from the faster developing areas of China, had no golf course at this point in time. However, Percy was a member of a club some five and a half hours down the expressway towards Beijing, so one Saturday he arranged a tee off time for us at 1:00 p.m. We agreed that in order to allow for delays, we should leave Taiyuan at 6:30 that morning. Percy arrived with Carrie, his long-time fiancée, promptly at 6:30. He had borrowed an older "luxury" car from a friend that was larger than the typical Chinese VW, so that we Westerners would have more comfort and room. The car was a black Nissan (Cedric) sedan of 1988 vintage – probably owned by a Chinese official who could bypass the country's import laws. While Randy and I were settling into the back seat, Carrie undid her shoulder belt to turn and greet us. To her dismay, she discovered a long grease mark on her expensive white blouse. She did not bring another blouse to change into, and the only way to cover the marks was to don a jacket. We hoped this was not going to be an ominous start to the trip – the day was going to be extremely hot.

We started out, and with Carrie wearing a jacket, we decided that the air conditioning should be turned up. To our dismay, we discovered the unit only put out hot air. After about an hour of driving with the outside temperature rising, Randy noticed the temperature indicator was in the red. He suggested we pull over at the next service/food/toilet stop. Such stops are spaced about every 100 kilometers along the expressway. After five minutes we pulled into the stop and opened the car hood. The cooling system was completely out of water. We filled the radiator to the requisite level and then checked the oil. It was down a full quart and we discovered in the trunk a full gallon of oil so we filled the reservoir from this. During the stop, we purchased about three liters of water for drinking purposes, as the day was only getting hotter. This would prove a prophetic benefit.

Exiting the pit stop around 7:30, we still had about five hours to our destination. As we were in the mountains, our trip was downhill for the next three hours. However, after two hours the car temperature again rose into the red. We were between service areas so we pulled over to the side of the expressway, raised the hood and again found the cooling system empty. Luckily we had purchased the three liters of water and used this to partially fill the system. We again checked the oil and found it down about half a pint, so we topped it off also. The roadway was now leveling out and we had proceeded for another hour when the needle showed red again. We immediately pulled over to side of the expressway. We were three kilometers from the next exit which was, unfortunately not a service stop. Randy and Percy, carrying our three empty liter bottles, set out on foot to beg for water at the first sign of habitation. Carrie and I stayed with the vehicle to protect our interests. Many cars stopped to see if they could be of assistance, but none had any water in the volume we would need. The temperature outside was now 38°C, and with no shade, it was extremely uncomfortable for Carrie and I.

It was even more uncomfortable for Percy and Randy who, after the 3 km trip to the exit, found a farmhouse after another half kilometer walk. Not only did the farmer allow them to fill the three containers, he sold them an old plastic five-gallon container with water for 10 Yuan ($1.25 US). Percy and Randy now had a 3.5 km return trip under load. They returned and we again filled the system, checked the oil, which only nominally down, and stowed the excess water in the trunk. We continued on our way with one more stop to fill the radiator.

We finally arrived at the golf club by 1:30 p.m., arranged for a 2:30 tee time, and had a nice lunch including many refreshing beverages. It was now mid-afternoon, the temperature at 42°C (104°F) so we decided that nine holes would be enough golf. The golf course was as good as any of the top courses in North America and UK that I had played on. We were assigned young lady caddies who were professional in their duties and were each responsible for maintaining a specific hole. After the game, we men went to the clubhouse, showered, and changed.

It was now 6 p.m. and we were (in theory) about an hour away from the LiDo Hotel in Beijing where Randy and I were staying for the evening. Percy and Carrie were planning on staying nearby with friends, where perhaps she could get a replacement blouse. As I had filled the radiator again before leaving the club, we arrived at the LiDo just below the red line. I again refilled the radiator for Percy and then Randy and I checked into the LiDo. Plans were for Percy and Carrie to pick us up early the next day so that we could get to the golf course again by mid-morning for a full round of golf before the return trip to Taiyuan.

It was going to be another stinking hot and humid day. By 6 a.m., it was already 32°C as we entered the Beijing ring road system. The LiDo was located in the northeast area of Beijing and our exit towards the golf club was in the southwest. In 1996 Beijing had only one ring road, but by 2000 a third ring road had just opened up. We entered the third ring road, and after about three-quarters of an hour Randy and I noticed the sun had changed from being on the back of our necks, to our eyes, to one side, back to the necks and so on. We were lost in Beijing. Percy and Carrie were natives of Taiwan, very versed in high Mandarin but not familiar with the details of Beijing's road system. Percy called his own personal OnStar (Liu Min, in Taiyuan, who was familiar with Beijing). We were duly put on the correct routing and found our exit. We arrived at the golf club at 9 am on the red line for temperature. While Percy and Randy are pretty good golfers, I am a hacker. However for the first three holes, I hit the ball very well and was only one over. My girl caddy was all smiles as she probably thought that she was working with a real pro. The fourth hole revealed my real skill as my first two tee shots hooked into the water hazard some 50 yards from the tee. After the third shot of some 150 yards safely on the fairway, I proceeded to card a nine. The rest of the nine were not much better. After nine holes, both Carrie and I had enough and told Randy and Percy we would proceed to the clubhouse so they could play serious golf for the last nine. While at the clubhouse, I again filled the car's radiator, refilled our water containers, and topped up the oil. At noon Randy and Percy declared it was too hot to continue and showed up at the clubhouse and we soon departed for our return to Taiyuan.

The initial part of the return was on flat to gently rising expressway. Over this part of the road, we were obliged to stop every 125 km to refill the radiator. Each stop took at least 20 minutes for the car to cool down enough to open the cap and pour the water in. The total trip from club to Taiyuan was 450 km. It was going to be a long day, especially since the balance of the trip was a long climb in the mountains with the temperature at 43°C! After the third stop we got into the climb portion, and the temperature rose to the red line more quickly. We had proceeded only about 75 km when the gauge showed red again. Fortunately we were about 2 km from an exit to a service stop so we slowed down and made it to the exit ramp – when a loud noise ensued and steam erupted from the car's hood. We had blown something! Luckily the ramp was downhill and we were able to coast to the entrance of the service stop. However we were stopped about 100 meters short. Randy and I jumped out to push and were immediately helped by a throng of volunteers who helped us get the car to the small service garage.

Diagnosis: we had blown the bottom radiator hose, which incidentally is the most difficult to replace. Randy and I were novelties, as the villagers rarely had the opportunity to meet Westerners. After the excitement died down, the mechanic stated through Percy that they did not have the correct part to fix the radiator hose. Randy, in addition to his formidable other talents, is a hell of a mechanic. After much back and forth through Percy he told them that together they could modify one of the other hoses in the shop to fit. Randy showed the mechanic what was needed and they successfully modified the hose. After two hours – with a refill of the radiator and addition of oil – we were again underway. Total cost was only 100 Yuan (about $12.50 USD)!

We had no more radiator problems and arrived at the last toll booth entering Taiyuan at 10 p.m. Percy used this opportunity to phone his friend and tell him of the car problems we had encountered. The friend told him that the car had about 400,000 km on it and had never been on expressway roads and that maybe problems should have been expected.

I should note that both Carrie and Percy, being proud Taiwanese, were concerned with losing "face" with their Western friends due to the arduous and problem-filled trip. Both Randy and I assured them this was a great opportunity for team building and there were no issues. However, this trip is still much talked about amongst many of our friends. Another adventure in China!

Carrie and Percy dropped Randy and I off at the Shanxi Grand around 10:45 that night. I usually called Cherie in the mornings given the 15- or 16-hour (depending on daylight saving time) time difference between China and Portland. However, this time I decided to call her that evening. When I called she said that she'd just had a nightmare that something serious had happened to me. She had woken up suddenly to a sound that sounded like a huge cutting machine. She rolled over in bed, checked to see that the alarm system was engaged, then glanced toward the dresser in our master bedroom and saw what appeared to be me. My apparition sighed a huge "AHaaaa," then faded away. She said it was a particularly creepy feeling and she was somewhat frantic, wondering what she should do, if she should call my boss and say she had just seen my ghost. After relating in detail our day's traumatic experience, she was much relieved.

By mid-2000, we were making significant progress in all areas of the plant operations, most notably in training, education, and loyalty of employees; safety and housekeeping standards; quality improvements; and recommissioning of equipment. We were now producing at the rate of 9.9 T/D, but again, it was mostly export business.

The new international airport in Beijing opened in September. This was a very modern world class airport with smoking only allowed in a few enclosed rooms. What an improvement.

Randy made what was to be his last visit to SCW in October–November of that year. Autumn is generally regarded as the best time of the year weather-wise in Taiyuan, with the highest probability of clear days. One clear early morning as we were driving to work, Randy suddenly got very animated and exclaimed, "There are f***ing mountains all around!" In his previous two visits, heavy pollution had shrouded the city, obstructing any visibility of the surrounding mountains.

Unfortunately, Taiyuan is known for its serious pollution problems. It is not uncommon to be able to taste the air! As Shanxi is the major coal-mining province in China and virtually all the electrical power is generated from coal burning, the city is one of the ten most polluted in China: fine dust is constantly in the air and on the ground, necessitating constant sweeping to remove the dust. The sweeping is done by retired workers of both sexes. Where the dust is deposited after sweeping up is anybody's guess.

After 42 years with Esco Corporation, Joe Burdett had retired that September and I asked his brother Dan to come to SCW and continue Joe's work. He arrived at the same time as Randy's last visit. Like Randy, Dan had expertise in a broad range of foundry operations and proved a valuable asset to the operation.

As the weather in early November was pleasant, on one Sunday afternoon Randy, Dan, and I walked many miles around the Taiyuan. We entered parts of the city where very few "round eyes" had been seen. Young people seeing us would say "hello," turn away and giggle. Older workers would stop whatever they were doing and openly stare at us. We would smile and say "Ni Hao" ("hello") and they would smile at us. Again, we were curiosities!

A river had run through the city dividing it east and west until about 1985, when overuse caused it to dry up. (Taiyuan now gets all its water from aquifers.) In year 2000, however, the dried river bed had been resurrected as a canal by diverting water from the Yellow River, which is the major river in northern China. A park was created along about two kilometers of the canal, traversed by five new bridges. Since the park had recently been opened with much fanfare, in celebration of the 50th anniversary of the founding of the PRC, we decided to end our two-hour city exploration with a stroll along the river park.

———

Year 2000 closed with SCW operating at an average of 9.9 T/D, with a growing reputation for quality and reliability. Both foreign and domestic visitors were impressed with the spotless facilities (the cleanest factory toilets in China!) and the general work ethic and cheerfulness of our employees. Most importantly, we were finally beginning to receive inquiries for castings from domestic customers. In addition, our reputation overseas was such that we were also receiving more and more inquiries from abroad.

Even with the steady progress, after two-plus years in operation we were still not making money as a business. In fact, to our dismay, we learned that over 200 tons of export castings did not meet dimensional tolerances and had to be scrapped. This was caused by poor pattern construction by our outside suppliers, something we'd have to find a way to address.

It was a milestone year for me, as well. I had spent 190 days – more than half the year, the most time logged thus far in China – at SCW, while still retaining my global duties as VP Manufacturing for Esco Corporation back in Portland. I ended the year tired, but invigorated by our achievements!

Early in 2001, we replaced Fang Ho, our sales manager from Singapore, with Philip Liu from Taiwan. This was a move to greatly accelerate our domestic business in China while continuing to increase our export position. The management team now consisted of Percy as GM, Annie Chen as finance DGM, Philip Liu as sales DGM, and Liu Min continuing as plant engineer and technical manager. Still, we didn't have anyone on the management team who was a Taiyuan native.

But university attendance had increased dramatically since the mid-1990s, and Taiyuan universities were beginning to graduate English-speaking students with technical and business degrees. This enabled us to increase the number of English speakers in our operation. This helped greatly in our inside sales area, where we had daily dealings with our global customers and other Esco Corporation operations. Hiring technical, locally educated personnel who could generally understand written English despite their limited speaking abilities was an excellent first step in building a local base of talent for the future of SCW. Over time, most of these new employees showed rapid improvements in their English communication skills.

Much to my chagrin, my inability to speak Chinese persisted, despite all the time I'd spent there in the previous three years. Various Chinese friends tried hard to teach me Chinese, as I taught them English usage, but they all failed. They would give a word or two and say it 10 times – each time I'd say it 10 different ways, all seemingly the same to me. I eventually learned about 300 words, but only my closest Chinese friends can understand me when I say them.

Going into 2001, we were receiving many inquiries for business both domestically and for export. In recognition of the potential increase in business, we continued with the process of recommissioning more of the production areas and equipment that had been idle since the JV's inception. In addition, the demands for new patterns exceeded the capacity of our outside suppliers (whose quality was also a problem). In response, we decided to construct an internal pattern-making capability. This facility became operational in early January. Although by now at 12 T/D we were still far below our target production rate of 40 T/D, we could see the future was bright. We were receiving inquiries from an ever-increasing potential customer base, which necessitated the construction of about 40 new patterns each month. In addition, the new business required the introduction of many new alloys, new molding procedures, new heat treatment procedures, new welding processes, and many other unique processing procedures. All training of the workforce still had to go through Liu Min as our only technical English/Chinese translator. Poor Liu Min was overloaded, since he still had to attend to his other engineering duties.

Since we were getting busier, it became clear that we were lacking sophistication in two main areas: production scheduling, and purchasing raw materials and supplies. To introduce modern scheduling techniques, we invited Tiffany Watts – Joe Burdett's daughter, who was the lead scheduler at our Port Coquitlam foundry – to visit for a three-week training and education process. Coincidentally, Dan was planning another trip to the JV and he was also Tiff's uncle, so Dan was able to guide her through her first visit to China. This was a great start to solving the scheduling situation.

Regarding our lack of professional purchasing expertise at SCW, we had many discussions and potential candidates in Esco's global operations, but none were immediately available to come to China. What to do??? The solution fell into our lap. One evening around 6:30 p.m., I was back in the hotel lobby when Percy phoned me.

"John," he said excitedly, "I have just interviewed the most intelligent person I have ever met and I want you to meet her tonight."

Percy and the lady in question, whom he introduced as Wei Yu, showed up at 7:00 p.m. She was 30 years old, about 5 feet one inch tall, and very trim and beautiful. She had been introduced to Percy through another lady (Bai Ling Mei, or "Stella" in English) I had hired who was a classmate of Wei Yu's.

Percy explained that although Wei Yu's English was very good, she had not used it much recently and if she felt uncomfortable answering my questions she would first ask him in Chinese to be sure she understood the question. However, her demeanor and confidence would not allow her to do this and the interview was conducted in English. I found that she was a university graduate in business with import/export experience at an SOE. She was married and her husband was also a graduate who worked in the same firm. Both Percy and I were so impressed with her credentials and potential that we offered her the position of purchasing manager on the spot. She informed us that unfortunately she had to refuse, as she and her husband needed to work for a further six months at the SOE in order to qualify for an apartment. However, after much further discussion, she agreed that she would come to SCW for free in her spare time to set up and train a new purchasing department. She started the next week. Six months later, Wei Yu became a permanent employee of SCW. Over the ensuing months, she was able to make significant improvements to the SCW purchasing process. In addition she was a valued addition to our taxed English/Chinese translation "department." (Liu Min was thrilled.)

From winter through mid-summer of 2001 we chugged along with education and training of personnel; introduction of new alloys, patterns, and procedures; and upgrading and modernization of production equipment. I remained the main conduit through which all training occurred and I continued to enlist the help of individuals with the essential skills from other parts of Esco Corporation's global operations. That year I had decided I would visit China less often but stay for more extended time periods in the hope this would increase my effectiveness.

In March of 2001, after living in the U.S. for 10+ years, Cherie and I became U.S. citizens (while retaining dual citizenship with our native Canada). The wait time for me was very long because my time spent out of the country had to be deducted from the normal five-year waiting period. At the swearing-in ceremony, I was asked if I was prepared to adopt the ideals of America and defend the country in times of peril. I answered "Yes!" even though I thought, "With my two artificial knees – I could only volunteer as a slow-moving target!"

Normally during the third week of September, Esco Corporation's senior management team and corporate executives from around the world would meet in Bend, Oregon, for annual planning sessions. I, as an executive, was to be an attendee as usual. However, at this time we were undertaking some critical new work at the JV and I decided to opt out of the meetings and return to SCW. We also decided that Percy, as GM of a fairly new Esco Corporation facility, should attend the meetings in Bend. In essence, we were sending China to America and America to China!

I arrived in Taiyuan right after Labor Day and proceeded with my regular duties. I was sound asleep in my room at 10 p.m., on 9/11/01 – which was early in the morning that day in Bend, Oregon – when the phone jarred me awake. It was Percy calling from Bend telling me to turn the TV to CNN, as something serious was happening on the East Coast of the U.S. I turned the TV on; just five minutes before the plane hit the second tower of the World Trade Center. I remained awake the rest of the night watching the horror and progress of this terrorist attack on our soil. Our son Brock, now with a family of his own, lived near Pittsburg and my sister worked at Pfizer in downtown New York. Luckily I was able to get through to them by phone and confirm they all were safe.

It was a long and agonizing night. I had not thought about it at first, but my room number for this stay was 911. This time there were no American expats at the hotel, so the only people I could relate to were some Europeans who expressed great sympathy for the United States. My Chinese friends, with little access to outside world news, would not hear the details of the attack until the Chinese government filtered the news to its liking. As a result, my colleagues found what I was telling them somewhat unbelievable. True to form, the Chinese news media published their versions of the terrorist attacks three days later. In all cases, though, the reports were factual and sympathetic to the U.S., and denounced the terrorist attacks.

In early October, we planned on holding our third annual picnic/BBQ at SCW. By now we had the BBQ operation down pat, and the employees always looked forward to the festivities. For the upcoming occasion, we had invited Fred as an honorarium to come back to SWC for a two-week visit. At the party, Fred was welcomed as a long-lost friend. He had the forethought to bring tee shirts for the Esco Corporation team silkscreened with the words "God Bless America." Mark Mallory, Liu Min, Percy, Annie Chen, and I proudly wore the shirts. After translating the sentiment to the employees, these were a big hit.

During the BBQ, Percy introduced a new addition to the SCW team: Liu Yu Feng (Francis) was a technical graduate from Dalian university who spoke passable English. Francis was a native of Taiyuan, so we finally had a local member on the team! He was to become another understudy to whom I could transfer my technical and manufacturing knowledge. We were gradually building up our English-speaking base. Francis was assigned the mandate of attaining ISO 9001 certification (internationally recognized quality standards) for the SCW operation with a target date set for mid-2002. Initially Francis was shy and, typical of Chinese education, his knowledge was not broad. Over the ensuing years, his growth has been incredible and he is a valuable employee: his English and knowledge of idioms is excellent, his technical skills have greatly expanded, and he continues to grow in all areas.

Figure 3 Francis and his daughter

After 75 days at SCW, I returned home just before the Thanksgiving holiday. I had spent 230 days total in China so far that year. Though it had been another year with a grueling travel schedule, some changes were in store. Esco Corporation and I had agreed to a modified employment contract for me beginning in 2002. The contract would finally relieve me of my global responsibilities to allow my full concentration on the Chinese JV. The contract was for three years, wherein I would work in China at 80 percent of normal hours for the first two years, tapering down to 70 percent for the third year. In addition, during my out-of-China time, I would maintain the necessary contact with the operation and critical resources within Esco Corporation via computer and conference calls. Cherie questioned what the 80 percent meant, as my normal yearly hours averaged around 3,200 hours. Cherie, correctly as it turned out, sadly predicted that it would not change the amount of time I spent in China.

Although SCW continued to operate in the red, we *were* making significant progress in all areas that were necessary to achieve world-class status: production for the year averaged 12

T/D and projections for 2002 were for a healthy 25 percent increase in volume.

Upon my return home, I received some bad news in the form of an e-mail from Wei Yu, stating that she had decided to leave SCW in order to further her education. She was to attend Shanghai University to attain a master's degree in commercial law. She assured me that she would consider returning to SCW in the future if that was in the cards.

Business in 2002 was picking up and we needed to continue with improvements in all areas of operations – but especially in the purchase of quality raw materials and supplies. It was evident that both the Chinese and global economies were picking up steam, primarily driven by China's rapid industrialization, infrastructure improvements, and increased demands for consumer items from an emerging and growing middle class with disposable income. China was beginning to require an ever-increasing portion of the world's raw material and power resources. In addition, the U.S. was entering into a higher-than-normal growth rate and the European Union was also experiencing significant growth – both situations also placing pressure on global demand.

The competition for the world's resources was beginning to cause shortages, leading to rapid and significant price increases. Raw materials such as melting scrap, iron ore, and pig iron all showed pricing increases of 60 percent or more by the third quarter of 2002. Ferro alloy prices were showing even more significant increases with FeMo (ferro molybdenum) topping the list by mid-year at eight times the price only months earlier. To meet the increased raw material demands, many mines in the U.S. and Canada that had been shut down for years due to low mineral prices were resurrected. As a result, many suppliers of equipment (including Esco Corporation) received additional orders to put these mines back into operation. Good news for us!

In China, even though the country had doubled electrical power production since 2000, power demands had increased threefold. This caused severe power rationing and affected our SCW operation, as we were a major power consumer. We were able to compensate for the shortage and meet our growing demands by melting (a heavy power hitter) on the night shift, when power was more readily available, and at cheaper rates. With our Chinese workforce being flexible in regard to their work schedule, this was easier to do than in our other global operations. (There are labor hours mandated by the Chinese government, but no laws pertaining to what shifts can be worked, and the Chinese were accustomed to doing what they are told.) In addition, with the institution of modern procedures and practices, we were able to reduce the melting power consumption by 80 percent since the JV's start in 1998. In short, we were able to make the steel twice as fast with less power consumption and could satisfy the current market requirements on one shift per day of melting. Now we were getting somewhere!

Early in 2002, we received a very large order for 66 sets of 1,000 mm ball joints for the dredging industry. Each set consisted of 4 finished castings totaling ~ 10 tons for a total of 660 tons which was a substantial order to say the least. The order was placed by one of Esco Corporation's good dredging customers in Belgium and was largely due to the dogged efforts of another Esco Corporation employee: Wil Hulst of Holland, who had been technical sales manager for many years serving the global dredging industry for Esco Corporation-designed products. Wil convinced the customer that with SCW's demonstrated capabilities and quality, we were competent to supply the castings to the required quality at a very competitive price. This type and quality of castings for export business had never before been supplied from China.

This was a multimillion dollar order and the specifications were extremely demanding for SCW. The order was for a brand-new design and was at the time the largest-diameter product designed for this industry. The job would also entail high-specification machining operations, which would have to be performed by outside suppliers.

We decided that we would need to hire a machining expert not only to search for qualified suppliers but also to educate us in the necessary casting dimensions prior to the machining operations. Percy interviewed and hired James Wu, an English-speaking Chinese from Xi'An, a city famous for the Terra Cotta Warriors in the province next to Shanxi. James had previously worked for both GE and Caterpillar in China. He also took the position of purchasing manager vacated by Wei Yu.

James was tasked with purchasing higher-quality materials in order to make the high-quality castings for this order. This was especially true for the steel scrap requirements we needed. The local scrap supply was always suspect in quality and purity, and we needed to find a supplier that could provide clean scrap of known analysis and quality. James Wu identified a large steel plant that had good documented scrap available and was located in Han Dan, a city of one million people about four and a half hours towards Beijing along the expressway.

Almost all dealings with SOE companies were done through middlemen. James contacted the appropriate people and they arranged to pick us up in Taiyuan and drive us to the plant to inspect the scrap. It was June and the temperature was at its usual high of about 35°C. At 7 a.m., the two middlemen picked us up at my hotel in a brand-new VW Passat and we drove the expressway to the Han Dan cutoff and arrived at the steel plant without incident about five hours later. We inspected the scrap, which consisted of crop ends from angles, channels, rounds, and heavy plate from the rolling mills: all segregated into alloy categories. We estimated there was at least 500,000 tons of good scrap potentially available. An unexpected treasure!!

On the return journey to Taiyuan we again were in the uphill portion of the expressway and it was even hotter outside. Not to worry … we had a modern vehicle with powerful air conditioning! At the 75 km marker from Taiyuan, the oil pressure indicator suddenly dropped to zero. The owner pulled over to the side, stopped and discovered all the oil had leaked from the oil pan due to loosening of the oil pan bolts. The driver called for roadside assistance and was told it would be three hours for it to arrive. Just my luck again!

I noticed that the next exit was 3 km up the road, called Percy on my cell phone, and asked him to meet us at the small village that would surely be located near the tollbooths. He said he could be there in about two hours. I then told James we would walk the 3 km to the exit and onto the tollbooths.

"It is too far and too hot," he exclaimed.

I replied, "You are a young man of 37 years and I'm an older man of 62 – if I can do it surely you can!"

Off we went with much grumbling on his part. We arrived at the village about 40 minutes later, where again I was a novelty. These villagers had never seen a foreigner before either. Through James, they asked many questions. Many wanted to put their hands on me, but resorted to peering closely into my face and round eyes. They were very kind and offered several different refreshments and food stuffs, which I refused. Percy arrived about an hour later to fetch us, and we arrived back in Taiyuan without further incident. And I added another Chinese roadside adventure to my roster of stories.

I had evidence of China's rapid growth right in front of me at the Shanxi Grand. By 2002 there was a significant increase in the number of expats residing in the hotel – especially Europeans, but also a number of Americans and Canadians. There were a number of massive projects taking place at the time in Shanxi and Taiyuan. One of the major stainless steel producers in China, a SOE of some 25,000 employees, was entering into a $300 million capital improvement program. Consequently, many of the major world contractors were involved and set up residency in the hotel. People from Germany, Italy, Austria, England, France, and many other countries, including Japan and India, were involved in these capital projects.

As this was a typical SOE with poor management, much of the needed work in the initial stages simply did not get done. It was very frustrating for the foreigners who suffered through endless meetings and then saw progress go nowhere. I could relate! When the original completion dates were over a year late, the SOE management finally woke up and started to help make things happen. The result was a 24/7 work schedule for all the expats. Two busses with about 45 expats would leave the hotel each morning at 7 and return at 7 p.m. Another two busses would leave at 7 p.m. and return at 7 a.m. What a cost! It was also frustrating for the foreign companies when it came to collecting money for their respective work. Over time I had the opportunity to meet and become friends with many of these people. I enjoyed the ever-lively atmosphere at the Shanxi Grand with this influx of interesting people.

———————

By mid-year we had attained our ISO 9001 quality certification. However, we were struggling with the scheduling and production of the dredging order, especially in the area of developing capable and reliable machine shops to perform this high-specification work. It turns out that James Wu was not the expert in this area that he was purported to be! James was fired shortly thereafter.

We were now operating at a rate of 17 T/D, but it was still below our prospectus. Inquiries for new business, both export and domestic, were being received on an ever-increasing basis, with many requiring development of procedures for the production of new alloys unfamiliar to the SCW employees. This in turn entailed more efforts on my part for education and training of the personnel.

The fourth quarter of 2002 proved to be the turning point for the JV, as the operation finally began to make a profit! Our hard work was paying off. The forecast for production demands in 2003 was for a healthy 50 percent increase to 25.5 T/D.

It was also during my latest tour that I began to read and hear in the media about an outbreak of what was termed "atypical pneumonia" in Guangzhou and Hong Kong. All news reports were optimistic; generally stating the situation was well under control.

When I returned home in late November, I had spent another 220 days in China!

Year 2003 began with me again supposedly on an 80 percent work schedule, so theoretically I would be spending less time in China than I had in earlier years. Events beyond my control also kept me away.

During a trip to Taiyuan at the beginning of 2003, I continued to hear from the media about the ongoing "atypical pneumonia" in the south of China, which was, apparently, still under control. On my second trip of that year, in March, the "atypical pneumonia" although spreading, was still determined by the Chinese Government to be under control. Whether or not I believed the reports, I was not very concerned, as the problem was far away from where I was working.

Two weeks after journeying in mid-April to our vacation home – on a five-acre beachfront site on Quadra Island in British Columbia – the world press declared the "atypical pneumonia" was now termed SARS. China was embarrassed on the world stage and heads would ultimately roll. The initial action in China was to create quarantine zones and special hospitals to deal with this now-deadly disease. The outbreak was not confined to China, but had spread to other parts of the world including Vancouver and Toronto in Canada. Fear engulfed people around the world due to the unknown causes and high death rates associated with this disease.

Fifteen days after my return to Canada, Cherie and I stopped at one of the local coffee shops: when I paid and tipped with U.S. dollars, the owner asked me where I was from. I told her I worked in China in Taiyuan and had returned 15 days earlier. She quickly backed away from me as if I had the plague: the newspaper headline on the bar counter read, "SARS hits Taiyuan in Shanxi Province of central China." Until this news, nobody on Quadra Island other than close friends had ever heard of Taiyuan.

I was due to return to China for my next trip in mid-May, but Percy and the SCW managers had been locking up or quarantining themselves in the plant. They and the employees would go to work each day, sterilize all the facilities, work, eat their brought-from-home food, and go directly home after they were done. I told Percy that I was willing to risk the trip but he said not only did they fear for my health but that I may bring the disease to them via Beijing. I accordingly delayed my trip.

While banned by the SCW team from visiting China, I kept close watch on the SARS news. By the first week of June, new cases had dropped significantly and I figured that it would be essentially over by the second week. I decided to leave for China on June 9, and arrived in Beijing on the afternoon of June 10. Apparently this was the day that China announced the SARS threat was under control. Upon arrival, we were surrounded by health professionals wearing gowns, gloves, and masks, requiring health data sheets, and taking temperatures of all arrivals. I passed the test, but as there were no flights to Taiyuan that day due to the not-yet-lifted travel restrictions, I proceeded to the LiDo for the evening. I was greeted at the entrance with more gowned, gloved, and masked health professionals demanding to take my temperature before allowing entrance to the hotel. This treatment had quite an effect on businesses; the LiDo was reduced to an occupancy rate of 15 percent. When I arrived in Taiyuan the next day, we were again subjected to temperature testing at the airport. Apparently if any one of the passengers had a high temperature, the whole planeload would have been subject to quarantine in the Bingjou hotel (which was old and rated only two stars). We all passed and I proceeded to the Shanxi Grand, which was almost empty. Taiyuan was something of a ghost town – almost all restaurants and businesses in the city remained closed.

During my absence, China had instituted draconian measures to control SARS. The main areas affected by the outbreak were Hong Kong, Guangzhou, Beijing, and Taiyuan. Special hospitals were set up in these cities to quarantine suspected victims of the disease, whole school districts and universities were closed, restaurants were closed, and even some entire districts in each city were closed to outsiders. Since China had lost face on the world stage by initially "hiding" the seriousness of the SARS outbreak, the incident rattled the government at high levels: many officials were found wanting, and at the very least removed from their lofty positions. At worst, they received severe prison terms.

SCW operations were certainly affected by SARS, as I mentioned earlier. Taiyuan had been designated as a SARS area and as such there was reluctance on the part of suppliers to deliver to the plant. Percy had to organize a drop-off system wherein the supplier would drop off the shipment outside the city and a city truck would then pick it up. The same situation occurred with our finished product deliveries to our customers, only in reverse. From the time of China's official recognition of SARS until the lifting of the alert, SCW was closed to all outside visitors and technical help.

———

Though the SARS epidemic had the biggest impact on business in 2003, SCW was also weathering changes in its management team. In January Annie Chen, our finance leader, had announced that she would be leaving to marry her fiancée in Beijing. Annie was a valued member of the Esco Corporation team and was difficult to replace. However, a local Taiyuan lady (Julia Fan) proved to be the best candidate for the position: she had top financial experience in a foreign firm, her English was excellent, and she and her family were from Taiyuan. Another native! Julia was offered, and accepted, the job of DGM Finance. Also at the beginning of the year, Phillip Liu had announced he would be leaving SCW to pursue other opportunities, leaving the DGM sales position vacant. The SCW management team now consisted of Percy as GM, Julia Fan as finance DGM, Liu Min as plant engineer, and Francis Liu as Q/A and technical manager. The balance of the team consisted of the two TZ nominees: Zhang Ying Tao and Luo. Zhang was becoming a valuable asset to the operations, while Luo's contributions were more minor; he preferred to play politics.

Soon, though, we experienced more shifts in personnel. Percy Chang had now been immersed in the SCW operation for a full five years and our original agreement was to move him along after that time period. Accordingly, in the second quarter, SCW was now seeking replacements both for the GM and DGM sales positions. We employed a headhunter to identify candidates for both positions.

In the meantime Wei Yu was in the last stages of her graduate degree in commercial law at Shanghai University. I had kept in contact with her over the past year and half. I suggested that although she lacked the experience for general management, her drive and intelligence could allow her to achieve at SCW. In short, I felt I could work with her and develop her into a first-class general manager. In March, Cherie and I traveled to Shanghai to meet with Wei Yu to see if she was interested in returning to SCW. We hosted her and her husband Mark for dinner at TGI Friday's. Mark is quite a catch: he is well educated, tall (at six feet one inch), good-looking, and his English is very good; however, I was surprised, watching him fumble with the knife and fork, that he was less than sophisticated in the use of Western utensils. They are a happily married couple and well adjusted but Wei Yu claimed that Mark was lazy and that she was pushing him to further his education by taking an MBA at Shanghai University after she graduated. One month later Wei Yu graduated with a master's degree in commercial law and the top marks in the class, despite being the only non-lawyer in the group.

Figure 4 Mark Wong, the author and Wei Yu (Shanghai 2003)

After Wei Yu expressed interest in returning, I presented the case to Mark Mallory and Percy, both of whom had been impressed with her earlier performance while at SCW. They did express concern at her lack of experience, but were willing to interview her, especially when I offered to spend another two years working with her on developing management skills if she was the successful candidate. Percy also said he would stay on in transition for a further six months. As part of the hiring process, Steve Pratt, Esco Corporation's CEO, met Wei Yu in Shanghai. It must have been quite a sight: Steve at six feet four inches tall and Wei Yu standing "tall" at five feet one inch. In short, she duly impressed Steve and other Esco executives. When I interviewed Wei Yu, I asked her what her and Mark's intentions were regarding children. (This question could not have been asked in any other Esco operation in the world.)

She stood up and replied, "I am 30 years old, very strong, and we will have our child when I am 36 years old!"

We offered her the job in mid-March, which she would start immediately upon graduation in April. We now had three members of the Esco Corporation team whose family roots were in Taiyuan. Next up: finding a candidate for the DGM sales position. Although no one that we interviewed was a local, He Meng Lin was selected as the most suitable. Percy always found it necessary to help us Westerners with Chinese pronunciation, and in the case of Mr. He, Percy said "not a he but a her." Meng Lin had work experience with two foreign companies both selling manganese steel crushing products and at the same time both competitors and customers of SCW. I knew *meng* as one of the tones in Chinese, which meant *manganese*, and Mr. He (her) forever became known as "Mr. Manganese"!

By spring, Wei Yu and Mr. Manganese were on board. Despite the impact of the SARS epidemic, raw material and alloy prices continued to rise at an alarming rate, and business opportunities continued to increase. Early in 2002, we had locked into some long-term contracts with OEM companies in China, the U.S., and Canada. With the dramatic price increase in raw materials, we found it necessary to revisit each contract and try to negotiate price increases. With Percy's help, this was to be Wei Yu's initiation to the new job – go out and obtain significant price increases. Over the ensuing months, she was extremely successful in attaining the required amounts. She also was able to initiate policy that ensured all new business would be quoted at reasonable profit margins, taking into account all cost factors including tariffs, duties and logistic costs.

During the years 1998–2002, we had been able to build a business from essentially nothing to a point where SCW was recognized as the best steel foundry in China for capability and quality. This situation was achieved through a determined effort on behalf of Esco Corporation to bring our worldwide expertise in steel technology and manufacturing to the SCW operation. We had progressively introduced new alloys, new procedures, new tools, and recommissioned inactive equipment and buildings on as-needed basis. Since during all of that time (1998–2002) we were not yet profitable, we were cash short, and out of necessity we concentrated on only critical items such as safety, quality, housekeeping, and productivity improvements. Virtually every visitor, whether Chinese or other customers from the developed countries, expressed surprise at the cleanliness and apparent productivity of the SCW operation, "the cleanest foundry in China." With the exception of our clean toilet, employee shower, and change-room facilities, we did very little to improve the exterior of the brick buildings or replace the numerous broken or missing windows in all the buildings, which were built circa 1960.

But since we were now in an ongoing profitable situation and were now able to accumulate cash, we embarked on a three-year capital spending program. This spending would include upgrading buildings and facilities, purchasing and replacing some of the older equipment with modern new equipment that had state-of-the-art control systems, and computers to run the modern business required by our global network. In addition, I renewed efforts to develop seminars for education and training in all facets of the business: steel metallurgy, modern electric furnace melting, molding and core making processes, heat treating, welding and casting processing, inspection and quality assurance, and basic business management practices. By mid-2003 I had spent some 150 hours developing the suitable material for presentation and over the next two years would spend some 200 hours of in the classroom instructing groups of 15–100 people. Some sessions were two hours long, while most were either one- or two-day seminars run on weekends, complete with examinations. Francis and Wei Yu were now my main translators.

We were starting to get pressure (no pun intended) from Har Bin Valve Company, a domestic company that manufactured high-pressure and temperature valve bodies for the China power market. We had been a supplier of their lower-pressure carbon steel requirements since 2000. At that time they also requested we quote on a much higher pressure and temperature specification valve requiring a very-difficult-to-manufacture martensitic stainless steel alloy. Har Bin had tried five other suppliers to provide these castings and all had failed miserably. Esco Corporation had successfully produced this alloy composition in the past and had well-developed procedures and processes for the production of this product. Earlier, in 2000, I deemed that SCW was not nearly ready to take on this challenge. But times had changed.

It was now mid-2003, and we were successfully producing and delivering the large ball joint order for the dredging customer in Belgium to the required quality specifications. I was convinced that with Esco Corporation's expertise and the current status of capability at SCW, we could undertake this latest challenge. To even consider the successful production of this alloy required the recommissioning of another piece of production equipment idled since the start of the JV: the AOD process. Again I was able to call on one of our specialists, Chris Oldfather, to develop the operating procedure for the alloy and come to SCW to help me in the training process. Chris, although a metallurgist is a down-to-earth (again, no pun intended) person and has developed great rapport with operation personnel around the world. He was well received not only on this visit but also on subsequent visits. Although Chris had been to Japan on numerous occasions, he had never been to China. On this his first trip, he was arriving from

Japan. When he arrived in Beijing he had about a four-hour wait for his next flight, and decided to order dinner at the Beijing airport. Unaware of the difference in the two Asian cultures, he ordered five courses – and to his great surprise found that each course was a full meal, so he was overwhelmed with food.

After bringing the equipment up to operating standards and finishing the necessary training of the crews, we accepted an order for one trial valve body. Needless to say the first attempt was a success. We continue to the present to do much business with this customer and remain the only successful supplier of this alloy.

Since our success with the manufacture and delivery of a significant portion of the 1,000 mm ball joints, we began to receive inquiries and orders from other international dredge companies for similar castings of slightly smaller dimensions. We were now getting really busy in all aspects of the business.

By the fourth quarter of 2003, the management team of SCW included Wei Yu as GM; Julia Fan as DGM for finance; He Meng Lin as DGM for sales; and Liu Yu Feng as Technical and Q/A manager. With the exception of He Meng Lin, we now had a top management team of people who grew up with their families in Taiyuan and really wanted to have their careers in this area. Meanwhile, Percy and Liu Min had moved on to Shanghai to begin planning for a wholly Esco owned green field foundry operation. This endeavor was based on the success of our JV operation in China. Honoring my commitment to continue in China to help counsel and educate Wei Yu in sound general management principles, in October, I had announced that I would continue, with Cherie's permission, for another two years – but on a reduced time involvement. I also resigned from the SCW board of directors and recommended that Percy replace me. The SCW board now constituted of the following Esco Corporation employees: Mark as chairman, Percy, and Ray Verlinich. Mr. Gao, the CEO of TZ, continued as the vice chairman and Mr. Du of TZ continued as a member. Zhang Ying Tao and Mr. Luo continued as TZ-nominated members of the management team.

In November, Wei Yu asked me if I would be willing to speak with representatives of a local newspaper. They apparently wanted to interview a foreigner who was spending so much time in Taiyuan, which was a great honor for me. Unfortunately, the Chinese version cannot be displayed as permission was denied by the editor-in chief to use the article. The paper is controlled by the communist party and is a further example of Chinese beaurocracy and failure to make a decision without consent from the very top. The English translation appears in the appendix at the end of the book.

During the year, we continued to hire local graduates with English-speaking skills both in our sales department and in the plant technical areas. Most of these new people became my protégées.

Late in 2002, we had sold our large house in Portland and moved into a 900-square-foot rental apartment about two blocks away. During 2003, I had occasion to spend only a total of 13 days in the apartment, a result of my long stays in China coupled with the off-time essentially spent on Quadra Island. Cherie and I decided that the apartment was unnecessary: I moved into a postal box in Portland and Cherie moved back to Canada as a permanent resident.

Completing my assignment for 2003, I returned to Quadra Island the last week in November after a total time in China for the year of 190 days. The next year was supposed to be different, with my new contract calling for less time spent in China, but continuing while at "home" via communications networks. Year 2004 was shaping up to be an even busier year with the forecast for a further increase of 28 percent in production volume, to 33 T/D. I believed with the previous and continuing improvements in all facets of the SCW operation, we could handle the increased volume. We would see.

My new contract stated that my work days on the job in China would be a nominal 120 days per year. To provide continuity, this would require five trips per year with each trip lasting about 35 days in total door-to-door time. In addition, during my off-China time, I was required to maintain the usual communications with SCW and other global Esco Corporation operations.

Because of our hard-earned reputation we were now receiving so many inquiries for new business that we were developing a bottleneck in processing and providing timely feedback to our customers. Additionally, when we were successful in receiving an order, our communications process was proving too inefficient, and there were many delays in getting the information back to the customer. To improve the follow-through in these two areas, we decided to form a team of cross-functional experts from selected parts of Esco's global operations and bring them to SCW for a two-week intensive education and training session with critical SCW personnel.

The global team was formed, created the required training material, arrived in SCW in late January, and, being experts in efficiency, finished their mission two weeks later. Some improvements in performance resulted, but Chinese culture being what it was, no orders of any magnitude or improvement occurred.

Also in January, Mr. Manganese decided to leave, as he felt that he had better opportunities elsewhere. His chances for success and happiness there had been slim all along: he was not from the local area, had not moved his family there, and did not like the living conditions in Taiyuan compared to Beijing or Shanghai. With some resistance from Mark and Percy, Wei Yu decided that she would not replace this position. She felt that between her own personal drive and the elevation of two of our more senior inside sales to assistants, she would be able to serve the various markets in a professional manner. We decided to give her the chance to prove it.

The year progressed, and in March, Cherie once again came to China for a visit. Her usual habit was to spend time visiting a local middle school, where she had become adored for her work with various classes helping the students to be more confident and competent in conversational English. She also would come to SCW and hold lunchtime classes for different groups of our now-growing number of English speakers. Our two new technical hires, a young man and woman from the local university, participated in one of the classes; in the matter of encouraging conversation, Cherie asked the young man, "Do have a girlfriend?" After a moment of embarrassed thought he answered, "Yes!! But it is a secret, or in Chinese, *mimi*."

Both of these young people were from villages where their parents did not have knowledge of their activities while they were away from home. They subsequently moved in together in Taiyuan. This was a new trend in China! (In January 2007 the pair tied the knot, and I attended one of their receptions for their SCW coworkers.)

Early on, it was clear that 2004 was developing into a very busy year with the planning for, ordering, and installation of new world-class equipment, continued improvements in our facilities, and of course, increased education and training of employees both through the seminars and on the job. SCW could pride itself on its excellent management team and well-trained, responsive workforce with equipment, facilities, and processes that were rapidly becoming world-class. SCW continued to be recognized as the best foundry in China; however, competitors were learning and beginning to make rapid improvements in their operations. At SCW, we stressed the need for ongoing and continuous improvement in all facets of operations. The slogan "It's not how fast we run, but how much faster than the competition we run that is important" became our battle cry. We talked the talk and walked the walk!

In mid-year, Esco Corporation was enjoying increased business in its global facilities, especially for its patented proprietary products. There was a recognized need for increased production to serve the growing markets. The newly planned foundry near Shanghai would not be ready for start-up until late 2006. SCW had the capacity, but had not considered the production of this different line of proprietary products. Again we had an idled facility that would have to be quickly recommissioned and modernized to meet the new production demands. This project would entail much time and effort from the resources at SCW. Plans were to be in production by mid-2005.

With five trips spaced over the year, time seemed to blow by, and during my last trip in October, my assessment of 2004 showed the following: continued improvements in quality, productivity, delivery performance, and profitability; raw-material price increases continued but were offset by an aggressive pricing policy; installation and start-up of new modern equipment; increased employee participation and input into the decision-making process; and an increase in business volume. Production volume averaged 33 T/D and the forecast for 2005 was for a 40 percent increase to 46 T/D. If we did that, we would exceed one of the goals laid out when we first began the joint venture: 40 T/D. On another front, I had not quite hit my mark: even though I was only contracted for 120 days, I had spent 170 in China that year. Where did the time go?

I arrived in Taiyuan on February 4, 2005, for a 36-day tour. The plant was extremely busy and I plunged into my usual routines: seminars, procedures, modern equipment installation and training, etc. The future for our business was looking up. I was also spending increased time coaching and counseling Wei Yu in the business process. Luckily she believed in my merits as much as I did hers; she referred to me as "the best customer relations asset that SCW could have." Her strategy was for me to meet with virtually every customer, whether new or repeat, and present an overview of our operations from a Western point of view. In addition, Wei Yu used my experience to impress key customers, especially in the domestic market. Apparently, the presence of an American on the premises guaranteed good quality to these customers! Additionally, Wei Yu, sales people and me visited many customers in different parts of the country.

With the ever-increasing demand, we now saw that SCW would need to ramp up from our original goal, what now seemed a nominal capacity at 40 T/D, to 70 T/D. Due to power and heat treat gas shortages, the plant was having difficulty meeting its customer delivery requirements. To improve the situation, creative scheduling was the order of the day. Heat treating capacity could be expanded by working Saturdays and Sundays. Melting power, although technically only available on the night shift, was sometimes available for short periods of variable times on day shift. To take advantage of the possibility of producing an extra 13 tons a day three times a week, we had a standby crew at all times on the day shift.

My three-year contract would expire on my 65th birthday, on March 15, 2005. This was also to coincide with my retirement. True to my plan, I duly retired on this day, signed all the necessary paperwork to collect my various pensions – then immediately arranged to be rehired 45 days later in a new role. I was now a technical consultant for foundry operations. This change from Vice President to advisor was a big role change for me. I would work on a half-time basis – essentially one month on, one month off. This annual contract would still, however, require between 160–170 days in China during the year. If the work was still interesting to me and Cherie accepted my working (and still being away so much), I would continue on a year-to-year basis.

Yet I would not return to SCW until the first week in June, due in part to the imposed 45-day retirement, and pressing duties on Quadra Island for the first weekend in June. Cherie is a glassblower and the first weekend in June on the island is an annual studio tour; I needed to help her get ready, as her studio was a highlight of the tour, which attracted 500–600 visitors over the course of the two-day event. It takes a lot of effort, and this was a chance for me to help Cherie with her work.

I planned my trip to China for June 7, with the return home planned for July 14. I arrived after this rare three-month absence, and immediately immersed myself in the operations. We were now in the start-up phase of production for the proprietary products for Esco Corporation. Engineering design and tooling for this product was all done by CAD in our Portland headquarters. Next, all data was digitized and downloaded to sophisticated machine shops to create the necessary patterns and core boxes for the manufacturing process. All tooling was then measured on a digital, computerized multi-axis coordinate measuring machine (CMM) to determine accuracy. The tooling next would typically be sent to the producing plant, where trial castings would be made to check out both the tooling and process control. In short, tooling was developed, sent to SCW for trials, castings produced, and sent back to Portland for measurement. Normally the first time through the trials would be successful, but occasionally, tweaking would have to be done to achieve the desired dimensionality.

To help with the start-up at SCW, we encouraged the Esco design engineer, Bill Blakely, to bring his expertise to China. Bill not only works in design but also is a hands-on member of the team in the production area. Bill is another "people person" and he is well accepted by all the people he works with at SCW.

Both 2005 and 2006 continued to show excellent progress towards achieving a world-class operation at SCW. We were now known worldwide as a supplier of quality castings both for export and for the domestic Chinese markets. And, importantly, SCW remained profitable on a consistent basis. We were still struggling to obtain high-quality, certifiable raw materials for our processes and were still plagued with both power shortages and heat treat gas shortages. But these were expected to be remedied by mid-year 2007, since China expected to have adequate power and gas by that time.

In the winter of 2006 Wei Yu informed me that she and her husband Mark had decided that she should have their child sooner rather than later. Cherie had earlier said that she figured Wei Yu would do something like this to ensure I stay longer at SCW than my intended time frame! (I would have to be there while she had her 3–4 months maternity leave.) I informed Wei Yu that it is not always easy to plan such an event; in response she stood up and said, "I and Mark are strong and healthy and it will happen!" At the time of my writing it has not yet happened – and I am still in harness to SCW!

I have learned much about doing business in China. One thing was clear: we as a JV will always have to operate under stricter rules than do the SOEs. For example, SCW is held to higher standards regarding safety and environmental standards. We are also required by law to pay workers 20 percent higher wages than the equivalent jobs at the SOEs. So far this has not been a problem, as we also have incentive systems and our workers are significantly better trained and more productive than their counterparts in the SOEs. Finally, SCW has also been required to pass many levels of regulation in obtaining permits for importing critical supplies and materials; this is time-consuming and inhibits our ability to act quickly. During the early, cash-poor years we found it virtually impossible to borrow "cash flow money" in China.

But we have worked hard at making do with these impediments, and have always kept moving forward. One very happy result: the new Esco Corporation foundry in Xuzhou near Shanghai poured its first steel in late December 2006. And although more training and education and debugging continues, the operation is up and running. I was gratified when the SCW melting Supervisor was invited to spend one month at Xuzhou in mid-2007 to train the new crews in metallurgy and melting practiced. He used all the training I had inured in him and was very effective in the transfer of knowledge since his presentation was done in Chinese. All my training and education efforts over the years were being passed on!

So ends the saga of building a viable business from scratch in China! Over the past ten years I have experienced both highs and lows, with the highs thankfully outnumbering the lows. I have learned much personally, including how to be a patient person! And I am proud to note that impressive progress and results at SCW have allowed the operation to produce castings in a safe and environmentally clean facility to world-class standards. SCW continues to grow, going into 2008 with an output of 45 T/D.

Of course, there are still challenges. The management remains somewhat weak in the areas of planning, prioritizing, executing, and controlling of major events and capital projects – resulting in significant delays in getting such projects up and running. Perhaps this failing results from the Chinese culture, where, as I mentioned earlier, "thinking out of the box" is relatively unknown or practiced. The Chinese in general are great copycats, but poor innovators.

I am continuing in my current role as technical consultant at least through January 31, 2009, and will continue working on these hurdles. In retrospect, Esco Corporation has accorded me an opportunity of a lifetime in my continuing employment post-"retirement." It is a great way to "go out gently" while continuing to contribute to the successes of our Chinese operations.

PART II: ESTABLISHING PERSONAL RELATIONSHIPS

Chapter XI: Kids and Families

Beginning in the fourth quarter of 1998, I began to meet some local Taiyuan children, and subsequently their families. In addition, through my business dealings and visiting customers, by traveling throughout China, and from my long-term residence at the Shanxi Grand Hotel, I enjoyed various opportunities to meet a wide cross-section of Chinese people.

Overall, I have found that the Chinese people are invariably friendly, inquisitive, and enjoy a good time. They show an eagerness to engage foreigners in conversation, and enjoy large and noisy gatherings – especially at lunch and dinner with large extended family groups and friends. Over the course of the past ten years, I have made numerous friends while in China and both Cherie and I have been invited many times to their homes, especially on festive occasions to participate in meals with their extended families. This alone has certainly made my experience here much more personal, and interesting, than that of just a businessman setting up shop. I thank my friends deeply for that and hope I have managed to sufficiently represent and honor them in the ensuing chapters.

———

Although Esco Corporation had purchased three apartments in the city, and I was offered one as my residence, I opted to stay in the hotel – as it was both more central to the center of the city and closer to SCW, and it was a hub for Western culture. At the Shanxi Grand, I would have the opportunity to meet others of my ilk during my long stays.

What I didn't initially anticipate is that hotel life would connect me with so many interesting locals, particularly children. Perhaps the first child I met was Simon, when he introduced himself to me that Saturday back in October 1998, in the hotel lobby, presenting me with his card and asking me if I would speak English with him. When I agreed to talk to Simon, he had asked for my business card, which he immediately put into a card holder containing perhaps 150 other foreigners' business cards. At the time, I had no idea I was going to develop a long-term relationship with Simon and his family. I also had no inkling that I would get involved with so many more kids and their families through my relationship with Simon.

Simon's father (Wang Zhi Meng) is an entrepreneur who owns several small businesses, while his mother is a doctor of traditional Chinese medicine. As such, they are a relatively well-off family by Chinese standards. Neither parent speaks English. The family is able to afford more than one apartment, has a modern car, and can pay for Simon's instruction at the best schools as well as special English-language training classes. I find it interesting that in a Communist society, people still pay extra for the best schools.

After our initial introduction and talks, Simon would come to the hotel almost every Saturday and most Sundays to see if I had time for him. He was such a charmer that rarely did I refuse him the time! Initially he was very inquisitive about what I was doing in China and what my thoughts about China were. However, I had a little problem finding out from him what his parents did in China. As time went on and he became more fluent in English, we would get into deeper conversational topics. During each trip, he would ask how long my intended stay would be and when my next return trip was scheduled.

One Saturday evening in the spring of 1999, Simon asked if I would go to "English corner" with him and meet his headmaster from the special language school and some of his friends.

"English corner?" I asked, puzzled. "What's that?"

He replied, "That's where we go to meet other people and practice our English."

Although somewhat reticent, I agreed to go with him and his father, who drove us down Yingze St. to a large square in the center of town. It was about 8 p.m. on a pleasant evening. When we arrived at the square I was amazed to see an extremely large crowd of kids – ranging from about six years old to late teens, with adults accompanying the younger ones. I looked around and did not see any other foreigner in the whole square. Uh-oh, it was all up to me. Indeed, I was soon swarmed: I felt like a honeycomb surrounded by bees!

I soon found myself seated on a cement bench with at least 60 kids facing me and peppering me with questions: "Do you like Chinese?" "Where are you from?" "Do you like China?" "Do you like Chinese food?" "Do you ...?" Each kid asked the same questions, one after another. It was as if none of them heard what the others had asked, or my answers. All their questions were of an objective nature. I asked a group of the older teenagers what they thought of Mao and the Cultural Revolution. In chorus they replied "We do not care about that, we just want to be rich like you." I replied "Why do think I am rich?" They said "because you are from America."

During this first time at the corner, I met two of Simon's best friends: two girls about two years older than him and two grades ahead. Apparently, they had all met in the special language school on Saturdays. Although he was younger and considerably shorter than the girls, they both considered Simon a "cool cat." (By the time Simon was an older teen, however, he had grown taller than the girls, and was a handsome, charming, and polite young man.) The girls' names were Han, Ting Ting (Jane) and Li, Xin (Gaylene). I was to subsequently develop a much closer relationship with these two and their families as well.

Figure 5 Kids and John at English Corner

After about two hours of constant questions and answers at English corner, I was exhausted, and we prepared to leave the scene – which was still growing with more and more kids arriving at the square. As we were leaving, Simon introduced me to the headmaster of his special language school. Amazingly, his spoken English was so poor that I could barely understand him – hence the reason Simon's parents supported his learning efforts so much and took him to the Shanxi Grand to practice spoken English.

Figure 6 John at English Corner

Figure 7 Cherie at English Corner

I had subsequent visits to the English corner, sometimes with Simon and both the girls and sometimes only with Ting Ting (Jane). Cherie has visited the corner on occasion and I have also taken colleagues to experience the corner. One evening, I took Randy. The usual swarming took place, and we were led to separate concrete benches about 30 feet apart. We could not see each other – we were that engulfed by eager children – but on occasion we could hear each other. We lasted about an hour before our heads were buzzing from the incessant questions. How determined these children were. On another occasion in 2004, the 3 kids and I took Ed and Addy Perkins (my cousin's teenaged sons from Canada) to the corner. They were great hits especially Addy with his long hair.

My last visit to the corner was in the summer of 2006. I noticed in particular that the newer kids had greatly improved English skills – indicative of improved teaching standards. Since I first started traveling there in the late 1990s, China had begun to allow many more foreign English teachers into the country.

———

The first week of October is a National Holiday in China celebrating the formation of the People's Republic of China

(PRC). Almost all business and banks shut down for the week. I was in Taiyuan during this time in year 2000, but the plant was shut down, so I was essentially idle.

This holiday week is typically a time for visiting family in China. Both of Simon's parents came from the same village (Wen Shui), about 70 km from Taiyuan, and they were planning a trip there. The family invited me to accompany them to visit the village and meet their families. We left the morning of October 2, driving the 1.5 hours on a two-lane country road and arriving at the village around 10 a.m. We entered the village through a gate on a muddy road. Wen Shui is a farming village where they grow mainly corn and giant sunflowers. The major portion of the acreage is communal but each resident is allowed to farm a small portion for profit.

In China, it is customary for married women to keep their family name, although all children retain the husband's family name. In the case of Simon's family, both parents have the same family name (Wang), although the families were not (at least before their marriage) related! This can be a rather common experience, as there are relatively few family names in China, for a country of 1.3 billion people. Simon's mother's family lived in a compound right across the muddy road from his paternal relatives' compound. When I visited, each compound consisted of a courtyard with date/nut trees, a small vegetable garden, and a series of individual, small one-story rooms. Unlike Western-style homes, these rooms were not connected by doorways. Each room was entered/exited through one outside open doorway, hung with a heavy quilt to cut down on drafts. Heating was supplied by small pots burning coke cubes, thereby necessitating the open doorways. Coke, which is made from coal, is readily available in China and is used for both cooking and heating. Because of this, China experiences many deaths each year from carbon monoxide poisoning. In the case of both Wang families, who were supported by Simon's parents, each extended family member had his/her individual room. Simon's parents had provided each compound with a clothes-washing machine, as well as bottled water on a weekly basis. These luxuries boosted both families into the upper echelon of the village.

The courtyard in Wang, Zhi Meng's family area had a communal cooking area, and very close by was an outdoor toilet facility: in this case it was quite clean and emitted no smells. The cooking area was about eight feet by ten feet and included a wooden chopping board built into a small table, one cold water tap from a well, and a small stove fired by coke. As water is in short supply in China, there was a large wooden barrel full of well water that was used to rinse vegetables and fruit as they were being prepared.

Accompanied by Simon, I was led from room to room in his father's family's compound to meet each inhabitant: Simon's aunts, uncles, cousins, grandmother and grandfather – and even his great-granny, who was 85 years old. In this village, I believe Simon was the only person that could speak English – and he was only nine years old at the time. Thus, he was my only link to the outside world! When we entered his great-granny's room, she was wearing a head scarf and sitting on her bed which, other than one small table and chair, was the most prominent piece in the room. No other furnishings were in the room. She was smoking and flicking the ashes on the dirt floor. She was fairly small and very well preserved for her age. I noticed a large number of posters and photos on her walls, all very sexually risqué for China. Simon introduced me, and with his interpretation we talked for about 15 minutes on various subjects. I think she thought I was brought to the village as a special visitor for her. While we talked, she inhaled about 12 cigarettes.

Figure 8 Simon's Great Grandmother's room– risqué pictures!

After visiting and talking to all residents in this compound, Simon led me to his mother's family home, where we went through a similar routine.

As we were to have a large lunch with Simon's father's family, we went back to their area while the meal was being prepared. I was first led to the kitchen to watch the initial food preparation. Apparently any female relative over the age of 8 years (including great-granny) helps in the preparation.

After a few minutes Simon took me back to the largest room in the complex, where his grandfather and grandmother lived. This was where the lunch would be held. Their room also had a dirt floor, and the doorway had the usual quilt to close off the drafts. The room was furnished with a double bed against one wall, a sofa, and two small wooden chairs against the opposite wall. Between the sofa and the bed was a small round table about four feet in diameter. Three more wooden chairs and three small stools were then placed around the table, which provided elbow-to-elbow seating for eight people!

This was going to be a big celebration: I was the first foreigner to ever set foot in Wen Shui! The various extended family members (aunts, uncles, cousins, etc.) that I had met numbered more than eight, and other guests had been invited, including Simon's maternal grandparents. Only Simon, his mother, father, his grandfather, and I would be seated at the lunch for the duration: all other invitees would be doing shifts. The table was laid out with bottles of the obligatory Chinese white liquor and bottles of cold beer which were essentially for me (the family had been clued in that I prefer beer).

Food was continuously delivered from the kitchen and the first sitting got underway with the five permanent sitters and three others, one of whom was Wang Zhi Meng's brother – who bore a striking resemblance to Wang Zhi Meng. I was to learn that an older brother of theirs had been killed in an auto accident while driving under the influence. With all the white liquor on the table and the inevitable toasts, I informed the party that Simon's father was not allowed to drink as he was my driver for the return trip. Not to lose face, Simon's mother took on the job and handled the toasts for her husband. Many faces turned red as the toasts wore on. About every 15 minutes three guests would leave and be replaced at the table by three new ones – all wanting to know my history and impressions of China. The meal consisted of many different dishes and courses and included various vegetable and meat dishes, vegetable dishes all cooked in a wok. There were also noodles, some fish dishes, nuts, and fruits. Although I had some trepidation regarding the cold dishes (remember the barrel of water for washing the vegetables), the food smelled and tasted excellent – and I did eat the cold dishes with no ill effects.

A little later, a father brought his three-year-old son into the room. The boy was about two-and-a-half feet tall. He had been coached to come in and greet me. I crouched down closer to his level. For a good two minutes, he did nothing but stare at the floor until finally his father got him to look up at me. He said one word – "Hello" – then immediately looked down again. During the 1960s, Mao feared that the U.S. might invade China, and the Communist party line to the villages was that if it happened, the Americans would eat the children! Although this line was not currently preached, apparently in the more remote villages this legend persisted, so this youngster greeting me was a big deal. I had a previous experience where parents tried to get a three-year-old to speak to me, but after seeing me he ran away and hid.

About 2 p.m., most of the family decided it was nap time: time to sleep off the white liquor. Simon's mother patted a position on the bed and said I could sleep there, but I told her that I do not take naps. While the rest of the family slept, Simon and his grandfather took me on a tour of the village outside the compounds. Other villagers would hear of our coming and run to the nearest corner where we would pass to have a good look at "the foreigner"! The corn had been harvested and the cobs placed on every available rooftop for drying, while the sunflowers were in the process of being harvested. Simon's grandfather showed me the communal pond and explained through Simon how all the villagers had worked together to dam up a small stream for irrigation purposes. They were really proud of the accomplishment. Later that day we said our goodbyes to the village, and I thanked Simon's parents for including me in their family gathering.

In addition to the trip to Wen Shui, I had the honor many other times of being invited to Simon's family's house in Taiyuan for meals, especially on Chinese national holidays when most businesses were closed. We had established a close relationship that I valued much during my time in China. There was one event in particular that was very special.

In October 2002, Simon was 11 years old on the Western calendar, but 12 years old by the Chinese calendar. Apparently in certain Chinese Provinces this birthday is extremely important, as it marks the official transition to manhood. As Simon's parents are relatively well-off, they hosted an extremely large party for the occasion. Guests included all his relatives from the village, who were driven by bus to the large restaurant where the party was being held; six of Simon's friends, including Jane and Gaylene, and their parents (all one-child families); Simon's headmaster and some other teachers; some former army officers and policemen (Simon's father, Wang Zhi Meng, had once served in both forces); me; Cherie, who was visiting Taiyuan; and Liu Min. The party was a luncheon affair, and I estimated by the number of tables that there were at least 250 people in attendance. I recognized about 60 or 70 of the attendees from former functions with the family.

The event was celebrated by having a large but lightweight lock called *Chang Min Suo* (long life lock) hung around Simon's neck. As the day wore on, and when all his presents were received, the lock was unlocked. This act is called *Kai Suo* (opening of the lock) and symbolized Simon's moving on to manhood. He still had a boyish streak though – I think his favorite present of all was some Lego bricks!

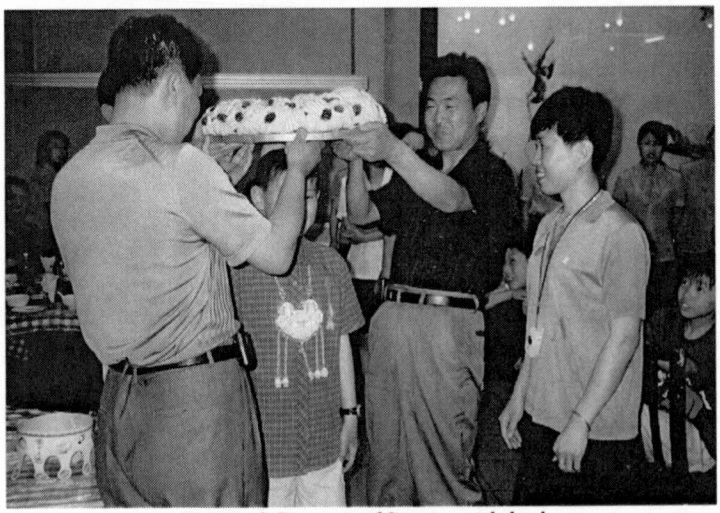

Figure 9 Picture of Simon with lock

Cherie and I were the only non-Chinese-speaking people at the party. We were seated with Liu Min, Jane, Gaylene, and several of Simon's English-speaking school friends at one table. Our table was next to a table of 15 with Wang Zhi Meng's family, including great-granny who kept grinning at me! All the tables were set up with bottles of Coke and Sprite and Chinese liquor. The family had taken great care with the details: my table had only soft drinks for the kids and beer for me, Liu Min, and Cherie. There was a good deal of food, including both cold and hot dishes, fruit, candies, and a large cake for Simon. Liu Min advised Cherie not to partake in the cold foods as most likely they had been prepared hours before and therefore may upset her stomach since she was an occasional visitor to China and her stomach most likely would not be accustomed to potential mild food poisoning.

After lunch was served, Simon gave a 10-minute speech in English followed by a 20-minute speech in Chinese. He then had to bow to all the elders and vow to honor and respect them as he grows up. I also gave a short speech, translated by Liu Min, extolling the virtues of Simon and his family. Even Cherie was obliged to deliver a short speech! Being included in Simon's birthday greatly enhanced my understanding, and enjoyment of, (regional) Chinese culture.

Simon, through our numerous discussions, learned I was an avid fisherman, although it was difficult for him to completely comprehend ocean fishing for salmon and halibut, which is a common activity where I live in the Pacific Northwest. In the fall of 2003 he and his family invited me to accompany them on a fishing trip just outside of Taiyuan. Of course I was game. It was a fine clear early October day. We drove some 50 kilometers to a reservoir of several ponds of stagnant water laid out for fishing. Upon arrival we were met by a retired colonel (reportedly an expert angler) who had been Wang Zhi Meng's superior in the army. Simon's father had thoughtfully brought along several cold cans of beer to quench our thirst while fishing. His mother also provided cold pop and some munchies. The rods we used were about twelve feet in length and very flexible, with no reels. The line was approximately 15 feet in length and led to a float with a further four feet of line that ended with two sets of hooks. We set up our gear in appropriate spots, baited our hooks with corn meal, cast the lines into the water, and intensely watched for a bite. We had many bites – but every time lost the fish. (I thought our bait was too mushy to stay on the hooks.) Still, we kept trying. While we were out there many of the other anglers came around to us to inquire who the foreigner was and offer advice on how to hook the fish. In one instance an older man came to us and asked the family who I was. Apparently he spoke one of the many different Mandarin dialects and Simon could not understand him. We fished for a couple of hours and much to the consternation of our "expert angler" none of us ever kept a fish on the hook. Many of the other anglers were more successful, and Wang Zhi Meng asked one of them for his fish. He wanted to take them to a restaurant and have them cooked up for our lunch. The angler proudly gave up two of his; carp of some sort. Our group then proceeded to a fine restaurant where we were met by four other guests who Simon's father had asked for lunch. Many dishes were served, as usual, including the two fish, which I declined to eat! There was no problem with my not partaking of the fish as most of my friends in China were aware that fish was not one of my favorite foods. In addition there were so many other fine dishes to choose. Simon and his parents on prior and future occasions would attempt to find different ways to keep me entertained. This surely was a different fishing experience for me, but I thoroughly enjoyed the day and the company.

Ting Ting's (Jane) father, Han Guang Ling, is a senior manager in a large SOE pharmaceutical firm in Taiyuan. Her mother, Zhao Xuan, is a homemaker. Mr. Han's father (Jane's grandfather) is a cardiologist and a doctor of traditional Chinese medicine. Jane and her family live in a very nice penthouse apartment while her grandparents (on the father's side) live on a lower floor in the same building. Both Cherie and I have had the pleasure of dining on several occasions with the Hans in their apartment, and on many other occasions with them in some of the excellent restaurants in Taiyuan.

During the traditional Chinese New Year celebration in 2003, the Hans invited me to their apartment to shoot off some fireworks from their roof, which was fun, then we went to Guang Ling's business for the real show. We arrived at the pharmaceutical company, passed through the gate, and parked inside the compound. The complex was immense – it covered a whole city block. Guang Ling led Jane and me into a concrete-block building in which the fireworks were stored. This building was about 20 feet square (6 by 6 meters), with a ceiling perhaps 15 feet high (4.5 meters) – and it was crammed full of assorted fireworks. While inside, I noticed several Chinese smoking cigarettes; I quickly grabbed Jane and her father by the sleeves and exited the place. Many Chinese die each year either in the manufacturing process or during fireworks displays themselves. Promptly at 8 p.m. the fireworks display began. Magnesium pyrotechnics were strung along the entire roof line of the block-long property. The string was lit at both ends and the dazzling display lasted 15 minutes. Over the course of the next hour and a half, a continuous fire rocket-and-loud-bangers display took place. The noise was constant and the air pungent with the smell of cordite. It was a spectacular display, with thousands of residents lined up on the street watching. When it was over, my ears were ringing and my neck stiff from gazing upwards. I had finally experienced a real Chinese fireworks display.

Over the ensuing years, I have many occasions to dine and meet with the Han family and my relationship with them continues to the present time.

———————

Li Xin's (Gaylene) father, Li Jun Wen, is the senior sports photographer for Shanxi Province and her mother, Ai Shi Jing (a beautiful lady!), is a commentator for the local Taiyuan TV station. Both Cherie and I have established close relationships with Gaylene and her family. We have had the opportunity of not only dining with them in their apartment, but also in some of the finest restaurants in Taiyuan. We had our first dinner at their apartment in 2004; there was a lavish display of many Chinese foods set on the table, and Cherie asked Shi Jing who had prepared the food. "I did!" she replied. Gaylene then told us her mother had taken the day off work to make the dinner preparations – some dishes, especially dumplings, take hours of preparation. Their apartment, which was supplied by the government was fairly small, about 60 square meters (540 sq. ft.), but very neat, tidy, and nicely decorated. It had the typical small

Chinese kitchen with a two-burner carbon monoxide stove. All cooking was done in a wok. In March 2007 I was invited to visit their new apartment. What a change! It is 140 square meters (1230 sq. ft.), with three bedrooms, a large living room, two bathrooms, and a study room. The kitchen is about twice as large as their former one and very modern. Jun Wen had also just purchased a brand new Ford Focus car. I believe the state provided both the apartment and the car to a higher level government employee/What a change in life in China! This was another example how the Chinese middle class has grown and become more wealthy. Diverging a little, I should also comment that when we first encountered Gao Zhi Jin (CEO of TZ) in 1998, he was riding a bicycle to work but now is supplied by a luxury car and driver.

Although I have met many more Chinese kids, not only from my relationships with Simon, Ting, and Xin but also through work and other avenues, the relationships are not nearly as close as that which I have with these three families. It is interesting that early on even though the parents of these three kids were acquainted, they were not close friends. But over the years, the families have become friends, as almost every Saturday evening they would bring the kids to the Shanxi Grand lobby to meet me. We called this the "inside English corner."

Perhaps these three families are the extreme in terms of the lengths they go in seeing their children attain the highest standard of education possible in the city. However, other families I have occasion to talk to also push and support their kids in obtaining the fullest and best education possible. This does not necessarily apply to the more rural areas where although the government is espousing to improve the school system, schooling is in general limited to elementary grades. In the time that I have known them, Simon, Jane, and Gaylene have attended the best city schools in their area for up to 10 hours per day, with extraordinary amounts of homework assignments on top of that. They also have attended special private schools on Saturdays and Sundays to enhance their English, math, and science skills to give them an advantage in attending university. The two girls are also accomplished pianists; however, the only time they could practice is after all their homework was finished – typically around 11 p.m. School would begin again at 7 a.m. Both girls have played the piano in the hotel lobby for Cherie and I and some of our friends. Simon and the girls have also won many English-speaking contests in Taiyuan and throughout China.

Apparently, each year in China approximately eight million high-school students write entrance exams for less than 3.5 million places at university. The total emphasis in their young lives is on education, and the kids cheerfully comply. It is sad, however, to see that this system does not allow for any extracurricular activities and the kids are not as well-rounded as children would be in the West, where they partake in sports, playtime, and other hobbies. (Organized sports at the high school and college level is a relatively recent phenomena in China) In addition, the Chinese kids all seem to suffer some form of sleep deprivation.

Seeing this, Cherie and I realized that there was one thing we could do for our friends Simon, Jane, and Gaylene. Accordingly late in 2003, I discussed with the three families the possibility of having the kids visit Cherie and I at our place on Quadra Island. This idea was received with great excitement, and over the next few months it monopolized our conversations. I had one caveat: when in Canada they were not to speak Chinese – or *no food*! This was to be an educational experience, and the best chance they might have to develop superior English-speaking skills. We decided that July 2004 was the best time for the trip, as they would be on break from school.

The first step in the process was for the kids to get their Chinese passports. This proved easy enough and they were obtained in about one month's time. The next step was for me to write letters of invitation for each of the kids, to present for an interview at the Canadian Embassy in Beijing for a visa.

Despite being told that getting a visa for the kids was unlikely – at the time China and Canada had no formal visa agreement – I went ahead with the invitation letters. I outlined that I worked in China for an international corporation and returned to China frequently; that I had a home in Canada; that I knew the kids and their families, and the parents were very supportive of the proposed journey; and that Cherie and I would be responsible for them while in Canada – and we would see to it that they would return to China. The next step was for each family to visit the embassy in person with their letter of invitation. On the first such visit, each of the kids was refused a visa.

However, I was pleasantly surprised to receive an e-mail from the Canadian Embassy stating my letters of invitation were very interesting and if I could provide two additional elements of information, it may be possible to obtain the desired visas: notarized letters from each parent giving Cherie and me legal custody of the kids for the time frame in question, and a guarantee that we would provide medical coverage for the kids while in Canada. Three of our grandchildren had also sent e-mail letters to the embassy saying they wanted to meet Granddad's friends. With these new letters in hand the families then traveled back to Beijing and met with the appropriate embassy official. Visas granted! We were all extremely pleased, especially Cherie and I, since we had been told by actual Embassy workers that fully 90% of applications are denied.

As I planned to be in Taiyuan from June to mid-July of 2004, we decided that the kids would travel to Canada with me on July 17, and then return to Taiyuan on August 6 for the beginning of the new school term. With help from both Wei Yu and Francis, the kids got tickets on the same flight as mine, and we were able to get them seated together.

Finally the day of departure arrived. I flew to Beijing from Taiyuan in time to catch our Air Canada flight to Vancouver at 4 p.m. Han Guang Ling had the use of a large company van and drove the kids and one parent each to Beijing. They left Taiyuan at 5 a.m. to allow time to get to the Beijing airport. They were not about to miss that flight! But this was to be a long day for all concerned – it would be the usual 26 hours in door-to-door travel time. Lots had changed in China over the years, but not my commute time.

Upon arrival in Vancouver we quickly passed through immigration. Cherie had ticketed the four of us on a float plane to get us from Vancouver west over the Strait of Georgia to the city of Nanaimo, on Vancouver Island. The float plane dock was situated on a river about five miles from the Vancouver international airport. The day was sunny and warm. We were able to catch a shuttle bus to a depot about one mile from the float plane; we then had to walk, towing our bags the rest of the way, the kids were real troopers. We arrived at the float plane dock about two hours before flight time; it was 1 p.m. and we were hungry. There was a bar/restaurant nearby, so Simon and I left the girls at the float plane dock and walked over to buy a take-out lunch. Simon was greatly surprised that he could not accompany me into the bar to order the food. In China, there are very few restrictions regarding minors in such premises. With food and (non-alcoholic) beverages in hand, Simon and I returned to the girls.

The 20-minute flight to Nanaimo harbor was a delight for the kids who could look out the windows and see clear skies, the clean water of Georgia Strait, and all kinds of boat traffic. Cherie met us at the landing dock. After hugs and kisses all around (even from Simon) we stowed the luggage in our Chevy Tahoe and departed for our home some two-and-a-half hours away. It was about 3 p.m., and we had a drive of 150 km (90 miles) to the town of Campbell River, where we would catch our local ferry for the final 10 minute trip Quadra Island. All three of our guests immediately fell into a deep sleep as the car pulled away.

Figure 10 "The kids" and I arriving in Nanaimo B.C.

Exiting the ferry we had a 25 minute drive and arrived at our home around 5:45 p.m. Everyone ran to the beach, since it was low tide and about 80 m (250 feet) of sand was exposed. Some of the kids had been to beaches in China but none had experienced the cold clear N.W. Pacific waters and such tidal sand. After a short run around the beach, we unpacked the car, served a quick dinner, and let the kids flop into their respective beds. Their tired condition was not only from jet lag, but from serious sleep deprivation from the exhausting exam schedule prior to school season's end the day before we left Beijing.

For the duration of the kids' stay in Canada, we had planned one "down" day at our base (home) for each two days of sightseeing. Working to this plan we took several boat trips around the enchanting Discovery Islands (of which Quadra Island is one); visited my 90 year old father in Victoria; visited Cherie's 86 year old mother in Nanaimo; toured the campus of the University of B.C.; explored the delights of Vancouver's Inner Harbor; and visited our daughter and her family in Vancouver.

The kids' senses were awakened to some simple pleasures that we typically take for granted. When we took the kids to one of the local lakes for a swim, they were greatly surprised that such clean water existed! China, as perhaps the 4th largest country in the world area wise, is deficient in fresh water lakes and rivers especially in clean and clear water. During their stay with us, Simon "discovered" sandwiches, which are not common in China; he developed a habit of eating them between meals (making his own sandwiches). As a result of eating well and catching up on lost sleep while in Canada, and considering he was thirteen at the time he put on a growth spurt and was 3 inches taller by the time I returned to China on my next trip in September. Prior to their visit, both Jane and Gaylene had recently learned to cook from their mothers. So we visited a very large Asian grocery store while touring in Vancouver, bought appropriate ingredients, and the girls cooked us a fine Chinese dinner at our house.

While on Quadra, the girls had a bedroom on the lower floor, while Simon slept in an upstairs bedroom. Every morning at 6:30 I would stand at the top of the stairs and yell "PRC (People's Republic of China) girls – time to get up!" After a few minutes and plenty of groans they would make their appearance for breakfast preparations. After one week Simon thought it would be cool to move over to our guest house to sleep all by himself. When I woke up at my usual 5 a.m. the first morning he was there, I looked over to the guest house and observed that every last light was on in there. I think he was spooked by the wolves! We had told the kids that there was a pack of wolves on the island, and even occasionally a cougar or two. More than likely, this was the first time he had ever been left alone overnight and he was a little apprehensive with the situation. He did better on subsequent nights.

One day we had a good neighbor take the three kids up Chinese Mountain, a local peak on our island. Dave Varley was about 62 years old at the time but very physically fit. He literally ran the kids up and down the mountain. When Cherie and I returned to our house later, the kids were sprawled out on the living room carpets, completely dead to the world. School kids in China with their long school days and rigorous homework did not regularly participate in exercise regimens.

Figure 11 The kids "baffed out" after their trip up Chinese Mountain

A humorous incident occurred when we visited Nanaimo. We took the kids and Cherie's mother to an all-you-can-eat-for-$9.95 Chinese buffet. When we entered the restaurant, I noticed an immensely overweight woman in line ahead of us, and I told the kids that when she was finished there would be no more food for us. Collectively their jaws dropped and they tried in vain to stifle their laughter. In 2004, they did not see too many obese people in Taiyuan.

We also took the kids to Victoria, the capital of B.C., to visit my father who at the time was 91 years old. The complex where he lives has a piano in the lounge area and the girls sat down and played. Soon there were 20–30 of the residents gathered around enjoying the music. While the girls played the piano, Simon and I played pool on the fine table there. It was a nice, spontaneous moment.

We took a ferry ride from Nanaimo back to Vancouver for a visit. While on the boat, Cherie noticed a Chinese couple, who she realized were speaking Mandarin. She asked the man where he was from. He replied, "From Belleville." (Belleville, Ontario in Eastern Canada.) She said, "Before?" He answered, "You wouldn't know – in northern China." Cherie then replied "Shanxi?" He nodded. Cherie then added "Taiyuan?" The woman began crying. Her mother still lived in Taiyuan; in fact she lived in the same block as Simon and his family – what a small world. Simon later made contact with the woman's mother.

The man and wife had immigrated several years earlier and worked for Nortel. After being introduced to the kids and hearing where they came from, the man wondered how they were able to get to Canada. In 2004, only about 30,000 Chinese nationals were able to obtain visas to visit Canada. We explained our successful process, and then the girls indicated they were starry eyed with all facets of their visit and commented that would like to attend university in Canada in 2007. The man blurted a strong no! He said, "It is tough to adapt to a new country and totally different culture especially when you are naïve and have close family ties. It is better to get an undergraduate degree in China first, and then consider an advanced degree in another country when you are older and more mature." We will see what the kids decide in the future, but clearly the trip left a strong impression on them, and opened their eyes to many more possibilities in their lives. We hoped we were not creating high expectations and potential problems for the future.

On August 5, the kids departed for Beijing, arriving mid-afternoon the next day. Their parents met them on arrival and drove to Taiyuan, getting there around 10 p.m. They started the new school year at 7 the next morning. What an end to their vacation!

Both Cherie's and my relationships with these three families continue to grow. Although in single-child families the kids are often doted upon (each of kids has the biggest bedroom in their respective apartments, complete with their own desk and PC to facilitate good study habits; the girls both have a piano in small anterooms adjacent to their bedrooms), they are in general well-mannered, respectful and polite. The girls, as of 2008, are attractive young ladies, 18 years of age and in their last year of high school (senior 3 in China); they plan to go off to university next year. Simon, age 16 in 2008, is in senior 1 with two more years to go – and he continues to grow taller.

All three kids now can "think" in English and are fluent in the language. Knowing this, Cherie and I have asked Jane, Gaylene, and Simon to write about their experiences in Canada. Following are the impressions of the three kids, in their own words, of their trip to Canada.

Chinese Kids' Experience – Canada Visit

Xin's (Gaylene) Canadian experience below is unedited.

During the Spring festival, Cherie told me that John was writing about his experience in China and maybe he would publish a book of his own. I was excited when I heard the news. Then Cherie and John asked me if I could written a few passages about my life in Canada, I said I was willing to do it. Two years have passed by, when I'm trying to remember my summer holiday in Canada, it seems like yesterday once more.

John and Cherie are really ebullien friends. In 2004, not long after SARS broke out in China, they invited Jean, Simon and me to their home. At first we thought the visa and passport would be hard to get, But Cherie said constantly 'well let's try'! Then finally, the first opportunity for us to go abroad came.

At the Beijing Capital Airport, my parents kissed goodbye to me. I guessed they were worried about me. They didn't know if I would miss my family so mush, and if I could adapt to the new environment soon. But later I knew we needn't worry about that.

During the first two weeks in Canada, we lived on Quadra Island. John and Cherie's house faces the Ocean a there's a forest behind it. This time we really touched the nature.

One day Cherie told us 'Let's go swimming in the lake and we didn't need to take a shower after that'. I hesitated a little at the beginning because I have never swum in a lake before, and I was afraid the fish in the lake would bite or eat me. But when I saw Cherie throw Christine into the water, I went down fearlessly. The water was crystal blue and clear, I tasted a little, how fresh! No salty at all! I lay on the lake, enjoying the hills around me. It was just like I was in a picture. I sycetized with nature, I thought I dropped into a fairy tale world.

In China, it takes me a few seconds to go to a neibour's home on foot, but in Quadra, we need several minutes to get to the neibour by car. Once, we paid a visit to a neibour's house, we rowed a canoe from the beach in front of John's house, and then turned a big bend, passed by from a hill, and finally we saw the house. Because the destination is always far from where we stared, Jean and I often had a sleep on the way, and everytime we opened our eyes, always green. In the green, I founded myself very comfortable.

There are more wonderful memories in Quadra. On Saturday Market, we helped Cherie to sell her glasses, Cherie has a nice craft, the glasses she blew were beautiful and attracted many people. There were many more people there selling things they made on their own. There were two girls playing the violin to make pin money. Their show won a lot of applause. The people on Quadra have taught me that I could use all my advantages to make my life better and more interesting.

In one shop, I saw and tried a environmental way to buy and make pop. That is, clean the used bottles, pour the pop in and seal up the bottle again. Maybe only by getting together those small things did make the Island such a wonderful place to live.

The place that impressed next was on modern city-Vancouver.

The following days, we lived in John's daughter Mary's house. During the first day, we arrived, we tried to traval on a yawl and played water trampoline. After a exciting beginning, we quickly used to the life there. In thecity, the shops and supermarkets are similar to Chinese. One place that gave me a deep impression is the history museum, I thought it must be a show of pictures and photos before we set out. To my surprise, the actors and actress there acted out the history of Canada from acient time to now. How amazing! It was the most wizardly museum I have ever been to.

Another kind of restaurant was also afresh to me. The car could drive throw the place and park right there, then a waitress came, we ordered the dishes, later, the waitress put a long table between the windows and then put the dishes on the plate, so we could eat in the car.

There are so many more things we did for the first time in Canada. The first time to travel in the sea plane, the first time to feed goats, the first time to take the fairy boat, the first time to make glass plates...

To us who grow up in a city where there are buildings made up of steel products and cement everywhere, these first times opened our eyes and minds and gave us wealth. I like the place and I like the people there. Thanks to my friends, Hardworking and friendly big John, Sonsy and beautiful Cherie, easygoing Mr. and Mrs. Weber, lively Jaoanna's family,gentle and quit small John, brisk and pretty Christine, smart and lovely Jeneva...

These friends brought me 'Quality time' and warm memories.

I can't write down all of my experience abroad at a time, but the memories are deep in my mind. I will treasure them. I think one day, I will go back again.

Ting's (Jane) Canadian experience follows in her unedited words.

A beautiful memory always supports me to overcome difficulties because it contained my dreams and my unbelievable fairy tales. It was my journey to Canada.

Before knowing that I could visit my friend John's in Canada. I seemed to be given a big break. When I true set my foot in Canada, I really didn't how to describe my feelings. The world all around me is likely to be a very big surprise. The beautiful scenery told me that I exactly came into my dreaming world.

Both the beautiful girls with guns at the airport and the handsome men with dogs at the getting luggage department are very kind and warm-hearted, and the bus in Canada is like a brick of bread. And I was in a plane. I seemed to be a seagull. Besides the big noise gave me a very deep impression.

John's home is on Quadra Island. His home looks like some toy building blocks in the forest which is also really close to the sea. I could see through the big glass window by sitting on the rocking chair, and eat Canadian corns with all my friends together.

What was my feeling for the Journey to Canada I want to use three letters to describe it. They are "F. W. V."

"F" stands for Food. I tasted different kinds of Food there. Food in Canada doesn't contain too much oil but always together with different kinds of sauces. Sandwish, hotdog, bacon and BBQ, which made me at a loss. It's hard to refuse their good taste, so they made my body bigger than before. Finally, I want to say, there was a spectacular food in my memory, the super big ice-cream with three big cream balls and the blue bubble-gum taste. After finishing it, be careful, don't look in the mirror, or you find a blue monster appearing in your eyes.

"W" stands for work. I did a lot of work there (For example) I washed the dishes, dried them, cleaned the carpet and cooked Chinese food. What an industrious girl I am! However, I learned how to make a glass plate from John's wife. I designed several glass plates by myself. Finally I found I have some art cells.

"V" stands for "visit', I visited two famous museums, and went to feast my eyes on a big plan park with so many huge trees, beautiful flowers and strange bugs in it. I also climbed up Chinese Mountain. It made me really tired. After spending several days on the island, we went to John's daughter's home in Vancouver. To my surprise, I met some Chinese from Taiyuan on the Fairy to Vancouver. What a small world it is! Except meeting John's dad and his wife's mom, I also went to an old people's home and played the piano for them. Their smiling face made me proud.

This journey indeed gave me a lot. It made my English has big progress. It helped me to inform that I have become an independent girl. I could take good care of myself. And I realized what life I want to give my parents in the future. From this trip I know that care and love among people really precious. Smile to the people around us, and say cheese to our future with a great confidence.

Thank you John. Thank you for giving such a great dream like Shagri-La. Remember, we are friends and you are my special granddad. You have a family in china. We are family forever.

Love you!

Ting Ting Han

Wang Gochen's (Simon) Canadian experience follows in his unedited words.

The sun rose earlier and set later. It was dawn by three in the morning and twilight lingered till nine at night. The whole long day was a blaze of sunshine. That is the place we have stayed for more than two weeks ------------Canada.

After flying sky for more than 10 hours, we arrived in a different country. I felt really exciting because of everything there: high architectural complex, different cars, strange people, different foods ----------------

One thing I can't imagine before I came here is about crossing road. As we all know, in China, when you are trying to cross the road, you have to stay at the former place and waiting for the car goes away you won't be safe if you don't do that. But in Canada it's really different. If you try to cross the roads, the friendly driver may stop for you and waiting for you.

Later on, we arrived in a beautiful island. That is the island we lived ----------- John's home is part of there.

Not very far from the house lies a seashore in front of. That is my first to see the ocean. I felt really exciting and joyful.

Accustomed to the clamor of the city, I can't visualize how tranquil here it is. I enjoy everything here; oceans, forests, hills, seashore and sunshine. But what I like to do best is waiting for the sunrise in the morning.

Because of the time difference between China and Canada, so I was up before the sunrise on the first day there. It's really amazing: peeping down the spread of light, the sun raised it's shoulder heavily over the sea level. Later on, sky becoming same color with the sun. Yet before floating impress of the woods could clear itself, suddenly the gladsome light leaped over the forest behind. Enjoy in the beneficence that nature gave.

Staying this charming island for more than 7 days, we did a lot of things, such as climb Chinese mountain, kayaking, fishing but without catching anything --------- not even an old boot. After having spending whole mornings on John's boat, we go home with an empty bag. But I still very happy because I'm not really interested in fishing. I am only interested in sitting on the boat eating sandwiches that made by myself and enjoy sight of the ocean.

We went to Vancouver for the last three days trip. It's really a nice and clean city. We also can meet many Chinese people there. They are all kind and friendly.

The thing is really unbelievable is that one day when we were on the ferry, we saw five or six Chinese people, and we decide to have a conversation with them. After we asked them where are they from, everybody amazed because we are from same country, same province and even same city ----- Taiyuan. Small world!

I think this is really a great opportunity for me and everybody. After this trip, we know a lot and make big progress on our English study.

After I finish this trip, I couldn't help feeling excited, encouraged, and urged to go forward! I will try my best on my study and never give up.

Aside from my close connection to Simon, Ting, Xin, and their families, I have had the opportunity over the past ten years to get to know many other interesting people – both Chinese and other expats – outside of the scope of day-to-day business. Cherie has befriended many of them on her visits as well. Following are stories of some of my favorites …

———————

One Saturday in September 1999, Randy and I were sitting in the lobby of the Shanxi Grand when we noticed a young lady standing outside the line of flower pots separating the lobby bar from the main lobby. She was barely two feet away from where we were sitting, and we could see that she was dressed in not especially clean brown cords, her hair was not washed (at this point in time most residential apartments suffered frequent water stoppages), and she was trying to get our attention! We tried to ignore her but she was persistent, and we finally made eye contact.

Finally she asked, "Can I practice my English with you? I am a teacher and have an English exam on Monday and need to practice."

After hemming and hawing, we told her we could give her a few minutes of our valuable time. She told us her name was Bai Ling Mei (Stella) and she was 32 years old. Her English was fairly good, although she was excitable, giggly, and talked very fast. After about two hours of chatting we informed her we had business to do and must end the session. She fairly begged us to see her again on Sunday and we reluctantly agreed to meet her the next day at 1 p.m.

Stella showed up on time, dressed in the same attire as on the day before. Both Randy and I gradually warmed up to her and spent a further four hours talking conversational English with her. She also informed us that she could read and speak Japanese.

This was of great interest to me for two reasons: first, we were woefully short of English speakers at SCW, and second, we also would often deal with Japanese customers.

Stella reappeared the next Friday evening. She came over to where we were seated and declared that she had passed the examination with the highest marks possible. She said she wanted to reward us, even though we told her that her passing was reward enough! Stella insisted it was the Chinese way and said she wanted to show us around Taiyuan on Saturday morning. We finally gave in and agreed. This was still fairly early in my time in China, and I had not yet completely explored Taiyuan.

The next morning, Stella met us in the lobby and we set out onto the streets of Taiyuan. It was a pleasant September day and she told us she was going to take us to an antique street market about 1 km away. Off we went! After about 20 minutes we came to a large square on Yingze St. and from there we entered a small alley system with both sides of the road lined with vendors selling everything: swords of unknown origin and vintage, trinkets, jade, posters, books, nail clippers, pottery, coins, and more. Stella was a little dismayed when I admitted that I had previously been to this market on my own – she'd been hoping to show us something new. Not to be daunted, she informed us that she had a special treat for us – she was going to take us to a renowned antique collector for whom she had done some translating work. She led us further into the narrow road/alley system – indeed, further than I had explored on my own – and we eventually came to a gated apartment complex with many black Mercedes and BMW cars parked inside the compound. Randy and I had no idea what we might be getting into!! Stella spoke into the intercom and we were bidden to enter.

We walked up to the fourth floor, found the correct apartment and knocked on the door. After noisily unlocking numerous locks, the collector opened the door and greeted Stella. She introduced us "foreigners," and we then met several of the collector's family members – none of whom spoke English. The collector proceeded to pull statues and artifacts from various boxes and cupboards to display for us. Neither of us knew anything about antiques and we were perplexed as to the reason we were even there! Did he expect us to buy?? He showed us old books authenticating the antiques. We *oohed* and *aahed* all the while, looking for the escape hatch. After a couple of hours and us not purchasing anything, we finally made our exit and continued on our walkabout with Stella. The collector was probably frustrated that he had spent so much time with these two "rich" Westerners with no sale!

Stella kept in touch with us, and near the end of the month, she invited Randy and me to her aunt's apartment to celebrate the Moon festival, which occurs each year when there is a second full moon in one month. Here we were presented with a table full of fruits, candy, nuts, drinks, and various samples of moon cake. Moon cakes are made especially for the Moon Festival. They contain a sweet filling, often with a stamp in the pastry depicting a moon. They are a dessert that I find icky – too rich and too sweet for my tastes.

Stella's aunt worked as a technician with Taiyuan City water works, (she assured Randy and I that the water in Taiyuan was safe to drink) and her uncle was an instructor at one of the local universities. The neat and tidy apartment was typical for China, at about 400 square feet in area, including a living/eating area with a TV, a small bedroom, a tiny bathroom, a tiny kitchen with a two-burner CO (carbon monoxide) gas stove, and a small half bedroom.

After a few more visits with Stella, I advised her to see Percy to determine if she could add value to SCW. We hired her to work in our inside sales area and she did a credible job. And, Stella is the one who eventually recommended Wei Yu to Percy, so we have her to thank for that. Unfortunately, Stella eventually fell victim to the politics of our human resource manager, Mr. Luo, and she left the company after six months. She did well for herself, however: she moved to Shenzhen, near Hong Kong, and attained a MBA from a university there. She then used her education to get a good job as an assistant GM for a Taiwanese firm in Shenzhen.

Both Cherie and I continue to maintain contact with Stella. We have visited her in Shenzhen and she has visited me in Taiyuan, where her parents live. She has been recently promoted in her firm and now works in Shanghai. She is now a well-dressed, good-looking woman. It is amazing to me sometimes to think of how many long-term, caring friendships I have made in China, by just making myself available to speak English with strangers.

———

My travels often led me to meet surprising people doing interesting things in China. On one of my numerous trips to in 1999, while waiting for the flight to Taiyuan in the Beijing airport lounge, I made small talk with another gentleman sitting beside me who came from France. His English and my French were at about the same level (low) but we were able to hold an understandable conversation. It turned out that he was a master vintner who had developed five vineyards and wineries around China, and he was on his way to visit his winery near Taiyuan. His name was Gerard Colin and his wineries were named Grace. On two subsequent trips in the same year I again encountered him, and he invited me to visit his winery outside of Taiyuan. I thanked him and said I would surely visit him in the future.

In the fall of 1999 I contacted Gerard and asked if it would be a good time for a visit, and if so, I could bring Liu Min along. He replied, "Oui!" Shortly thereafter, Liu Min and I secured a driver and set out on the 75 km journey to the winery. China was a little short on road maps at the time and we had only general directions to the facility, so as we got closer we had to make frequent stops to ask the locals where the Grace winery was. After a few false turns we finally saw the entrance road, through an identifiable arch. Along the approximately 700-meter roadway to the winery we observed cart after grape-filled cart being pulled by one-lung tractors. Apparently this was the first harvest of grapes for the winery and they were on the way to be crushed and processed into Pinot Noir. We passed the carts, and proceeded to the winery, where we were warmly greeted by our host.

We were given the royal tour of the facilities and were hosted to a grand lunch complete with wine tasting. In spite of my limited French and Gerard's nominal English, we were able to learn that the goal of Grace was to become recognized as the leading winemaker in China. He did acknowledge that the drinking habits of the Chinese would have to change to make wine drinking popular. (They were quite hooked on their white liquors.) He also informed us that the facility would be replete with a hotel/chateau in the near future. Since the visit I have bumped into Gerard on other occasions, but have not yet been back to the finished facility. However I have ordered Grace wine and the quality now is quite good. They may yet make their goal of popularizing wine, as more people in China are embracing Western customs.

———————

In 2001, I met another interesting "foreigner." That year the Taiyuan local TV station began approaching foreign-controlled businesses in Taiyuan, including SCW, to participate in a forum dubbed "Doing business in Taiyuan." We decided this might provide a good chance to publicly present some of the problems of operating a JV in China, and we agreed to participate. Accordingly, Percy, Julia, and I showed up at the appointed time and place. After entering the TV station, we were met by a promotion person who directed us to a seating area where the nine participants would meet for introductions. Here I met a man named Finn Torjesen who was with the Evergreen Family Friendship Service. Soon we nine participants were led to a studio where the interviews would be held. They informed us about the format expected during the interviews – everything was to be out in the open. We were all happy with that; we wanted to share our struggles in the hopes of remedying them. During the interviews each participant was asked to describe the pros and cons of doing business in Taiyuan: all in Chinese. Percy presented SCW's case. When the others spoke I was surprised to learn that Finn spoke fluent Chinese. Unfortunately, when each presenter started to discuss the problem areas the host quickly changed the subject. What a sham! China did not want to hear about our problems, only praise! The whole show took about four hours of everyone's time. And as far as I know, it was never aired – a complete waste!

I did, however, learn more about Finn and his organization. His grandfather, Peter, was a missionary who traveled to China in 1918 to set up a Christian ministry and school in a remote area of Shanxi Province. Peter's wife, Mor, joined him in 1920. They set up in Hequ, a small village in Shanxi very near the Mongolian border – it was extremely primitive and poor. After opening a school there, and after much struggle, they were able to gain the trust of some of the peasants. In 1926 civil war broke out in that part of China, however, and Peter and Mor were evacuated back to Norway until the unrest died down in 1928. Over the years, with significant hardship, they were able to convert some of the villagers to Christianity.

The Japanese invasion caused increased hardships for the family (now with children), as the area was constantly bombed. On December 14, 1939, a bomb hit the rudimentary house where the family lived and Peter was killed. After much discussion with the village representatives it was agreed that Peter could be buried in a plot in the village. Mor stayed on and by May 1940 had established a church building and meeting place in the village. Around this time the Red Army, in cooperation with the nationalists, took over the area and the Japanese hostilities were no longer a factor. Yet after a trip out of Hequ during early 1941 Mor and the family found it impossible to return to Hequ, as the political situation regarding the Japanese had changed again. Mor was then asked to establish a ministry in Chefoo in southern China. In the summer of 1942, after the attack on Pearl Harbor, the missionaries were taken as Japanese prisoners and transferred to a former Presbyterian compound where other prisoners were being held. (In an interesting side note, Eric Liddel of *Chariots of Fire* fame was also interred in this camp.) Finally, After VJ day the camp was liberated and the family returned to Norway via Canada, then eventually settled in the U.S.

Surprisingly, after many years away from their calling there, what was left of the Torjesen family was invited back to China and Hequ in 1988. In 1991 many Torjesens, including Finn, his wife, and their twins, were in Taiyuan and Finn was invited by the vice governor of Shanxi to set up a permanent mission in Taiyuan. After much soul-searching and governmental red tape, Finn and his family moved permanently to Taiyuan and set up the Evergreen Family Friendship Service (EFFS). Because of problems regarding Chinese translation it became necessary to change the name to Shanxi Evergreen Service. Some of the ongoing services provided by the group include consulting, English-language training, medical work, community and agricultural development work, and the Shanxi Evergreen International School. What a story and family legacy! Since our original meeting both Cherie and I have met Finn and his wife on several occasions.

Beginning in 2000 the word had spread that the Shanxi Grand hotel lobby was the place to be on Saturday nights. Simon and the girls began to bring other friends to meet me and some of my expat friends. And then the parents of the new kids would often accompany the kids. On some Saturdays, the group could number as many as 20 kids and parents. Occasionally parents and kids would show up unannounced and just sit expectantly in the lobby near where my friends and I would be sitting.

One of the most interesting kids was Wu Jin (Jenny Wu): she was nine years-old, cute as a button with one dimple, a bundle of energy, and the best student of English out of all the children I met. She could not stand still – bobbing to and fro, shifting her weight from one leg to the other – and she spoke very fast. I learned she was homeschooled by her mother and had already won many English-speaking contests around China. On several occasions, I had dinner out with Jenny and her parents. We have not seen Jenny or her parents for the past three years; Jenny had told us at one point that her parents were moving to the UK.

The Shanxi Grand lobby and English corner are not the only places we've befriended Taiyuan's youth. As I mentioned earlier, when Cherie comes to Taiyuan she makes a point to visit a local middle school and spend time in many classrooms to speak conversational English with the students. In 2003, one day she returned to the hotel and told me she was "blown away" by a 13-year-old girl in one of the classes. Cherie had asked the girl to sing partly out of curiously and politeness, but she immediately felt the girl was extraordinarily gifted. The girl's voice sent shivers up Cherie's spine – her vocal range was tremendous. She sounded like the young Welsh singer Charlotte Church. Her name was Wang Zi Wei. When Cherie had asked the teacher about her, she was told that Zi Wei came from a single-parent family of limited means and probably would not be able to continue on to high school. Cherie asked if she was taking voice lessons; the teacher replied no, as the girl's mother could not afford to pay for lessons.

Since I was intrigued by Cherie's account of the girl's talent, we invited Zi Wei to sing in the hotel lobby, where there was long-term duo (a violinist and a piano player) who provided music every evening. The entertainers, Mr. Zhang and Liu Li, had become friends; when I asked them to evaluate Zi Wei, they readily agreed. After she sang, they both agreed that her voice was extraordinary and that she could become an accomplished singer if she received lessons. Cherie and I made a proposal to Zi Wei and her mother, Ms. Li: we wished to sponsor the girl for singing lessons. We even had an excellent connection; when we had mentioned our intentions to my colleague Francis, he told us that his father was a professor at a local university with a music school. His father found us a retired music teacher who took on Zi Wei.

We have continued to sponsor Wang Zi Wei's lessons and she has moved on to much higher qualified and famous teachers. She has won scholarships to help her continue through high school and she planned on attending university in 2008. In the spring of 2006, Zi Wei won first prize in the 8th level (out of 9) in all of China for her singing.

Figure 12 Zi Wei winning a singing contest

In March 2007, Zi Wei traveled to Beijing to write special university entrance exams for the prestigious Beijing University; she came in seventh, but there were 10 positions at stake. Thinking she had qualified, both she and her mother were aghast when envelopes and/or keys to expensive cars were proffered to the examiners by others. She and her mother had nothing with which to compete. Unfortunately money and influence count in China – even regarding university education. She subsequently was refused entry and was devastated.

We invited Zi Wei to come to our place in Canada in summer of 2007. I began the process of preparing the necessary paperwork for her visa application. Undoubtedly the majority of embassy employees are dedicated and perform with a high of integrity but some of it was beyond our rational. Unfortunately, on two separate attempts, we ran into some mindless minions in the Canadian embassy that have denied her the visa. Their decision appears to be arbitrarily based on their feelings that as a single, very pretty young adult, she does not have strong enough ties to return to China. They have deemed her a flight risk! Despite several appeals for reconsideration, we did not even have the courtesy of a reply. We still hope that she can come visit us there someday.

We do still see Zi Wei when she comes occasionally to the hotel lobby and sings for us and our friends. The expats claim that when she sings "Danny Boy" without accompaniment, they are so touched the hair on their arms stands up!

(In the epilogue you will find more details; she did get accepted to another university and was finally granted a visa to visit us in Canada.)

Here I invited Cherie to write some of her thoughts and comments about children, education, and Chinese family life, since she has unique perspective from her time spent volunteering in local schools and socializing with our Chinese friends.

Children

Astrologically, 2007 was the best year in 60 years to have a baby – projections were for a 20 percent increase in babies in the Year of the Golden Pig. And, indeed, the prophecy came true! Aside from the fact that there is relative stability and a good economy, would-be parents prefer to have their babies in an auspicious year according to the Chinese calendar. In addition there is careful consideration given for the timing of babies – for example, it is good luck to have the child born when fruits and vegetables and good temperatures are in season.

I have been surprised to meet young parents who seem to have very little understanding of babies. Mothers are routinely in their thirties when they have their first child. But I suppose it is natural that expectant parents have had little experience with babies: in a one-child country, where few people have siblings and teenagers rarely babysit, there is just not much exposure to young children. The young children we know who have cousins, call them "brothers" or "sisters." Eventually, if the one-child policy continues, no one will have cousins either.

Some of our young professional friends do object to the one-child policy and say the wrong people are having a second child. [Only peasants and those of ethnic origin are permitted to have a second child, and only if the first is a girl.] Some professionals we know are considering having a second child, but would have to pay a large fine to do so. We have been told the fine can be up to $20,000 USD. Consequently, they have concern about the cost and about the censure they might get from friends and co-workers. There doesn't appear to be much of a shift in attitudes toward this policy; in fact, there is still quite a stigma attached to having more than one child, except in the case of twins. Twins garner a special status in a one-child country.

Since parents only get one chance to raise a child, Chinese children are dearly loved and indulged. They are usually beautifully dressed in darling clothes. We chuckle at young friends who have two washing machines in a tiny apartment: one for the baby and one for themselves. They do not want to contaminate the baby's clothes! Diapers are not usually utilized; the pants have a split bottom. I love babies but always have to be careful picking up Chinese babies that are not wearing diapers. I have seen mothers hold a baby on the store floor so the child can have a bowel movement. The clerks do get annoyed and hand out tissues to clean the mess. It is a poop and scoop rule. As the middle class has grown in China, more parents are using disposable diapers, but the peasant population is still significant, and they, for the most part, use the old methods.

There are many customs involved in bringing up a Chinese baby. There is a naming date – at 100 days – at which point the baby's head is shaved. The shaving is supposed to promote a healthy head of hair. The babies are rarely taken outside when young. Parents, if they have a car, seldom have a car seat or any other child restraint. I have not seen car seats for sale and not seen any babies in car seats, other than in expats' cars in Beijing and Shanghai. The SCW company lawyer, Nancy Zhang, recently had a little girl. She imported a car seat and receives much derision from her friends over its usage. I was always terrified driving in Beijing with Annie, Liu Min's wife, when her four-year-old son Chin Chin was playing all over the car, totally unrestrained. Annie is a good driver, but ... I am just uncomfortable in a car with an unrestrained beautiful bright wonderful child! I would rather he was in a car seat!

Because more and more women have careers, Chinese grandmothers are expected to be the caregivers – of all of the young Chinese women we know, almost all of them have the grandmother(s) looking after the baby. Good thing I am not a Chinese grandmother! I dearly love my grandchildren, all five of them, and would give anything for them but I want my children, *their parents, to do the childrearing. I did my bit. I like my freedom.*

Education

I have spent much time teaching conversational English to a multitude of classes at Number 12 Middle School, the Shanxi Grand Hotel, a pre-school, and at the SCW foundry. Number 12 Middle School gave me a name that sounds much like Cherie but its translation is archaic and obsolete. Xi Rui in Pinyin means "erudite" and "wise." How can I go wrong with that name?!

The following is how Xi Rui is written in Mandarin (note the Chinese words need accent marks).

Teaching me my new name certainly eliminated any possibility of an ego trip, however! It also helped me relate to my students who struggled with English. All the squiggles and wiggles of the script, and then to say something that is supposed to sound sort of like "Cherie." With all the squiggles went many giggles. In Pinyin (the anglicized version of Chinese or Putonghua) Wo shi Xi Rui means "I am Cherie," only every word has to be said with the correct tone; otherwise shi can mean either "ten," "shit," "be," or "to try." One has to be careful with tones or shi ren nankan – it can be embarrassing! Listening to me bungle my Chinese name helped loosen things up – it was easy to have fun in the English classes. We laughed to the point that one of the kids commented, "Our regular teachers are not so much fun."

Many of the children and adults have English names, but one that set me back was a boy at school who told me this English name: Peja Swjakovic. OK! I asked him where he got that name, and like all other Chinese, he said he got it from a book! I'm guessing his name needs an accent mark too!

At university I was a geography/English major with some credits and experience in teaching ESL (English as a Second Language). When we lived in Portland, I did a number of classes in talk time at several of the community colleges. The students came from diverse ethnic backgrounds, and I was told that I was good at getting people to relax and talk. So, teaching English in China seemed like a natural choice, as well as being fun for me and something to occupy my time and to try to be helpful.

The conversational English sessions that I taught for SCW and at the Shanxi Grand Hotel, were attended by adults from a wide mix of education backgrounds: from formally educated to very little instruction! Their strengths in English are mostly commensurate with their education. A number of the participants had very good English and just needed to do some listening and practicing to get some confidence. Many of them also had VERY strong grammar skills. The big problem in China is the English teachers are not conversant in English. One friend from China immigrated to Canada and was stunned to take the English placement test and score so poorly. She was embarrassed. She had been a senior English teacher at a middle school in China.

There is a fanaticism to speak "standardized English." Their attempts at obsessively correct English made the students freeze up in silence. My Chinese students were reluctant to be less than perfect, so I tried to make them relax and have fun. At the hotel and at the foundry it was relatively easy to point out Americans, Canadians, Australians, Europeans, and other Asians who had a great variety of accents. I tried to convince them that the most important part of communicating is to have a good time.

*By the way, there is a famous Chinese teacher of English,
Mr. Leong, or as he is known, "Mr. Crazy English." Mr. Crazy
English holds huge lectures, often 30,000 people, and charges
huge fees. He has a marvelous marketing system selling himself,
his videos and his books. He is making millions by saying "don't
be shy, just try." He is rumored to have a number of villas in
China and to have a wife and daughter who live in Vancouver.
He told me that his daughter does not speak Mandarin as she
finds it too hard. I had the incredible experience of joining him in
a lecture to all the hotel staff. He played and bantered with me, in
English, using me as part of his lecture. He seemed to be a very
nice man and it was a great fun to be part of the lecture.*

*An interesting tidbit: The Chinese newspapers say that there
are more people in China studying English than there are
English speakers in the world. There are wonderful television
shows teaching English. I have actually sat and watched, trying
to learn in reverse: English to Chinese. The programs are akin to
Sesame Street, but without puppets.*

*Even on our first trip to China, little children would say
"hello, Lady" and then titter in shyness. To encourage "talk
times" in my classes, my tactic was to show family pictures; this
helped relax students and pique their interest in talking to me.
Everyone was interested in family, children, forests, cities,
scenery and western holidays, my cat, wildlife.*

*People loved glimpses of our life, which enabled questions
and conversations. Regardless of their English level, most people
could understand some of what I was saying and could hear the
music of the language – and that is a good place to start.*

*The first picture I would show was of my mother. She was 89
years old at the time, and the photo depicted her sitting at her
computer. The concept of a great-grandmother at a computer
was so foreign, that the picture produced many "ooh's" and
"aah's." The pictures of our granddaughters' classmates was
always received with great interest, too, as there is a broad range
of ethnic diversity in their U.S. and Canadian schools. Two of our
granddaughters attend private schools and wear uniforms; the
other grandkids go to public school and wear civvies. Two of our
granddaughters have blue eyes, and one is a blond, there are not*

too many blond and blue-eyed kids in China, so these pictures elicited interest too! One picture of a large Thanksgiving turkey had the kids sucking wind ... more oohs and aahs!

At the factory we worked with words and phrases that people had trouble saying, for example, "trousers." One of the men could not believe when I told him to forget "trousers" and just call them "pants." I don't think that he believed me that the words mean basically the same thing. He really could not say the "trou" sound. His mouth and his tongue could not go in the correct position to form the sound. I tried to recall my linguistics instruction, the grouping of words, the pathways to forming the sounds, the position of the mouth and tongue. But inevitably it was easier to solve the problem by calling trousers by the alternate, pants.

In the factory we went over technical words, fortunately, over the years, I have absorbed many of the steel-making terms and was able to help with the pronunciation. I often asked the people what their position was at the foundry. One of the men, Mr. Luo, told me his job. I looked at him blankly. Mr. Luo repeated an incomprehensible mix of sounds. One of the office women understood and wrote on the blackboard: Human Resources Manager. We all tried and got everyone to say it. The "hu" sound comes out like "shu." It took some effort. That is a hard grouping of sounds, just like "trousers" or "trowel." Eventually, we were able to get everyone's job title correctly pronounced in English.

John had mentioned that several of the men in technical positions were in a position to go to North America for training. I asked if they ever thought they would travel outside China and got a resounding "NO!" They had no concept of ever traveling. Undaunted, I said they might want to know how to eat with a knife and fork. They did not think so, but while we had talk time we used knives and forks that I had borrowed from the hotel to cut up and eat wonderful huge Asian pears and mooncakes.

About six months later, two of the men were sent for training in Ontario and British Columbia, Canada. During the trip, Mr. "didn't want to use a knife and fork" and three others came to our home on Quadra Island for the weekend. I asked him again if he had ever dreamed he would travel outside of China. He laughed and said "NO, never, in his wildest dreams!" He was in sensory overload and culture shock from his experiences. We took them out to a nice restaurant for dinner and they were astounded with the size of the portions but they functioned effectively with our utensils. Likely he was better than us with our first attempts with chopsticks.

The moon cakes I had used for my cutlery lesson at the factory were from the children at the school. They often gave me dozens of these cakes, which are very yummy. There were big ones, small ones, homemade ones, store-bought ones – way more fattening moon cakes than we could eat in a lifetime (especially since John doesn't care for them). The Asian pears, the largest I had ever seen, came from a farmer who wanted to talk to us through a translator. He wanted us to help him pay bribes so that he could immigrate to Canada. We told him that that is not the way that Canada works – you can't pay bribes. He has four daughters in a one-child country. Unfortunately, we had to tell him we could not help him. He left, shuffling away sort of hunched over, looking very dejected and sad.

I once had occasion to visit a private preschool in Beijing. Our friends Annie and Liu Min's son Chin Chin attended the preschool, which was in a converted Russian Embassy. Chin Chin, at four years old went there Monday morning and stayed till Friday evening. (Chin Chin seemed to have a nanny, a relative from Mongolia). Annie, his mother, would go to visit him once during the week. The preschool/day care had a spectacular play area with massive jungle creatures in mosaics, climbing walls, and balance bars. The classrooms were clean and bright. When we went in, unannounced, the pre-kindergarten children were eating lunch. They were all in T-shirts and underpants eating spaghetti, with a fork. I assume it was Chinese noodles! The children, to a one, all looked up and said with no prompting, "hello lady." They appeared to be happy and stimulated. These were not the children of poor parents.

I also loved my experiences teaching at Number 12 Middle School; the children are a great delight. The first time I went to the school it was to meet a select group of top students. They *were all dressed in white shirts/blouses and dark pants. I, with great unawareness, assumed that their garb was normal. I also assumed that the 25 or so students were one class. I was treated with great courtesy and respect. The questions were polite and uniform: "Do you like China?"; "Do you like Chinese food?"; "What is your favorite festival?" and "Why have you come here?" I was the first foreigner that they had ever met, so it was a big deal. A number of the children brought me gifts. (I had to politely tell the teacher after the class that I did not want to be given gifts.) With the translator's help, I established a good rapport with the kids.*

Over the next half a dozen years, each time I went to the school it seemed there were more and more students squeezing into my classes. The norm was about 60 kids in each class, but sometimes as many as 120 stuffed themselves into a classroom, each bringing a small picnic style bench as a seat. The kids were noisy but polite, affable, attentive and had a delightful naïveté. As with the adult groups, I showed pictures, but never of my home or personal effects. I did not want to flaunt my lifestyle. I have so much and many of them have so very little. They loved my pictures and asked many questions.

One young boy asked if I would adopt him and if he could go to school at my house. I said no, I live too far from a school on an island. To start a conversation, I asked one tall kid at the back of the room if he played basketball. I guess he was the school star and thought he was super cool and was the class smart ass. He asked me for a kiss, and to much hooting and derision, I strode to the back of the room and I gave him a hug and a big, loud, mucky wet smacker on the cheek. He turned a delicious rosy pink.

Figure 13 Which one is the basketball player? – nice kids!

That seemed to break the ice. After that, there were lots of questions about basketball and other sports, dating ... all the kid stuff. They had heard Western schools had dances and they wanted one. I told them they were on their own for that one. We were able to communicate and have fun. Almost always there was a blackboard of art welcoming me, as well as gifts (as hard as I tried, I could not get them to stop this custom).

The head of the school district came to pick me up at the hotel one day. He did not speak any English. I asked him what he did, through my little translation book. He looked up his job and pointed to "secretary." Secretary is a big important job, so it was a huge honor to have him pick me up! Frequently one of the parents, a wealthy one with a car would pick me up or, more often than not, the school driver would take me in the ratty school vehicle. I was treated well and appreciated.

Although earlier in the book John mentioned Zi Wei, I will give a few more details: Early on, in one of the classes in the auditorium, Zi Wei sang for me, and I was greatly moved by her incredible voice. We have since helped Zi Wei with voice lessons and she has been able to stay in school (kids pay for middle school and high school, which was difficult for her single mother to afford). Zi Wei finished school, has gone on to university, and has received accolades for being the best singer in her age group in all of China. She has been accepted by "the best voice teacher at the best academy in all of China" [her words]. Zi Wei is a very pretty girl, who is also very talented.

It has been a joy to help provide someone with the resources to fulfill a dream and to achieve, to go a step beyond. Her mother was all teary eyed when she met us. Momma wanted to know how they could repay us. We told her that someday, when Zi Wei was older she could help someone who needed some help. That was all the repayment we would accept. Zi Wei did not wait long. A few years later she organized a fundraiser, unheard of in China, to raise money for a classmate with leukemia. Zi Wei and her classmates raised 40,000 Yuan, which for China is a lot of money (about $5000 USD dollars at the time). As a result, a newspaper article was written about me saying that a lady had come from across the ocean and taught the true meaning of charity. The Chinese version, of the interview, as well as the English translation appears in the appendix of this volume.

Figure 14 Cherie (Xi Rui) being interviewed for a newspaper

One day Zi Wei asked me to have lunch with her in the school cafeteria. Against my better judgment, I agreed – she was so very keen and earnest! Zi Wei went to one of the many long lines and was quickly sent to the front and returned with a tray of lunch (Chinese food, what else). We sat and talked and I ate a wee bit! Actually it was good. After about 20 minutes my tummy said "get back to the hotel NOW!" Fortunately I heeded my tummy and just made it back to the hotel and was very sick. I had even taken one of my miracle prescription intestinal drugs in the taxi. I did not wait for the school driver. I ran! I had been in Taiyuan so much that drivers seem to know where to take me. I rarely have to show them my hotel card. I strongly doubt they understand my few garbled attempts at Chinese!

Speaking of upset stomachs, I should delicately attempt to tell about the school bathrooms. The staff bathroom is a squatter toilets in a cubicle. I prefer squatters, as there is no contact with anything, clean or otherwise. But, there is no place to wash hands. Toilet paper is BYO, "bring your own." As is the case in most of China, refuse is deposited in the garbage can, if one is available. The student's bathroom is a long concrete trough with a miniscule trickle of water. There are no doors on the open cubicles. There is no place for refuse, no toilet paper, no soap and no place to wash hands. It is not for the fainthearted. I have suggested that there be a waste receptacle in the girl's bathroom and a place for students to wash their hands. Nothing as of yet! As an aside, even in hospitals I visited, both in Beijing or Shenzhen, the public toilets did not have toilet paper or soap or towels of any kind. Nurses, and other staff, in the hospital dry their hands inside their pockets.

I loved my contact with the English teachers. They were so appreciative but also very shy and reluctant to speak English. They were uncomfortable that here they were teaching English and really could not converse or speak effectively, although I am positive their knowledge of English grammar is far superior to mine. Very early on, the "face-saving" technique of one of the teachers was to arrive at our talk time with a very obscure grammar question. I readily acknowledged she knew more grammar than I had ever cared to learn. As we got to know each other, most of the teachers loosened up and talked, and I think I helped them with their English as well.

The school board even gave the teachers money to take me out for lunch. I usually begged off and was then given a lovely book or other gift. I couldn't break them of the gifting habit, either! I have even threatened not to come again if they give me gifts. Finally we arrived at a solution: they have started to give me their favorite recipes, written in English and Mandarin, and those are wonderful. Still I was given months of mooncakes, dried fruit, fresh fruit, Chinese dates from someone's farm and many candies. Most of the food was re-gifted to hotel and SCW staff.

A number of the teachers have continued to send me e-mails and I hope that some of them will remain friends. Curiously, any time there is anything questionable said by them, my ability to return e-mail ceases and I get computer viruses and worms. I am always very careful what I say.

As our conversations went on over time, I have prodded the 22 English teachers to speak English in their office. The kids come in and out of the office to bring their homework: I suggested that they make the office an "English zone" in the school. Sadly, the teachers still lack sufficient confidence to make that change.

The schools are large and teachers live in apartments on campus. (The middle school and senior school were grouped together side by side.) Each school seems to have its own uniquely colored track suit, so, in effect, the kids do wear a uniform. I believe most of the kids have few clothes, compared to Western kids. Chinese students also wear a fatigues outfit, a military style drill practice outfit. It is very interesting to watch thousands of kids lined up for drill practice, to observe pomp, ceremony, the flag raising with uniforms, marching, saluting, the national anthem and lots and lots of national pride.

As the years have gone by the school day has been legislated to be shorter, although most schools have ignored the new legislation, due to parental pressure. In my chats with the teachers, we all agreed that the children were overworked, had too much homework, and need more time for fun. However, even after an official edict was passed, eliminating mandatory school on Saturdays and Sundays, the parents wanted extra classes for their children. Education is the way to the future, hence

*competition is fierce. In a one-child society, all the parents'
hopes are placed on their child's achievement. If only Western
kids had any clue of how hard the Chinese kids work. They would
be running scared.*

---

*A simple cultural difference once produced much hilarity.
We were invited by Ting Ting's (Jane's) father to go on a trip to
the Wu Tai Mountains. I wanted John to come, and Mr. Han had
expected John to go as well, as he supplied and paid for a driver
and a translator. John conveniently had work to do; his attitude
is "seen one temple, seen them all."*

*It was very nice to have an escorted day to the Wu Tai
Mountains. As I was leaving, John leaned into the open back
window and gave me a little kiss. This little "see ya later" kiss
caused a huge titter! I did not realize it at first, but the small kiss
even took aback my driver and my translator, as well as the
bellhop and the concierge.*

*We started off on our odyssey, through the city, to parts that
I had not seen before. My translator was telling me with quite
fluent English that we were going to the Wu Tai Mountains to see
a very large monastery. His background information was printed
on old-style computer paper with holes along the edges. He was a
doctor and wanted to practice his English. He worked for the
pharmaceutical firm that the Hans work for (they are also both
doctors).*

*Out of the corner of my eye I caught sight of a steeple. I
asked my translator if that was a church, which he confirmed. We
sort of sniffed each other out, getting a sense for what we could
talk about. He asked if I went to church. I said, "Yes, I do." I
cautiously asked if he had ever been to church. He answered that
he goes to church every Christmas Eve and Easter Eve and
spends the time singing and praying all night. I asked if he went
any other time of the year. He said no, that he got enough
religion for the year on those two nights.*

*It became clear later that the driver was a Buddhist. He lit
many candles in the temple and spun the prayer bells there. (I*

think because of the poor roads and weather.) We took a gondola to the top of the mountain to see the beautiful view and the interesting buildings. Shortly after, the Wui Tai Mountain staff closed the gondola due to a coming storm so we rode horses down the mountain. It was terrifying, as I had never ridden a horse before and to learn to ride a horse in a storm was quite a challenge. Just as we got to the bottom, to a tent restaurant area, the skies opened up with rain followed by amazing thunder and lightning. We ate lunch in a small restaurant with a cook wearing the dirtiest, greasiest apron I have ever seen. I thought I would likely die of everything known to medical science! But I was hungry and the food was good.

Several nights later, Ting Ting came with her father to visit us at the hotel. She was all tittery and giggly, as she had heard that John had kissed me. Ting Ting was about 13 or 14 at the time. She said she thought her parents might have kissed once before she was born. Chinese do not openly display affection. I enjoyed very much watching her father. He clearly understood the topic of discussion at her talk time with John and me. He speaks as a second language, Russian, but only a little English. Mr. Han's eyes are wonderfully friendly and expressive. Ting Ting was telling us that Chinese parents would prefer to have a boy, not a girl. From Mr. Han's eyes, there was delight, love and respect for his wonderful daughter. He laughed lovingly with his eyes, he did not want a boy more than his charming, naïve, very bright daughter.

Figure 15 Jane (Ting Ting) and her parents

Chapter XIV: Taiyuan and the Shanxi Grand Hotel (Home Away From Home)

Like most Chinese cities, Taiyuan grew from a series of small, ancient villages into the present metropolis of about 3.5 million people. Each of these early villages was self-contained and consisted of small one-story buildings lined along narrow and winding streets and lanes. Street lights were few and far between. Most vending was done on the narrow roads: clothes, vegetables and fruits, meats, etc., could all be found here; the garbage was occasionally swept up to keep vermin away. The average citizen did not travel outside his/her local area, as everything he/she needed was nearby.

Over time, the villages began coalescing into the unified city of Taiyuan. Even still, it is only in the last decade that Taiyuan has erected a modern city skyline. Prior to 1998, there were very few buildings higher than four stories and there were very few gas stations and even fewer car dealerships to be found in Taiyuan prior to 1998. That situation has changed dramatically over the ensuing years: construction is rampant and the city is burgeoning with high-rises. Sometimes I think I see more building cranes in Taiyuan than I do in all of Oregon and British Columbia.

Transportation and its infrastructure in Taiyuan have changed immensely in a very short time, as well, leading to quite a bit of disorganization. On our first trip to Taiyuan in 1994, Cherie and I noticed that only two roads were more than two lanes wide: Yingze St., running east-west, and the street that the Shanxi Grand is on, running north-south. By 1998, there were several other streets being widened. This was a difficult job entailing moving of residents, demolition of the single-story buildings lining the narrow roads, building multi-story apartments, new stores and businesses, and straightening up the winding alleys. An 'expressway' 30 km (18 miles) in length was constructed connecting the airport to the city in 1999. However this road passed through the city, with many crossroads and stoplights and the trip from mid city to the airport would typically take about 40 minutes. This was usually a hazardous trip due to the Chinese drivers' habits of ignoring red lights.

In 1994, there were few cars on the streets; those we did see, were almost all black Mercedes owned by the government, SOEs, or mafia types. Most of the traffic consisted of busses, trucks, scooters, horse/donkey/ox drawn carts, one-lung tractors, three-wheeled bicycles with boxes overloaded with produce or supplies, and some taxis. Of course there were also legions of two-wheeled bicycles. Interestingly, the Chinese did not seem to care or distinguish between the girl and boy bikes since I observed a significant amount of men and boys riding what we in the west consider girl bikes. The taxis were all two-cylinder VW "Bugs" that had a propensity to flip upside-down; the cabs were generally in poor states of repair and inside the taxis the exhaust fumes were overpowering due to leaky exhaust systems. The fragility of these taxis was brought home when one day early in my China tenure, when Randy Green and I were walking on one of the narrow vendor-lined streets. We saw a Bug taxi, while trying to make a u-turn, hit a bicycle. Taxi drivers in China are ever vigilant for fares, and the driver saw us on the opposite side of the road and figured we might be a fare. The bike and rider went down; luckily there were no injuries to the rider or damage to the bike, but the front end of the Bug had fallen off as a result of the collision. After a short discussion, the bike rider dusted himself off, picked up his bike and rode off while the taxi driver picked up his bumper, put it in his vehicle, and drove off.

By 1998, there was a noticeable increase in car traffic, which made the roads more dangerous. Riding in a car at night had always been a harrowing experience, especially because of the Chinese people's reluctance to use a car's headlights at night – we were told the Chinese drivers generally believe it runs a car's battery down.

By mid 2002, many more roads were in the process of being widened throughout the city to accommodate more the increases in passenger cars. At the time most of the streets, especially the smaller ones, remained clogged with vendors. All Bug taxis were decommissioned and sent to the "country". They were then replaced with Jettas, Citroens, and some Chinese-made cars. Now, almost all makes of cars familiar to Westerners can be seen on the streets of Taiyuan (even Humvees and stretched limos).

In early 2003 then Premier, Zhu Rongi, visited the city and met with many high officials, including the governor of the province and the city mayor. Apparently they were extolling the virtues of the city and patting themselves on the back for all the progress they'd made in modernizing Taiyuan. Zhu, we were told was not so impressed. He reportedly informed the officials that Taiyuan was one of the most backward cities of its size in China and ordered them to clean it up fast! It appears that the city officials took this order to heart. Subsequent to his visit and between the time I left for home and returned, approximately 45 days later, many of the narrow streets had been widened; many of the one-story buildings were torn down (leaving rubble everywhere), street vending was banned, and construction on many new high-rise buildings commenced. I was amazed – and even more so when most of the rubble was cleaned up during my next 35-day visit. Myriads of workers and much equipment were employed during the demolition and construction phases. Additionally traffic flows were adversely affected while the various projects were in progress.

Along the widened roads, many new stores and restaurants were opened, including small supermarkets. Cheap shopping was finished in Taiyuan, as there were very few street vendors allowed. Most people in the inner city had to buy their daily needs in new supermarkets or upscale stores. With all the new housing, comes the need for goods. Modern furniture, appliance, and lighting stores opened up, as well as department stores – huge stores, mostly with blaring music and sometimes clerks sleeping if there were few customers. Now all the famous designers and brands were available at prices similar to those in Canada or the USA. "Big box" retail had also arrived: Wal-Mart opened its first store in Taiyuan in 2006.

While the city streets were more modern then, all the construction and ever increasing traffic had introduced new hazards. The new, wider streets necessitated many manholes to access the newly installed services. Invariably the manholes had no covers, creating dangerous conditions. In addition, most Chinese drivers, cyclists and pedestrians ignore most safety rules of the road. For example: at marked crosswalks, passenger cars invariably sped up to get through an intersection before the pedestrians could bring them to a halt, and drivers start left turns prematurely on roads that had no dividers, even to the extent of moving into oncoming traffic. I witnessed such violations even when traffic police were present. It was not a rare occurrence for me to see some bicycle or motorbike squished under a bus or larger truck, multiple-car crashes, and pedestrians maimed or killed. Such accidents would result in many people arguing who was at fault. Police and ambulances would arrive to assess the situation and to tend to the victims. During this time there would be no attempts for traffic control and traffic would be tied up for hours.

One day, after having been a frequent traveler to China for several years, I decided I would write a letter to the local newspaper and the mayor, presenting my observations about these things as an expat who spent a significant amount of time in Taiyuan. I was gentle. I praised the progress that had been made in improving the city. I then broached the manhole and traffic violation situation. I received a reply from the mayor and had an interview with the local paper. Wow! I was surprised one man (a foreigner, at that) could elicit such a reaction. Within one month there were almost no manholes without covers – and the situation prevails today. However, the traffic violations continued, even though I did see police occasionally handing out tickets. But then in mid-March 2007, suddenly, stationed at almost every intersection, were two or three smartly dressed (complete with cute Kepi hats) lady police officers directing traffic and pedestrians. There is now improved order in the traffic situation regarding vehicles. Where pedestrians are concerned, a certain chaos remains.

Crosswalks are clearly marked at all major intersections but the pedestrian is always lowest on the totem pole. One of the most dangerous aspects of using a crosswalk is protecting one's backside from the cars turning from the entering street: the cars are so quiet one almost needs an eye in the rear end to see them coming. Even though I have seen numerous serious accidents all over China, it is a wonder that the frequency is not even higher.

Mark Nolan and I had an experience during one Lunar New Year National Holiday. We had been invited to Francis' family home at one of the local colleges for lunch. When we were finished, Francis' uncle insisted on driving us back to the hotel, some 10 km away. He was perfectly sober as no alcohol was served at the fine lunch. It was a Sunday in the middle of the holiday period, so the traffic was somewhat light. The uncle must have had an urgent appointment somewhere else. Once we were on a main road he immediately sped up to 90 km/hr, passing everything in sight. Turning onto the hotel road (divided except at intersections) he continued at the same pace. At an intersection approximately 1 km from the hotel he swung into the extreme lane of the oncoming traffic and continued against the oncoming traffic until we arrived at the hotel. Apparently this move was necessary. since he would have needed to make a more time-consuming left turn at the proper exit. This was one harrowing trip especially since the car had no seat belts.

Chinese drivers are puzzling. They drive poorly but are invariably patient and emotionally stable. Rarely does one see 'the finger' or road rage in China. If an accident occurs, especially to a pedestrian or cyclist, the driver is responsible for taking care of the injured to the extent of paying hospital costs. Under Chinese law, the driver is presumed guilty until proven innocent. This law and the responsibility for the injured results in many hit and run situations.

Since 1998, there have been immense changes to city amenities as well, and many of these have made my time there quite enjoyable. Chinese relish dining out and the city is blessed with numerous excellent Chinese restaurants. I have found the food in Taiyuan to be the best I have tried in China. One of our favorite restaurants is located a short walk down an alley from the hotel. We call the restaurant "dumpling house" not only because it serves delicious dumplings, but also because at one time it had a sign posted a la McDonald's, stating "over 4,000,000 sold." Patrons of this restaurant are mostly local residents, and the place is invariably crowded with throngs of people, probably because the food selections are numerous, tasty and relatively cheap. I have hosted as many as 15 guests for as little as 300 Yuan ($38.00 USD). Even in 1998 the restaurant was clean, with spotless tableware and dishes, and the toilets were clean, with no smell. Since we discovered the dumpling house we have returned many times and many expats through our "advertising" now frequent it. The waitresses are young girls imported from the countryside. Typical of all Chinese restaurants, the staff is numerous, including many greeters at the entrance dressed in traditional Chinese dresses. The waitresses are rather "un-cool" fashion-wise, in their very heavy tights and uniforms that stick to their legs with static. We were told that the restaurant houses these young girls in a dormitory close to the restaurant. Most of their wages reportedly go home to support family.

Where food is concerned, the incoming influences are not all good. Prior to 1998, there were no Western chain restaurants in Taiyuan. There was also very little evidence of obesity among the Chinese. Then the first McDonald's opened in 1998 and the first KFC in 1999. Now there are at least ten McDonald's restaurants and twelve KFCs around the city. A Pizza Hut opened in 2004, followed by three or four more. And, not surprisingly, now there is much evidence of obesity, especially among the younger kids.

Taiyuan city services have also shown significant modernization over the past nine years. Yingze Park, at the center of the city, is much improved. This park surrounds a man-made lake and has many paths and walkways throughout. It also features several bridges that cross the lake, and canals that connect different parts of it. In days gone by this park was very dirty with garbage lying around, and the recreational equipment was in disrepair. Now it has been almost tripled in area and the lake doubled in size. It is maintained regularly and is much cleaner. It has had many midway rides added and improved boats and floats on the water. Paths have been expanded, with many fancy gardens and trees planted. There is even a Western-style restaurant in the park called "1950." This place is decorated in the style of an old fashioned '50s restaurant, featuring western foods and music, and the walls are decorated with old license plates from the U.S. and posters of the likes of Joe Montana and Michael Jordan. During the daytime one CD of past western popular hits plays over and over. It seems that they have only one. In the evenings, a trio plays western style music that attracts young Chinese as well as foreigners.

Yingze Park is the hub for physical activities in the city as well. Many older Chinese arrive early in the morning to exercise before it gets too hot. Exercise takes many forms: Tai Chi, walking, badminton, Chinese games (Feng Hu Lu and Jian Zi), Ping-Pong, dancing, playing musical instruments, and much singing! Some people even bring their caged birds to the park as an outing. I regularly exercise there, too, usually walking around the lake and its arms twice on each visit, which is good for about one and a half hours. The park is a 15-minute walk from the Shanxi Grand, and I normally walk there to and from the hotel as well.

Taiyuan now has a golf course and clubhouse in full operation. (No long trips to Beijing anymore.)

Even the number of non-pollution days a year has improved each year. In Taiyuan, you can see blue skies about 50–70 days per year now.

In addition to all of that, there is no lack of cultural activities in the city. In 2005 the city, like many modern cities, opened a world-class museum. It is located in a new four-story building in the shape of an inverted pyramid. The theme of the museum is "Shanxi Province history over the past 5000 years." That's quite a bit of ground to cover. China is lucky to have such a rich history. The displays are well planned and laid out with very good English explanations at the entrances to each display. I have visited this facility on numerous occasions and am particularly impressed with the state of the art of bronze and copper castings from 3000 years ago. I also recommended visits to the museum to many locals as well as foreigners I have met during my stays in the city.

The city also has several other parks featuring ancient Chinese culture, one close to the hotel is a quiet place with ponds, flora and exhibits historical calligraphy.

———————

I should probably describe Shanxi Grand life. I learned and observed so much from living there over the years. As I stated earlier, I chose the Shanxi Grand as my home away from home, because it was the only four-star (clean) "Western style" hotel in the city during the late 1990s, when I first began journeying to China. It was also a "Western" hub where I knew I would be able to meet other expats.

The heart of the hotel is its lobby – where the expats converge and also scene of the new "English corner" (the inside English corner) for my Chinese "kids" and their families. The hotel lobby is entered through revolving doors directly opposite the reception area. In the middle of the lobby is a spiral staircase leading up to the second floor, where the Chinese restaurant is located. This restaurant features a large open dining area as well as numerous small and large private dining rooms. The staircase also leads down to the floor below the lobby, where the confectionary store and business center are located. The lobby bar, albeit small, is cozy, close to the piano bar, and provides a good view of all the lobby activity – an excellent vantage point to observe the coming and going of the hotel visitors.

The Shanxi Grand is also popular with the locals. It is a favored place for the wealthier among them to host their wedding receptions – decidedly festive and, as is typical of Chinese celebrations, noisy affairs. Almost every Saturday and Sunday there are receptions at the hotel, with as many as 250 boisterous guests at a time milling around inside the lobby waiting to be greeted by the bride and groom before proceeding noisily up the spiral staircase to the Chinese restaurant. While the guests arrive, typically a band will play cymbals and drums outside the hotel entrance. Most wedding celebrations are also accompanied by noisy fireworks to frighten off the demons. When the receptions are over one can observe the guests who have overindulged in the

Fen Jiu (strong white liquor) – staggering or being carried down the spiral staircase. Again this is a lively and boisterous process. Occasionally a fight breaks out but the other guests always seem to break it up before anyone gets seriously hurt. One particular Saturday two wedding receptions were held simultaneously and my estimate of the crowd was upwards of 500 people. I wondered if the second floor was built to hold that much weight. I thought it a good thing they were all Chinese and not Americans.

The Shanxi Grand is, not surprisingly, also a popular stopover for the numerous tourist groups that come to the city. These groups vary greatly in makeup: monks from Japan, Korea, and Taiwan come to visit the nearby Wutai Mountains, which are dotted with shrines and temples for religious purposes. The different clothes that the monks wear are extremely interesting. Some of the groups bring large crèches and icons to take to the shrines. European groups from Germany, Austria, France, and others come to visit the mountains and to visit the ancient city of Ping Yao. Usually the number of people in each group is between 35 and 40 – and there are many groups. The groups normally stay at the hotel for one night before proceeding to the mountains.

When I first began visiting, entertainment was provided in the lobby, usually by duos playing the grand piano and violin. In general, the quality of the entertainment was poor. But beginning in 1999, Mr. Zhang and Liu Li were hired as the primary entertainers. He played violin while she played the piano, and they were good. He also played violin in the local symphony and she was a recent graduate in music from one of the local universities. As such they played every night (with occasional substitutions) from 6:30–9 p.m. I and other friends would typically spend one or two hours several times a week listening to them play. Liu Li even learned the Star Spangled Banner to play on occasion for me. She would also play one of my favorites frequently – Chopin's La Grande Valse Brilliante.

For the first year, most of their music was Chinese traditional or Russian classical. However with much expat influence and changes in Chinese laws allowing alternative music, their repertoire considerably expanded over the years to include Western, pop, movie themes, and other popular world music.

They also encouraged our singer protégée, Zi Wei. In late 2003, Mr. Zhang left to pursue other interests and Liu Li took over the lead role in providing the entertainment each night. She brought in various other violin players to accompany her on the piano. Some of her accompanists were her former students, and Liu Li herself is now recognized as one of the top graduates in music ever to come from the university.

Over the years, Cherie and I became close friends with Liu Li. We also met her fiancé, and in November 2004, I was honored to be invited to her wedding reception. Wei Yu was also invited and we attended together. It was quite a show. Liu Li was dressed in a traditional red Chinese wedding gown as she and her husband, wearing a suit, stood at the entrance of one of the largest and most prestigious restaurants in the area, greeting the guests as they arrived. Once inside, Wei Yu and I were seated with young ladies who had on several occasions performed with Liu Li at the Shanxi Grand. After many Chinese dishes, speeches, and the usual toasting, Liu Li and her new husband visited each table in turn. She was now dressed in a "knock your eyes out" slim, slit down the side dress. What a beautiful lady! In November 2006 Liu Li took leave of absence from her work at the hotel, since she was pregnant, and her co-accompanists took over in the interim.

During the past ten years, I have witnessed many interesting incidents at the Shanxi Grand. On a Saturday afternoon in 1999, Phoa, Percy, Joe, and I were sitting in the hotel lobby. There were several Chinese sitting, smoking, and drinking heavily in the seats opposite us. One was even passed out in his seat. Sometime later he awoke, saw me and the others sitting and talking, staggered over to me and began yelling "Foreign devil!" in Chinese. Phoa and Percy interceded and directed him back to his seat and his friends. In the next 15 minutes he came back twice and repeated the same words with more vehemence each time, and each time he was escorted back to his place. The last time he was taken away he again fell asleep. About 15 minutes later, he woke up, called Percy over and told Percy he was a major distributor of Maotai, a brand of white liquor, and wondered if the foreigner would be interested in working with him to sell to North America. Fat chance!

I realized how well I was cared for by the hotel staff when one Saturday evening in 2003, around 10 p.m. after the "kids" and their parents had left, I was finishing off a beer and a well-dressed lady sitting at the far end of the lobby bar ordered me another beer. I thought she was a hotel guest who wanted to practice her English, so I invited her to join me. Before I could raise my new beer to my lips, two of the waitresses appeared. One, Song Annie (one of my favorites), took my beer away and said, "Bad lady," then escorted the woman out of the hotel. I had no idea I was being hit on by a call girl! The waitresses even told my wife about the "bad lady" almost the first minute Cherie arrived on her next visit to Taiyuan. She thanked them for looking out for me.

In the early years supplies of Western goods (beverages in particular) was quite erratic, and we had to make do with what we could get. I have already mentioned that on my first trip in 1998, when I arrived Fred was waiting in the lobby bar with a bottle of scotch whiskey. In those days there were very few expats staying at the hotel: Fred, Mark Nolan, and I were basically the sum total of long-term guests. For draft beer they would serve San Miguel. However, one day the hotel brought in a mini keg of Carlsberg beer. We three finished that off in short order. It took the hotel about two weeks to supply another and we finished that one off pretty fast too. It took the manager about six months of running out of Carlsberg to realize that perhaps we preferred Carlsberg and he should get an ongoing supply. At the time very few Chinese drank beer. This has changed considerably over the years. Incidentally the beer is 30 Yuan ($3.75 USD) for 500 ml in the bar, but on the street you can buy a 500 ml bottle for 2 Yuan. I had a similar experience somewhat later regarding Diet Coke. Both the Western restaurant and the confectionary suddenly were able to provide Diet Coke, which at the time was unavailable anywhere else in Taiyuan. We were able to enjoy Diet Coke for about two months and then no more. It took almost three years before the hotel re-established its supply. I found that in China while some changes happen rapidly, others take time.

Being permanent resident had its perks. In appreciation of our long-term residency in mid-1999, the hotel management wanted to invite Fred, Mark Nolan, and I for a lavish meal on the hotel. Mark had resided at the Shanxi Grand for three and a half years. At the time he was the longest-term tenant the hotel had had. In response to the hotel's invitation, we said that we would prefer to sit in the lobby bar and have a couple of beers and have a few friends join us. When we came home from work at 6 p.m., a place was set up for us in the lobby bar and they provided fruit, snacks and beer. We enjoyed ourselves and ended up inviting many of the waitresses and other staff who so ably served us to join the party. I think the bill for the hotel was significantly higher than what a full blown formal dinner would have cost. From my experience eating at the hotel, the cost would be ~1000 RMB. I do know that the cost of the beer consumed alone at market price was probably close to 3000 RMB.

I saw good things come and go. In the summer of 2000, Mavis Chen (the hotel's Western restaurant and lobby bar manager) decided to open an outdoor BBQ bar in the garden outside the lobby bar. She decided that the draft beer (local brews) would sell for 2 Yuan for 500 ml – street prices. And food and snacks were considerably cheaper in the garden than inside the hotel. As a result many Chinese and hotel staff could afford to enjoy the facilities. On opening night Mavis organized a contest and selected me as one of the participants. There were four Chinese contestants and me, with three pints of beer in front of each of us. It was a traditional boat race. What Mavis did not know was that in my youth I was a champion racer! I finished all three beers following the procedure of showing empty by holding each upside down glass over my head before any of the others even finished one. I won coupons for free BBQ food for one week. I ended up in an article in the hotel newspaper and was surprised when the manager saved it and showed it to Cherie on her next trip. "I thought you were over that stage in life!" she said. Unfortunately the government later banned outdoor barbecues. Ironically the reason for banning was given to reduce the pollution in the city. The last year for the outside barbecue was 2002, when the hotel mounted a large screen TV outside to show the World Cup games, which were being held in Asia. It was a great gathering spot and very interesting observing the Brits, Germans, French, Italians, and Brazilians boisterously cheering for their respective teams. Unfortunately for the Chinese, their team was not represented.

I also learned much from observing the comings and goings in the hotel. For example, I noticed that posing and posturing are very important to Chinese relationships. It is interesting to sit in the hotel lobby and watch this tradition. Any number of Chinese men will come through the main entrance doorway, proceed loudly to the lobby seats, immediately pass out cigarettes to each other, order one pot of tea for the group, and proceed to exchange and smoke numerous cigarettes over the space of an hour or two. Sometimes a few leave and others come.

The Shanxi Grand is clearly the place to be seen. There are two well-dressed Chinese men who regularly frequent the lobby bar. They generally come to the hotel in the morning, buy a pot of tea, and stay all day. I think they use the hotel as a prestige place to impress their friends. I have never observed them sitting together but they both are constantly on their cell phones. One day while Cherie was sitting in the lobby one came over to her and asked where she was from. She replied "Janada" (Canada). He proudly replied, "I am Chinese," and then walked back to his seat. The other Chinese fellow is extremely obnoxious – he is constantly clearing his throat and everyone in the lobby can hear him. One day Cherie was sitting in the lobby reading and he was really irritating her. She went downstairs to the confectionary and bought some throat lozenges and put them on the table in front of him. He looked at the lozenges, looked at Cherie, and continued on with his cell call. Later he asked one of the waitresses who had witnessed the scene, "What are these?" The waitress said, "She thinks you may have a sore throat." He continued with his annoyance! He eventually left the lobby and left the lozenges on the table.

Much as the Shanxi Grand became my comfortable second home, I did venture out – or sometimes, was coaxed out – to explore the city and have fun with my gracious local friends. One memory stands out in particular. I was in Taiyuan during the first week of October 2002, the national holiday week celebrating the formation of the PRC. As all banks, government offices, SOES, and many businesses including SCW were, as always on such holidays shut down, I found time to work on some seminar material. Many of my friends, concerned that I may be lonely, invited me to various functions but I declined most as I had much work to do.

But early in the morning on October 5, I was in the lobby finishing off a seminar segment when I received a phone call from one of our employees at SCW. Unfortunately, this employee's English was about the level of my Chinese – almost nil. The hotel lobby manager was able to translate for us. Apparently the melting supervisor Zhang Wei Tao and some of his crew were concerned that I was alone and wanted to invite me for a day of excitement with them. Through more translation by hotel staff, I was able to deduce that the plans were to go to Yingze Park for fun, go for a fine luncheon and finally finish off with bowling. I could not refuse. It was arranged that the group would meet me in the hotel lobby at 10:30 a.m. the next morning.

However at 9:15 a.m. the next morning I got a call from the lobby that there were 14 people waiting for me. I finished off my work and hurried downstairs to the lobby. Off I went with 14 people who spoke no English. The group insisted we take taxis for the short ride to the park, even though it was a pleasant, semi-clear fall day. On arrival at the park we walked around until we came to the amusement area, which at the time was limited in scope. After some minor games, we came to the bumper car enclosure. These people with me were aged 35–50, yet they got into the cars and acted like little kids, spending over an hour on repeated rides. This age group had very little opportunity as youngsters to experience what would be normal in our society, and it was an experience for me to witness their collective enjoyment.

We left the park, loaded into taxis and headed to the restaurant. Zhang had made reservations for a table of 15. During the taxi ride I was able to contact Percy who luckily had just returned to Taiyuan and he agreed to join us for lunch. Thus I had an interpreter. We arrived at the restaurant; it was packed to overflowing, but our table, although small for 15 people, was reserved. The table was the usual round table with a lazy Susan. When Percy arrived, we all had to shift and squeeze closer together - but there is always room for one more Chinese. With Percy's translation, I was able to express my appreciation for the nice day we experienced together and thanked them for the sumptuous feast and refreshments they had hosted for me. At the same time I begged off bowling citing I had much more work to finish off my seminar material.

Chinese New Year is always another boisterous occasion where I am warmly included in my friends' celebrations. Over the years, I have experienced all or part of this 15-day celebration at least five times. Taiyuan especially goes all out for this holiday. It is also the time for families to reunite, and is the biggest travel time of the year in China. The holiday begins on the eve of the lunar New Year around 6 a.m. – with firecrackers and sky rockets. Some of the bombs are 1.5 inches in diameter and 8 inches long. They are set up in "sixteens" in a square cardboard case, and fused together. The noise is deafening and the concussion can be felt from fifteen feet away. All over the city the fireworks are let off continuously for 24 hours. The paper from this largesse litters the streets and the pall of smoke that hangs over the city is a sight to experience. The good news is that the fireworks usually die down and are more sporadic until the fifth, tenth, and finally, the fifteenth day. The fifteenth day is the traditional "lantern day," where red lanterns made of cloth or paper are hung along streets, buildings, and doorways.

At midnight on New Year's Eve the hotel shoots its fireworks off and invites any guests who remain in China for the holiday to watch. After the fireworks display a dinner and refreshments are served. The dinner main course is special dumplings ("Jiao Zi"). One time I was there only five guests remained in the hotel: Mark Nolan, myself and three Japanese.

Including staff that was not on vacation, the dinner had 22 guests. It was a nice way to start the New Year.

The Shanxi Grand was an ideal place to meet foreigners on business. Some of these people were frequent visitors and both Cherie and I befriended several of them. In October 2002 Cherie came to Taiyuan for another visit. During this time Per Jensen, a glass designer and friend from New York, was at the hotel. Per makes frequent trips to Shanxi to visit various glassmaking factories to present his designs and order glasses to supply restaurants in New York and New Jersey. One evening while I was out, Cherie had dinner with Per and Tom Cottinger, of Waterford Glass in Ireland. Tom was head of quality control for Waterford Crystal. Subsequently Cherie had occasion to talk to both of them in the lobby. As Cherie is a glassblower, Tom invited her to visit Waterford any time she could get to Ireland.

In late February 2003, I was descending in the elevator and one of the guests asked where I was from. I replied "America" and asked him where he was from. He replied "Ireland." I told him that last year my wife had met some idiot from Ireland who had invited her to visit Waterford. He stated, "I'm that idiot!" I then told him we were planning on being in Ireland in late March of that year. "I hope you can come and visit us," he said. "I will set up a special tour for you – just present my card when you come." We did go, and had a spectacular and unique tour of all the facilities, including the glassblowing floor. Cherie was allowed to blow glass – apparently the first and only woman to ever do so at Waterford.

Because I am the longest long-term individual the hotel has ever had as a guest, I am treated with special care. I also seem to be the "go to" guy when any of the other foreigners have problems with the hotel. Cherie and I on occasion, have been honored with dinners hosted by the hotel management as a token of their thanks. That has truly helped make China my second home. Cherie has also visited on average twice per year, so she's quite cozy at the Shanxi Grand now too. We have celebrated many birthdays with our local friends, coworkers, and expats; we split celebrations between the hotel and local restaurants. Indeed, since 1999 I have had all my birthdays in China.

Figure 16 Cherie's birthday party, Zi Wei, Gaylene, Simon, Cherie, flowers and Jane

In 2004 I met another interesting individual, Harry Zilm, originally from East Germany. Harry is a minority owner of an overhead crane manufacturer who had a minority position in a joint venture with TZ. At the time Harry, fluent in both German and Russian, was difficult to converse with in English. As he spends many months in Taiyuan, we have become close friends. He and his family visited us on Quadra Island in May of 2005. Harry's wife and another couple who visited with them spoke no English; however we were lucky to have a German couple living on the five acres adjacent to us, and they happily obliged with the translations. Harry and his party hosted a BBQ for us, including our neighbors. We also spent time on my boat touring the many islands in the area. Harry has promised that he and his wife will visit us again in the future.

The Shanxi Grand Hotel, although restricted in size, has shown continuous improvement in its facilities, cleanliness, and services for foreigners over the years. Initially the hotel's general manager was a government official and was on the corruption list, where favors were freely given to other party officials. We foreigners referred to him as "Fat Zhang" or the 'waddling duck.' During his tenure there were numerous large free banquets for his colleagues. The hotel personnel and their needs came secondary to the largesse! Luckily he was promoted (!) to a position in Beijing in early 2004. His replacement, Mr. Liu, came from within the hotel (which was unusual), and he appears to be a good manager with the hotels' guests, and employees' interests in mind. Another top manager who is the real brains of the operation is Jane (Xue Bao Zhen), who provides great services for the guests – she is the one who resolved Brock's ATM problem. The service and lobby personnel are also helpful and generally happy employees. Not a bad place to call home.

Although I have mentioned Wei Yu throughout the book, I would be remiss if I did not provide a more comprehensive account of this remarkable woman. In 2003 when I formally interviewed Wei Yu for the GM job, I told her that this was a big step for her, and although we felt she was highly intelligent, capable and energetic it was somewhat a risk for the company to place someone with no general management experience in the position, but I would work closely with her to ensure her success. I then told her, she and Mark are a handsome couple and certainly would want to start a family in the future. She stood up to her full 5 feet and said Mark and I have decided we will have our child when I am 36 years old.

I had agreed with Esco Corporation that since Wei Yu was so young and inexperienced that I would stay on past retirement to mentor her. Over the next five years she and I became very close, like a father and daughter. Even though, Esco Corporation supplied her with a modern apartment, she determined it was too far away from the hotel to keep in close contact with me. She elected to move into an apartment owned by her parents that was some 3 blocks away from my hotel. Cherie and I became close friends with both Wei Yu and Mark. Wei Yu calls Cherie Mum.

Beginning in mid 2002, significant price increases in raw materials were occurring and even more dramatic increases were continuing into 2003. As SCW had signed long term contracts with many customers, these price increases were severely eroding profits. Accordingly Wei Yu's first priority as GM was to renegotiate all contracts with customers. She was extremely successful at this endeavour.

While she was brilliant, confident, intense, and effective in many aspects of the job, she also had some weaknesses. These included a stubborn streak and sometimes making decisions without proper background. She also tended to be highly opinionated. While we were very close, and my mentoring meant we had many educational sessions together. Many of these trying occasions involved shouting matches, cooling off periods, then reconciliation and finally progress.

Some three years later in early 2006 when I was considering retiring, Cherie stated "I bet Wei Yu will try to have her child sooner in order to keep you working longer." Sure enough, when I returned to China in January, Wei Yu informed me that she and Mark would have their child in the autumn. She explained that this was the best time to give birth because the weather was good in autumn and many fruits and vegetables were available then. I said "it does not always work out as planned." She again straightened up to her full height and stated "both Mark and I are strong and healthy and it will happen." However, it did not happen. In December of 2006, Wei Yu and Mark took a holiday to Sanya in Hainan Province – a world class resort area on the ocean in southern China. This was really the first real vacation she had taken since starting with SCW. Cherie figured this would be a time for relaxation and possible pregnancy. It did not happen! Later, we found out that Wei Yu's parents also went on the trip. As it is a Chinese custom, all stayed in the same room.

October 2008, was a period of both excitement and extreme tension at SCW. This was the 10th anniversary celebration for SCW, a big deal in China, which took a significant amount of organizing. At the same time significant management and board of director changes were announced, The SCW board meeting was held the day before the anniversary celebration. Wei Yu told Percy and me that on that day she had suffered a miscarriage earlier in the week. She was so fit, no one had noticed she was pregnant. Initially, Wei Yu considered the event as a personal failure but her friend Cherie told her it was not failure but the miscarriage (Cherie had several) was probably due to natural cause and that she was young enough to try again. Cherie stated "I want to have a Chinese grandchild to come and visit". After some time consoling Wei Yu, she seemed much relieved.

Beginning in January 2009, Wei Yu was formally moved to a new job, Sales Manager for all Esco sales in China. In March, she left SCW to manage a privately owned Chinese company.

While the Shanxi Grand was turning into my home away from home, China was becoming a destination of choice for family members. I have been blessed with many family visitors helping ease the long stints away from home. Sean, my brother; Brock, my son; later Brock and his family Mary, my daughter; later Mary and her family; and two of my *cousin's* teenagers have all journeyed to China.

In March of 2003, my brother Sean came to China. He is a PhD scientist in molecular biology from Canada. He had meetings scheduled at a scientific institute in Wuhan where several of the scientists had worked in his lab at the NRC in Saskatoon. Sean had studied mandarin in university but had not used it much in recent times. I flew to Beijing to meet him and we toured Tiananmen Square and the Summer Palace. The Summer Palace is huge. We also walked miles around Beijing marveling at all the new modern buildings.

After Beijing we flew to Taiyuan, where Sean spent a few days with me. We toured the museum and visited Pin Yao. I also gave Sean a guided tour of the SCW facilities where he met the staff who hosted a lunch.

We then flew to Wuhan together. Wuhan a city of ~5 M people is south of Taiyuan and thus is somewhat warmer and more humid than Taiyuan. Wuhan comprises three city districts: commercial, government, and university. The city is situated at the confluence of three rivers. We were able to visit, as guests of the institute, Mao's home on the lake where he spent much time. The walls were lined with pictures and memorabilia of all the people and meetings Mao had hosted at this home. We also saw the bed where reportedly he slept with many underage girls.

We walked many miles around the city visiting other sites, one of which was a very large and four storied pagoda called the

Yellow Crane Pagoda. The institute lodged us in their dormitory facilities; as such we were in a small room with two single beds. At least the facility was clean. But after bedding down for the night, we were awakened by the buzzing of mosquitoes in the room. It was a "Keystone Kop" routine of lights-on, lights-off while we tried to locate and subdue the pests. Breakfast in the morning was fairly Spartan: one fried egg and some Chinese porridge called Congee.

I left Sean to his scientific duties after two days and flew back to Taiyuan. While we were in Wuhan the temperature had been 25°C, and the evening I arrived back in Taiyuan wearing shorts, a cold front had come in and it was 5°C – Brrrr! Shortly after I arrived, my left leg began swelling just above the knee, then the swelling started to slowly progress downward. I wanted to keep the leg elevated as much as possible and would, with shoes off, put it up on a hotel lobby bar table. The waitresses at the Shanxi Grand noticed the swelling and were very concerned. Any time I came to the lobby bar they would run and bring me a stool for my leg. After a few days of this, I phoned Cherie and related the problem to her. She immediately called my orthopedic surgeon in Portland (I have prostheses in both knees). He thought I might have deep vein thrombosis. He ordered me to get a Doppler ultrasound. As Beijing had the closest medical facility with that capability, I flew there to have it done.

The Beijing United Family Hospital had several doctors from Britain, Australia, and the U.S., and had modern technology. The technicians were all Chinese – but very professional. However, when the Doppler probe was run from above my knee down to the prosthesis there was an excited chatter amongst the three lady technicians. They then moved the probe to my other knee and more discussion ensued.

"What's the problem?" I asked.

One tittered, "You have strange things in your flesh." Apparently, knee replacements are a rarity in China. After completing the ultrasound, the British Doctor concluded no thrombosis. He suggested I go back to Taiyuan and rest the leg as much as possible.

Three weeks later, after returning home, I had visits to doctors in Canada and many specialists in Portland – during which I had x-rays, more ultra sounds, and cat scans – yet there was no definite cause determined for the swelling. After a final check with a vascular specialist, it was concluded that a spider bite I had received in Canada in early February was the primary cause. It combined with all the exercise I had while with my brother in China caused the poison to spread. Shortly after all the doctor visits and tests the swelling totally disappeared.

Another memorable visit was in June 2004, Ed and Addy Perkins (my cousin's sons) aged 19 and 17, came to Taiyuan for a two-week stay and became acquainted with Ting, Xin, Simon, and their families. Both boys are fluent in French and play jazz.

Since the boys were new curiosities, I decided to take them with Ting to English corner on a Saturday evening. The boys are fairly tall and Addy, with his then-long hair was sure to attract attention. Sure enough, we were thronged and it was a full three hours before we could extract ourselves from the masses.

One day Ting and her cousin who is a college student in France accompanied Ed and Addy on a trip to the ancient walled city of Ping Yao. Ting spoke Chinese and English, the cousin spoke Chinese and French, while the boys spoke English and French. Ting's father who spoke only Chinese was the driver. There must have been some very dynamic conversations during the trip. It would have been an experience to be a fly on the wall.

On another occasion the boys were invited to Ting's home along with Simon and Xin. The boys played some of their Jazz while there. I must say that while the girls are accomplished classical pianists they did not particularly like Ed and Addy's jazz style.

Before the boys returned to Canada, I hosted a dinner party for 16 guests at a restaurant of Han's choice. Included were the three kids' families, the boys, Francis and Min Min (his wife), and Wei Yu and her husband Mark Wong. The Hans were in charge of ordering the various and many dishes. A special surprise happened when one of the chefs, an expert at noodle-making, appeared for a demonstration of the art and also encouraged the guests to try their skills. Kneading the dough and knife cutting the noodles was not overly difficult but then the chef demonstrated the technique of swinging the dough, constantly doubling the strands, to make hundreds of noodles of a very small diameter. It was a fascinating display watching his arms in action while the number of noodles constantly increased. No one in the group could make noodles this way. Everyone in the party enjoyed the food and camaraderie. Ed and Addy, along with their parents, Joanne and Ilted, would visit us on Quadra Island when the Chinese kids were there the following month.

My daughter Mary visited me in Taiyuan in March 2004. She held a very senior position in the B.C. Hydro Corporation. She came for only four days, first visiting Beijing and then on to see Taiyuan. I met her in Beijing and Liu Min and I took her to the Great Wall. It was clear and cold with icy conditions on the wall, making footing very treacherous. In the West the attraction would have been closed for safety and liability reasons – but not so in China. Mary was amazed at the number of street merchants hawking their wares especially in the cold weather.

The next day Mary and I toured the Forbidden City. When we finished the tour we exited the far gate and came into part of the city unfamiliar to me. Mary was a little concerned that we were lost. "Not to worry," I said, "as many police and young people are reported to speak some English." When I spotted a police officer I asked, in my incomprehensible (to him) English pronunciation, for directions to Tiananmen Square. He neither understood nor spoke any English. After several other unsuccessful attempts we kept walking in what I knew was the general direction we needed to head. We also encountered some teenagers who also did not comprehend us. So much for the many English speakers! Carrying on, we eventually arrived at our destination. The next stop was to a tourist hutong (a narrow street or alley) featuring many different shops. This was a designated foreign tourist shopping area and all merchants accepted visa or master cards. We walked and visited many of the shops. We continued to walk until the tourist area ended and we found ourselves in a real hutong, where the people lived in fairly primitive conditions. Mary was amazed at the living conditions and general run-down state of the buildings. There was no running water and all toilets were outdoor cesspools that reeked.

Figure 17 Wiring in Hutong in Beijing

After two days in Beijing we flew to Taiyuan. Mary visited SCW's operations, and met the management group, the families, and Wang Zi Wei, Cherie's protégée singer. She was invited to lunches and dinners during her short stay. Mary impressed enough that I was able to convince her that her family should collectively visit China in the future. As a result they decided to take a family vacation to China in 2006. The family Weber, accompanied by Cherie, came to Beijing in March 2006 to begin their vacation in China.

Figure 18 Weber Family on Great Wall

Our son, Brock, visited SCW in mid March 2007. He is CEO of a small manufacturing firm in North Carolina and has ordered high-specification castings from SCW. It is a small world. As a customer of SCW he was treated with much respect, and in between business discussions he was given a tour of various highlights around the area. At one point Brock found he was short of cash and as there was an ATM in the hotel lobby, he put his card in it and punched in 2,000 Yuan, withdrew his card, and the cash duly appeared in the slot. He had a satisfied grin on his face at his successful withdrawal; however, while he was still in the self-congratulatory mode, the cash disappeared into the machine. A look of astonishment crossed his face. When he explained the situation to Jane the brains of the Shanxi hotel management, she called the bank. After about half an hour, several armed soldiers showed up in the lobby, and an official opened the ATM, verified the paper work, and gave Brock his 2,000 Yuan. I should have known, as two years before, a Chinese lady approached me in the lobby and asked me to write a protocol for the ATM machine. She came to hotel because she knew I was there and could explain in English for her students how to operate the machine. She explained to me that you must insert your card and very quickly remove your card. When the cash comes you must remove the cash quickly or else the cash will disappear. I dutifully wrote up a procedure for her.

During this visit Brock and I were invited to the Li's (Gaylene's parents) new home for dinner. Dinner was cooked by both her mother and grandmother. Grandmother, daughter, and granddaughter are all beautiful women. The dinner as usual was delicious. After dinner, Gaylene played a medley of tunes on her piano for us. It was a very enjoyable evening.

Figure 19 Author, Gaylene's grandmother, and Gaylene

Figure 20 Galyene's parents, Brock and the Author

Brock's last day was a Saturday and we hired the hotel car and, accompanied by Mark Wong, were driven to Ping Yao one and a half hours away via an expressway; this famous walled city dates from 700 B.C. and is on the list of World Heritage sites. Cherie visited this city in 2000 and it was terribly run down, with no facilities for tourists available. Since then an American heritage group had donated some $35 million to upgrade the facilities. The area immediately outside the city was under construction with modern hotels and restaurants to serve the increased tourist traffic. The city itself has undergone much reconstruction and is slowly getting back to its original splendor.

Upon returning from Ping Yao to Taiyuan for my birthday, I hosted the usual three families, plus Brock and Francis, his wife and baby girl, to a lavish dinner at the most prestigious restaurant in Taiyuan. This is a theme restaurant. It is approximately three football fields in size with exotic imported trees planted throughout. There are streams and ponds complete with fish, seals, and even caged crocodiles. Numerous different-sized tables are nicely spread throughout the flora. Private dining rooms of different capacities are on both sides and the rear top floor of the building. The restaurant can seat 1,500 people, though our spacious room had one round table with, you got it, a lazy Susan, and seating for 14. The room was also furnished with sofas and arm chairs and a large-screen digital TV. While the rest of us sat and chatted, Brock with Ting and her father went to order the various dishes from the seafood aquariums. This process takes time since the variety of fish, shell fish, crabs, lobsters, snails, and other unnamed sea creatures is enormous. There is also a large price difference between some of the species, so the selections must be carefully considered from that point of view. We did have a hearty and tasty dinner complete with the usual birthday cake with fireworks and stupid hat. The baby liked the cake. This meal would be described as expensive by Chinese standards – the cost was 1550 Yuan or about $200. Other Chinese restaurants with the same amount of food and people would typically cost around 500 Yuan. Before he left Taiyuan, Brock and I discussed his bringing Jacqueline (his wife) and his daughters Lauren and Maddy, aged 14 and 11 years, for a visit. He agreed that this should happen while I am still in China.

———

Big men! Over time SCW has been visited by many Esco Corporation personnel. Three individuals in particular have had a significant impact on the citizens of Taiyuan: Dean Richards and Bill Blakely both from the U.S., and Archie Vos from Canada. These men all weigh somewhat near 300 pounds and are all around six foot two inches in height. It is uncommon to see a Chinese person of this size. Our people cause many stares. On occasion, while walking around the city or in the park with any of them, we get many second and third looks. Although I am 5 foot 9 inches tall and weigh 180 lbs, the Chinese must think I am the 'runt' of the litter.

One evening while Dean was visiting SCW, Cherie and me with Tian Jian (a very small and trim Chinese) from our Xuzhou operation hosted a dinner with Dean. The restaurant we selected was a 15-minute cab ride from the hotel. Cherie, me, and Tian Jian climbed into the back seat of the small "mid-sized" taxi, leaving the larger front seat for Dean. Dean, huge as he is, entered the cab rear first and slowly but steadily squeezed his body and shoulders into the cab, growing ever bigger in the space! The driver's eyes widened in awe and he exclaimed "wushi" – perhaps meaning "My God!" The same reaction was repeated by a different cabbie on the return ride to the hotel. Dean has traveled to many cities in China. He is a nice person and realizes in a humorous manner the effect of his size has on people. Recently he related to me that occasionally when entering a full elevator in China, he will stand with his back to the door facing the crowd. He claims he gets a kick out of the various stunned looks on the faces of some of the crowd.

All three of the big men immensely enjoy their trips to China and are well accepted by all the SCW employees and supervisors they interrelate with. More Chinese people living in the cities are getting more obese. This is especially true regarding young kids. This is probably the result of the availability of more foods with higher calories, but more so probably due to the increase of the western fast food availability. Needless to say, our big men will not seem so big as time goes on.

Part III: Exploring China — History, Future, and Impressions

Chapter XV: The Four Dynasties — China as a Giant Onion

Though China's long history of imperial governance was overturned early in the twentieth century, the subsequent years can be divided into "dynasties" in their own right. I've loved learning about China's past (see the list of suggested resources at the end of this book) and have felt especially privileged to witness the rapid changes in the country's most recent phase.

The Communist era in China officially began in the post-World War II years. After some years of co-operation in defeating the Japanese invaders in 1945, Mao and the Communists turned on the Kuomintang, finally defeating Chiang Kai-shek in 1949, and the PRC was formally founded in October 1950. In my opinion Mao was a great revolutionary – but a poor manager. He was burdened in the decision-making process by a cadre of hard-liners adhering strictly to the Marxist doctrine. During this first Communist "dynasty," the country and people suffered greatly under Mao's series of "5 year plans" and sweeping political purges. Innumerable high officials were expelled from the Communist party and at the least, imprisoned, and at the maximum, executed.

Perhaps Mao's greatest failing was allowing the disastrous Cultural Revolution not only to take place, but also allowing it to last so long. This failing caused the county to regress for a generation. Under Mao's tenure, other than Russian development, there was very little foreign investment in China. It was not until the early 1970s, when Henry Kissinger and then U.S. President Richard Nixon visited Mao, that relations between the West and China began to thaw. This was the so-called "Ping-Pong diplomacy."

Mao died in 1976 and Deng Xiaoping assumed the chairmanship, ushering in modern China's "second dynasty."

During his career under Mao, Deng was censured numerous times for his progressive ideals. Although he and his family suffered house arrests, perhaps the only thing that saved him from the fate of many other high officials was the fact that his party membership was never cancelled. Deng was still saddled with many party reactionaries during his rule; however he was convinced that for China to succeed it needed to modernize its industries. Accordingly, he spearheaded changes in regulation and laws to allow more foreign investment in the nation. Farmers were the first to be affected by changes in the regulations – they could now have small private plots and sell the excess produce in the markets. This change resulted in the farmers/peasants having significant improvements in their incomes. This policy greatly increased food production in China and for the first time in history, China was self-sufficient in terms of food supply – and there were no more mass starvations.

The Tiananmen Square standoff occurred in 1989 near the end of Deng's watch. This was a tense time in China, as there was much uncertainty regarding the smooth transition of leadership. Leaders who originally had been designated to take over for Deng were blamed for the poor handling of the situation. This resulted in an unlikely candidate, Jiang Zemin, being selected as the new chairman to replace Deng after he died.

Jiang Zemin assumed the chairmanship in China in 1991. He did not initially receive all the offices that either Mao or Deng had – these came to him over time. As the third Chairman of the PRC, Jiang had fewer old hard-liners in the party to contend with than either Mao or Deng had. As a result, in this third "dynasty," China was able to make much more progress towards modernization and the establishment of policies for the betterment of all citizens.

The "fourth dynasty" was established as a peaceful and smooth transition of power while Jiang Zemin was still alive. The role of chairman was passed to Hu Jintao in 2004. During the politburo meetings, many new, generally younger and formerly barred people were "elected" to decision-making positions in the party. Almost all old hard-liners had either died or were not "reelected." The government was now less hindered in domestic or foreign policy matters than it was under the former chairmen. The present government is expanding its foreign affairs involvement, enacting laws to protect the rights of individuals, expanding efforts to stamp out corruption, putting policies in place to ensure all Chinese share in the growing prosperity, and setting regulations for environmental protection.

However, I make the analogy that China is like a "giant onion" – peel one layer off and you get yet another layer. In my opinion, China has many layers left to peel before a truly world-class society is achieved! Primary case in point: China is not a democracy, nor is it a free market economy. Individual freedom and rights are not guaranteed. There is a recognized and formal legal system in China – but no one can sue the government. Citizens or groups of citizens may do almost anything in their daily lives without interference from the government; however, if they are perceived as a *threat* to the government, swift corrective action takes place.

Witness the fall of Falun Gong! Prior to 2003, I saw many gatherings of these people in the parks and public places. Ultimately they and their ideas were determined to be anti-government and the sect was banned. I never see any more gatherings of Falun Gong. While attendance at churches is growing [underground, that is] it remains to be seen how far the Chinese government will allow the open flourishing of these institutions. China has an open conflict with the Vatican on who chooses bishops and cardinals for the Catholic Church in China. In China "all is rendered to Caesar."

The government can and does move people! While the Three Gorges Dam was a vital and necessary project for China's development, it resulted in the relocation of millions of residents from the regions slated for flooding. The people essentially had no choice; they were informed that they would be moving on to better housing and better lives. The younger people were more amenable to the moves than were the older residents. All were subsequently required to move. There have been other instances of protests by villagers complaining that land has been appropriated for development without their input. After a short period of protests, the government moves in and quells the protests. Annually there are many protests around various parts of China.

The Chinese government, being totalitarian, can arbitrarily take actions for the "betterment" of the populace in general. In order to preserve the declining fishery, in 2003 the government cancelled fishing in the oceans around China for three years. In the interim they also permanently cancelled fishing licenses for millions of fisherman. The displaced fishermen were provided funds and encouraged to move to freshwater fish farming. Today some 65 percent of China's fish needs are grown this way.

The world is generally aware of some of the problems China has with its annexed province of Tibet. China has significant problems in another area vis-à-vis the Xinjiang Uygur Autonomous Region, or East Turkestan. This is an area with a large Muslim population, and reportedly Al-Qaida has been providing weapons and training to the indigenous rebels there. Recent reports in the *China Daily* indicate a large group of rebels was rounded up during a major army action; many weapons and bombs were recovered. I think this is one hotbed area of China that few foreigners would be allowed to visit!

The Chinese news media is also tightly controlled by the government. In the early 1970s China suffered a massive earthquake, resulting in the loss of life of around 300,000 people. Yet the government was able to keep this a secret for years: indeed the general public was not informed of this tragic event until well into the 1990s. Western hotels such as the Shanxi Grand are allowed to air CNN and BBC-type programs, but the average Chinese citizen does not get these channels, and the news for the papers is generally massaged before it goes to the citizens. For example, I happened to be in China for three significant events: the U.S. bombing of the Chinese embassy in Belgrade, the spy plane incident south of Hainan, and 9/11. In each case I saw the events on CNN as they occurred, and each time the reports did not come out in the Chinese media for three days – and then with a government slant. In the first event, the government blasted the U.S., rejected any apologies, and allowed

– even encouraged – countrywide protests against the U.S. For the second event – wherein a slow-moving U.S. surveillance prop plane cruising near Chinese air space suffered a collision with a Chinese jet fighter plane, with damage to the U.S. plane and loss of the Chinese jet and pilot (the U.S. plane made an emergency landing on Chinese soil) – I again saw it on CNN, and three days later it made the Chinese media. This time there was less anti-American rhetoric; protests were not encouraged or allowed, but strong diplomatic actions would be carried to the U.S. by China. In the third instance, of September 11, I stated earlier that I witnessed the whole thing on CNN – but it was not until three days later that the Chinese nation was appraised of the situation. The report was then anti-terrorist, favorable, and empathetic with the U.S.

The Internet is also monitored and controlled by the government. In 2006 there were 113,000 Internet cafes in China, mostly in the larger cities – 31 million is the number of Internet users according to government-released reports. A recent announcement in the *China Daily* stated the government had initiated laws to prevent new Internet cafes from opening. So much for progress, but it is clear that Chinese citizens will continue to be exposed to news from the outside world, and it will become more and more difficult for the government to control it. I continue to watch with interest the rapid changes in China, and wonder what shifts a fifth "dynasty" might bring.

I've noted in prior chapters how much improvement I witnessed in terms of infrastructure and amenities in Taiyuan and Beijing. I also noticed how quality of life has changed for the Chinese people I've come to know in the last decade – everything from their appearance to their habits and attitudes. For example, during our first trip to China in October 1994, other than in the major cities, most people, male and female, were dressed in drab Mao-era outfits. In hot weather men would habitually pull their pant legs up and pull their shirts up to cool down, exposing their bellies. The women wore their hair cut short and straight. Little kids wore quilted Chinese coats, but wore no diapers; instead they donned a unique Chinese "split" in the back and bottom of their outfit, for dumping purposes. This was accomplished by squatting and doing the job right there on the sidewalks or wherever else, with their little bare asses hanging out!

By 1998, there was evidence of some fashion changes, especially regarding the younger generation. Men were now wearing Western-style suits and casual clothes. Women were now sporting long hair and some perms, wearing fashionable skirts and dresses, and donning nylon stockings and high-heeled shoes. Change, when it happens, comes fast in China! It is interesting to note that many male bicycle riders wear suits, while more than a few women ride wearing high heels! Certainly by 2003, in Taiyuan many youngsters were sporting Western-style branded clothes such as those with the Disney logo. Many babies were now wearing diapers in place of the traditional Chinese splits. During warm weather, I usually wear shorts while out and about. I was an oddity for the first few years, as shorts were unknown in Taiyuan. But by 2003 men had discovered shorts as *the* way to remain cool during hot weather!

In 1994 there were no cell phones in evidence in China – and landline phones were few and mostly controlled by the government. Nowadays China is the world leader in the use of cell phones, with most people in the cities having one or more phones. The Chinese tend to want the latest in technology, and are constantly upgrading their cell phones as a show of newfound affluence. Chinese are constantly on their cell phones, and text messaging is popular to such an extent it is a nuisance!

The Chinese working population breaks down into three main social strata. My estimate of the current population demographics is 900 million farmers or peasants living in small villages in the country; 250 million people in cities working for the government, military, and SOEs; and 150 million entrepreneurs running small and medium-sized businesses. The farmers who were the first to benefit from Deng's policies have fallen behind during China's rapid industrialization. Their average family income is very low, reportedly at less than $400 USD per year. Many farmers send some of their children to the cities to work in restaurants to earn money for the family (as they do at the "dumpling house"). The building boom going on in the cities has also encouraged a significant migration of peasants to urban worksites. It is estimated that over 200 million migrants work in the cities. Although there are laws in place to protect the rights of the migrant workers, these rights are regularly ignored; in many cases safety rules are disregarded and employers often shortchange the workers' wages.

Overall, though, safety at construction sites has improved in recent years. On our first visit, and even in 1998, most demolition and construction in the cities was done by hand labor, and scaffolding was invariably made of bamboo. There was no protection to passers-by from falling debris. Work was carried on from dawn until dusk, as no artificial lighting was provided. But by the early 2000s scaffolding was uniformly steel, demolition done by machines, and buildings erected with the use of cranes. Almost all projects now had netting to provide safety to passers-by from falling debris. Project work now runs around the clock with the use of artificial lighting. Again, change happens fast in China!

Coal mining is one industry where workers still labor under dangerous conditions. It is estimated that 5,000–10,000 miners (mostly coal) lose their lives in accidents each year. In many cases the operations are small and run by local village officials to provide incomes for their people. In most cases such operations are not sanctioned by the government and are illegal. These mines have virtually no safety standards and are extremely unsafe to operate.

Yet there is still often an attempt at secrecy surrounding what happens there. In 2006 the *China Daily* reported that 55 people were killed in a gas explosion at a mine. The local officials had reported that only five miners were killed. The officials attempted to round up all the relatives of the deceased, pay them off and move them to a different location to prevent them from testifying. They failed, were arrested, found guilty, and summarily executed. This scenario is played out over and over again throughout the country. Many thousands of these illegal mines have been shut down by the government – but as with much in China, this practice still persists. At the time of this writing in March 2007, I quote the *China Daily* of March 24, 2007, as follows:

Coal mine death toll at 21
Rescuers have found the body of the last miner missing after a gas explosion in a coal mine in Jincheng, North China's Shanxi Province, bringing the death toll to 21. The rescuers found the body at 11:30 a.m. on Friday. The blast occurred late Sunday afternoon at Miaojiang Coal Mine of Jincheng about four hour's bus ride from the provincial capital Taiyuan, when 21 miners were working underground. Rescue work was delayed for 44 hours because the mine owner attempted to cover up the accident. Eleven people, including pit owner Wang Junjun, the contractor, the district work safety inspector and the official in charge of monitoring gas density, have been arrested for attempting to cover up the accident.

In a very short time the individuals mentioned in the article will have their trials and no doubt will quickly be sentenced and receive a death sentence. As I continue to write two more serious cover-ups have been reported, one in Beijing and one in Shanxi. In Beijing 15 workers were buried underground when the walls of the pit where they were working in collapsed on top of them. The officials in charge fled the scene, but were captured shortly afterward. In Shanxi another coal mine gas explosion killed 17 miners. After this latest episode, the governor of Shanxi Province announced a serious crackdown regarding safety in all coal mining in Shanxi: the legally sanctioned mines will have more monitoring, while an increased effort will be undertaken to shutdown the illegal mines. It is a difficult task when some of these illegal mines operate in remote villages and provide incomes to families that would not otherwise have income.

Almost every school kid knows that China invented gunpowder and fireworks. Indeed even at the present time China manufactures the majority of the world's fireworks. Firework displays in China are an important tradition not only during the national holiday periods, but also at weddings and openings of stores and factories. Apparently the noise is meant to scare off bad spirits. Here is another situation wherein many small villages operate illegal and unsafe facilities, in this case to manufacture cheap fireworks. The papers report that thousands are killed and maimed annually from massive explosions that regularly occur in these operations. In addition many deaths and injuries are reported during the annual celebrations. The government is clamping down, but this too is a pervasive and not quickly eradicated practice!

In the case of some SOEs, when an industrial death occurs in their operation a large payoff to the appropriate officials and the deceased's family usually prevents any further legal actions. The government is gradually clamping down in this area as well but, you guessed it – it is a big onion!

The 250 million people who work for the state have it much better than farmers or other poor migrant workers – they are generally paid nominal salaries and supplied with housing and pensions. Unfortunately, in the government and SOE hierarchy, success is still not guaranteed by performance but more generally by relationships and influence ("Guang Zi"). This system is fraught with corruption and bribes. Within this system some individuals have become very rich. One small example was related to me by a Canadian I met in the hotel lobby. He had a project in the modernization of a stainless steel plant and was working with a Chinese engineer assigned by the SOE. He told me that this engineer had given him virtually no help during the process; however, two years ago this engineer was riding a bicycle, then last year he rode a motorcycle, and now he is driving a brand-new BMW. Where did the money for these conveyances come from on a nominal salary? Who was above him, and how many others received so much more money???

The government is attempting to deal with this situation, but remember, it's a giant onion – peel one layer and you get another one! From January through October of 2006, the Chinese newspapers reported that 32,500 cases of corruption or fraud by ranking officials had been tried by the courts, with only about 300 individuals being found not guilty. The final penalty depends on the amount – at the least it ends in the loss of position and benefits, possibly imprisonment, and in general if the crime is valued at over $250,000 in U.S. dollars, the death penalty is imposed. This seems like quite a deterrent!

In addition to outright corruption, the SOE system is also plagued by inefficiency and largesse. Our joint venture partner, TZ, for example is only marginally profitable yet they spend over 1,200,000 Yuan annually on Mao Tai and Fen Jiu white liquors. In addition, for the 2007 lunar New Year's celebration, they spent 1,700,000 Yuan on fireworks. Much money is wasted on show rather than structure in China.

I must at this point stress that Gao Zhijun, the CEO of TZ, has been most helpful in assisting the JV in achieving its goals and ensuring that all contractual obligations are met. In addition many positive changes have occurred during his watch at TZ.

That being said, doing business within China has been difficult for SCW, for many reasons outside of our immediate control. To deal with the SOEs as customers, it is customary to try to influence officials and create "relationships," i.e., bribery. This is totally illegal in our Western society! To manage this situation we are forced to use middlemen, wherein we sell them the product and they make their own deals. Out of necessity, SCW personnel, including myself, visit the various customers on an ongoing basis. Last year one of our major customers had 14 of their top officials arrested for corruption and bribe-taking, and off to the courts they went. These people have all been replaced by new and younger personnel. Hopefully as personnel changes take place, and as China becomes more and more familiar with Western business practices, they will see the light and the system will change somewhat!

I think it is appropriate at this point that I expand a little more on "relationship" issues in China, since it has been one of the main cultural differences I've observed. "Relationships" are of utmost importance in Chinese culture, and most business is conducted on the basis of said relationships. Indeed, most friendships are based on relationships. But the practice of Chinese relationship-building is different than how it is generally seen in the West. In China, relationship-building involves gifting, large lunches and dinners, toasting, and passing around numerous cigarettes. In some cases, both in business and holiday celebrations, there is a contest to determine who is stronger and can survive the most Fen Jiu. I normally do not participate in these contests, but it is interesting to sit back and watch the action during the drinking bouts. I occasionally see people leave the table. I believe they are taking an antidote (barfing) and then returning to the action. I have observed Chinese turn white and/or red during these bouts!

I recently had a firsthand experience with the custom of relationship-building. I needed a follow-up blood test while in China. One of our inside sales ladies, Sun Yan, has a friend in a high position in the closest hospital to SCW. She contacted this person to see if I could get in for the test, as this hospital technically is not allowed to treat foreigners. When Sun Yan, Wei Yu, and I showed up at the waiting area of the hospital it was crowded with elderly Chinese people waiting for service. We only had to wait about ten minutes for the friend to show. The friend appeared and we were led to the front of the blood-testing line and immediately served. The stares I received were amusing. I wonder what the natives were thinking. Also, there was no cost to me! We did decide to donate a nominal amount of money to the hospital.

The remaining 150 million working people are entrepreneurs and the new middle class, armed with real disposable incomes. This class has grown significantly over the last six years, from about 10 million to the present number (by my figures). These people are creating real jobs and are driving the economy. They are the ones purchasing cars, new apartments, and furnishings. Perhaps indicative of the rise of this middle class is the tremendous increase in domestic air travel in China. In 1998 there were two flights daily in and out of Taiyuan city – one to Beijing and one to Shanghai. By March 2007, Taiyuan had 83 flights daily in and out, to 34 different cities. These flights are habitually full, as I have experienced myself. Once I was on my return from Shanghai Hongqiao Airport (one of two in Shanghai; both are now severely overtaxed). While waiting in the departure area for my flight the incessant noise from the constant announcements of departures and numerous flight delays made it almost impossible to conduct a conversation. My particular flight was delayed one hour before we passengers were finally allowed to board busses to be taken to our aircraft, which was parked about a five-minute ride away – since all gates were fully loaded at the terminal. I was shocked as we made our way to the parked aircraft. I counted 80 other aircraft, all lined in rows in the same area in the process of loading passengers. Already one hour late, we were loaded and then the announcements began: "Sorry for the further delays but due to air traffic, please be patient." We finally took off after a total delay of one hour and forty-five minutes. Beijing Airport has experienced similar growth in domestic travel, and delays are habitual. Clearly, the middle class is growing and traveling. When it comes to international flights the growth has been slower due to international agreements, but it too has seen inexorable growth with the percentage of Chinese travelers!

Compared to those in the middle class, the average factory worker in China finds it difficult to own a car. It would take four or five years of gross earnings to purchase even a modest vehicle – compared to a half year's gross earnings for a worker in North

America to purchase a car. Yet wages are increasing considerably in China, even for the lower classes. Many factory workers have been able to upgrade from bicycles to motorized bicycles and motor bikes. The labor policy is such that the Chinese government promotes trade unionism in the belief that it protects workers rights. For example, currently the Guangzhou government has taken issue with Western franchises such as McDonald's, Pizza Hut, and KFC for their apparent violation of employee rights. The government has mandated a minimum wage of 7.5 Yuan/hour ($ 0.97) for part-time workers. Yet it is reported that each of these chains pays the following: McDonald's, 4 Yuan); KFC, 4.7 Yuan; and Pizza Hut, 5 Yuan. In addition the government claims that the employees at these places are required to work excessive hours each week. Interestingly, the price of the food from each of these chains is almost identical to that in the North American markets. Someone is making a lot of money in China!

The Chinese one-child–per-family policy came into effect in the early 1980s. This policy has allowed China to stabilize the population at roughly 1.3 billion. The policy applies to government employees, SOE employees, armed force personnel, and most people living in the cities. There are exemptions for the 55 or so recognized ethnic minorities and for the rural peasants; these groups are allowed to have a second child if the first born is a daughter or disabled. The current government is concerned with the plight of these minorities. The 55 different ethnic groups number about 100 million or 8.4 percent of the total population. It is estimated that fully 11.7 million are abjectly poor and 20.5 million have barely only enough clothing and food for daily survival. The government has plans to divert more state funds towards improving conditions for this segment of population. That is if there are funds left after corruption is taken into account! Rumors are that in the early days of the one-child policy infanticide was practiced in the case of the first born being a girl or disabled. China, along with India, has a 110/100 male/female ratio. Sometime soon young Chinese males will have a lot of competition for female companionship! In most of the rest of the world this ratio is reversed. I have talked with numerous young couples regarding their choice of gender and they invariably say it does not matter; many say they would prefer a girl!

The one-child policy has also created much traffic in foreigners adopting Chinese babies. Over the years I have seen many couples, usually in their mid-thirties, from Europe, the U.S., and Canada in China to adopt babies and young children. The adoptees are almost exclusively girls. One month in 2002 there were at least 50 couples from the U.S. and Canada staying at the Shanxi Grand with their adopted daughters. In only two cases, Cherie and I saw couples from the U.S. with adopted boys: one with a severe clubfoot and the other with a severe cleft palate. In talking to these couples we learned that in both cases the husbands were pediatricians and would repair the problems back in the U.S. One of the boys, aged three, had been in an orphanage all his life: he was extremely underdeveloped and it was obvious that he had experienced no loving contact with caring humans.

Currently almost all of the parents affected by the one-child policy are between the ages of 20 and 45. These parents generally came from bigger families and have brothers and sisters. The current only child thus has uncles and aunts: what they have not figured out is that these children's children will not have such an extended family. In addition there will not be enough young people to attend to needs of their parents as the older generation ages. Some of the more affluent middle-class citizens are beginning to question the one-child policy.

Divorces, while discouraged, are fairly common in China. There are many single mothers in China who are in their early to mid-thirties. Most of these mothers were married in their late teens or early twenties, then later the husbands deserted the family. Now most Chinese are not getting married until their late twenties or early thirties. I have also had occasion to meet several Chinese men who keep "two families," since their work often takes them to different cities.

On the resources front, China currently produces over 400 million tons of steel annually – more than double that of any other country. The authorities readily admit, however, that only 35 percent of this production meets world-quality standards! The country is also now the major producer and user of cement in the world, and one of the world's major energy users.

Some of these resources are going into the improvement of infrastructure. China is currently building a massive "interstate" type road system connecting the major cities. (Which will accommodate all the new cars: private automobile ownership has seen a dramatic rise from 5 million in 2001 to 15 million in 2004, and the rate continues to rise.) The railway system is being expanded and updated significantly, too. Massive pipelines for the transport of natural gas from the western parts of the country to the energy-hungry east are being built. Major new power facilities including nuclear are being erected in all parts of the country. In certain flood-prone areas levees and dikes are being constructed. The aforementioned coupled with the current booming construction in the major cities has created the tremendous demands for steel, other metals, concrete and power.

While China has experienced rapid and dramatic industrialization and has moved into a real power position in world trade, there are many endemic problems created by this. Some of the more significant problems facing the new China over the next generation include a woeful shortage of fresh water; rampant pollution and general environmental issues; sustainability of growth to provide jobs for the have-nots; continued corruption within the government and SOEs, which widens the gap between the haves and have-nots; and enshrining human rights to its citizens. I will give my views on each of these areas in order.

I believe the largest constraint to China's ultimate success is the abject shortage of water – both in terms of total resources and safe water. China, with the world's largest population, has less fresh water resources per capita than most countries in the world.

It is reported that over 400 million people have no access to daily water either of adequate quantity or quality for drinking or cooking. There are measures in place to alleviate water shortages over the longer term; some make sense, while others seem frivolous. Industries are now required to reduce water consumption and recycle what water they do use. Beijing has banned the growing of rice, a water-intensive crop, but because of the increase in affluence of its citizens, personal hygiene and water use is on the rise. To serve its inhabitants, water is brought to the city from remote areas or other less-inhabited provinces. Unfortunately this water is transported in open canals and much water is lost to evaporation during its flow through arid regions.

As I've mentioned before, pollution and air quality are significant problems in China. Approximately 85 percent of the country's electrical power needs are supplied by coal burning. (The Three Gorges Dam and the Chinese nuclear program now supply about 15 percent of power demands.) The government policy is to shut down all inefficient and dirty power plants. In my estimation they have so far eliminated a significant number of the heavier polluters so that now about 15 percent of the coal burning plants are of high efficiency and are clean burning. Not only is the air quality affected by the heavy use of dirty coal, but it is also acerbated by heavy dust storms resulting from desertification of the northern Mongolian regions (due to drought, deforestation, and/or inappropriate agriculture). The government has instituted massive tree plantings in attempts to halt this desertification.

Waste disposal, both toxic and "normal" uncontrolled landfill material, contribute to pollution of the Chinese waterways. Toxic chemical spills in different parts of the country are frequently reported. In 2006 a major spill occurred in the Harbin area, resulting in a complete shutdown of all drinking water supplies for the city. Emergency bottled water supplies had to be brought in to supply the residents for two months – until the spill passed by. In addition this spill occurred on the ice on the major river that flowed into Russia, causing an international incident. "Midnight dumping" is rampant around China.

To alleviate the heavy pollution endemic to the capital city, and in anticipation of hosting the Olympic Games in 2008, the Chinese government in year 2000 began a program of moving all heavy industry away from Beijing. The industries required to move were mandated to meet world-standard environmental regulations and meet stringent water and energy conservation standards at their respective relocated areas. The moving of virtually all this heavy industry has no doubt reduced the overall pollution in the city, but the rapid increase in automobiles and the continued issue of the frequent dust storms still cause the pollution conditions to be less than ideal.

Can the Chinese government continue to oversee rapid industrialization while improving the poor environmental conditions endemic to most parts of the country? It will be a challenge, as it is absolutely necessary for China to maintain the current industrial growth rate of about 9 percent in order to provide jobs for the hundreds of millions who also desire to move up the ladder of success. In addition, as the SOEs drive towards more efficiency, they are shedding workers, and jobs must be created for these people also. Reports in the newspapers each year indicate that a high percentage of Chinese university graduates have difficulty in obtaining jobs. Can the government improve environmental conditions while still creating jobs?? I say it's possible but will probably take a generation to achieve.

I see significant problems for China once in the post-industrialized era. China is now in a position not unlike the U.S. after WW II, wherein most heavy industrial products are consumed domestically towards building a modern infrastructure; however most Chinese industries (especially the large SOEs) have not recognized the value of quality, speed, and service. The Chinese customer willingly accepts less-than-quality goods and unreliable deliveries. While the ISO certificate attained by SCW is genuine, a significant percentage of ISO certificates in China are bought, and therefore meaningless. Again, relationships and influence play a significant role. Another area of failure is meeting delivery schedules on orders received and conveying information in a timely manner. If China is to succeed in supplying sophisticated and high-specification products to the developed world, changes of several orders of magnitude will be necessary! This will also require significant cultural changes and deregulation. I am not convinced that this will occur in the near future. China will face significant challenges and competition from India, which seems poised to meet the standards required by the developed world. One of the greatest challenges for China to achieve world competitiveness will be the dismantling of the of the influence systems in the SOEs.

The Chinese government is working to improve conditions in all the aforementioned areas, but it is a big onion!

Chapter XVII: Visits to Other Cities

A bit of a travelogue; all learning experiences!

During my tenure in China I have had the opportunity to visit many of its cities and villages. Most of my visits have been for business purposes, but Cherie and I have also taken some vacation time while there to explore the country on our own. Even during my business trips, the customers I have met with have been most gracious – often insisting on showing me the local sites of interest; so I have been able to absorb much of China's culture even while conducting business. In this chapter I've included bits and pieces of what I have experienced in many of these places. I hope that, as a whole, it presents an entertaining and interesting introduction to the wide variety of people and places that form this fascinating Asian nation.

Hoh Hot & Inner Mongolia

During my first trip to China in 1994, while visiting the An Tai Bao (ATB) mine with Mark Mallory and Phoa, we stayed in the city of Hoh Hot in Inner Mongolia. We were lodged in an expat compound, and did not get much time to explore the city, but I did note that it seemed quite primitive, with no high-rise or modern buildings. Our group also noted the dearth of automobiles on the poorly paved and narrow roads. I never did make it back there; I wonder if it is the same today.

There was one place in this area that I got to know well. Between 1999 and 2003, accompanied by Liu Min, I visited a small village in Inner Mongolia several times to purchase hand-woven Chinese carpets for Cherie and several other family members. Liu Min knew a woman, Ms. Wu, who owned a small carpet factory in this particular village. To get to the village from Taiyuan, there was only 50 km of finished expressway to travel on; the remaining distance of 120 km was via two-lane road roads through small villages and mountains – and there were no guardrails along the drop-off. The road was populated with every conceivable conveyance, making travel all the more dangerous, and on each trip we witnessed terrible accidents.

On the first trip to meet Ms. Wu in early 1999 we had allowed two and a half hours for the trip in; however due to the difficult road and congested conditions it took almost four hours to get there. As a consequence we arrived just in time for lunch, and Ms. Wu took us to her favorite restaurant. Remember, this was a small village – and the water quality and cleanliness were extremely doubtful. But I was obliged to sample everything put in front of me. I was concerned that this would result in my first case of food poisoning! Luckily I did not get ill.

After lunch we followed Ms. Wu to her factory. All of her carpets were hand woven by what appeared to be mostly teenage girls, each seated at a bench in fairly primitive conditions. The wool carpets were woven with 200 stitches to the inch, which required much effort on the part of the weavers. I later learned that it took two girls almost nine months to complete the weaving on a 2 x 3 meter carpet. It then took another two months for two girls to tie all the knots. For a silk carpet of the same size with 600 stitches to the inch, it took three girls nine months to finish the weaving, and a further three girls another three months to tie the knots. In the warehouse, we examined many carpets of different sizes, colors and designs. In all cases the quality was superb.

We undertook this first trip to order a 5 x 8 foot carpet for my daughter Mary, to match the colors and design style of her home. After discussing this with Ms. Wu and ordering the carpet, we left for the return trip back to Taiyuan. When I returned 10 months later to pick it up, much to my horror it was the wrong colors; Liu Min, thankfully, decided that instead he would buy it for his wife. We then had a long discussion with Ms. Wu (she spoke no English) to help her understand the color scheme we required, and then we ordered another one. When it was finally finished I returned to pay for and pick up the carpet, making this now the third arduous and dangerous road trip. With relief, I saw that it was to the ordered specifications.

When my brother Sean visited me in 2003, Liu Min and I made yet another trip to the village, for Sean to purchase a carpet from the warehouse stock. At the same time, I ordered a second carpet for my daughter, with the same design specifications and colors as the original. I also purchased a carpet for Cherie from the warehouse. Incidentally, the price for a 5' x 8' wool carpet was a nominal $500 USD. Carpets of this quality purchased in North America would command a price at least 10 times greater.

Before leaving with my brother, I asked if Ms. Wu would deliver my daughter's second carpet to the Shanxi Grand when it was finished. She readily agreed. When she did deliver the carpet it was, disappointingly, slightly off on the color scheme, but I took the risk of wrath from Mary and accepted it. I resolved not to have any more trips to the village, as each time we got back to Taiyuan I thanked God that we had not suffered a major accident.

Cherie also wanted more carpets, and not wanting to subject her to the road conditions, I asked Ms. Wu if she could bring five or six carpets to the Shanxi Grand for Cherie to peruse. Fortunately she complied, and Cherie bought two more.

Figure 21 Carpet for Cherie's sister

Xi'An, the Capital City of Shaanxi Province

In the spring of 2000 Cherie and I had the opportunity to visit the old walled city of Xi'An, home to the famous Terra Cotta Warriors. It is about an hour and a half hour flight west from Taiyuan. This trip included some business; I was to visit a machine shop near Xi'An to inspect the machining of some initial pipe joint orders. We were accompanied by Ray Sykes from our Portland office, Tom Holly from Portland, James Wu, and Percy Chang. Cherie and I were registered in the Hyatt – a true five-star hotel. At lunchtime, James Wu, who was a native, took us to a restaurant that served ethnic food. It was a 13-dish Chinese spread, laid out on the typical lazy Susan. The entire spread, excepting the rice, came from either the sea or from fresh water. There was fish maw, fish skin, various kinds of unidentifiable fish and fish parts, jellyfish, sea cucumber and shrimps. The look on Ray Sykes's face, a longtime friend and finicky eater, when he saw the spread was unforgettable!

After lunch, we went to the site of the Terra Cotta warriors, a collection of 8,099 larger-than-life Chinese terra cotta figures of warriors and horses, a must-see in China! That evening we visited a world-class museum in the city, and afterwards we sampled food at one of Xi'An's many Muslim restaurants, in which lamb is one of the main offerings. (The city is also home to about 45,000 Muslims.)

After I was done with my business the next day, Cherie and I went to the top of the old walled city. The walls are about 15 meters high, 15 meters wide at the top, and extend for around 6 km. We rented bicycles and rode around on the wall; no cars were allowed up top. During our short three-day stay in Xi'An it was often necessary for Cherie and me to ride in the local taxis, which were built in the province. We were a little leery of the safety, as the fiberglass gas tank in each was located immediately behind the back seat – inside the taxi!

I had occasion to revisit Xi'An in March of 2006 to check on the delivery of a new arc furnace transformer from a manufacturer. My friend Mark Nolan was planning on meeting me there, and had agreed to be my interpreter, although I planned to travel to the city by myself. Just before boarding the plane I received a text message from Mark saying he had to cancel. Now what was I going to do?? I decided to wing it! Fortunately while boarding my flight I noticed a lady, Zhang Bing, who used to work at the Shanxi Grand who was traveling to Xi'An to visit friends. I had on occasion talked to her and her English was OK. I asked her if it would be possible for her to accompany me to the manufacturer and help me with translation, and lucky for me she agreed. Although she did not have the technical understanding, she at least could voice my concerns regarding the delivery of the transformer. Lucky again! Zhang Bing and her friend also insisted on taking me to see the Terra Cotta Warriors. It was well worth visiting the site for a second time. They also insisted that I go to the top of the city wall and ride a bicycle. I did not have the heart to tell them I had previously experienced that event too!

Village whose name I can't say or spell!

In the fall of 2000 I had occasion to visit a small village (I have forgotten how to say or spell the name) about three hours from Taiyuan. The village was home to a foundry that I needed to audit to determine if they could be an acceptable supplier of small ductile castings to SCW. I traveled by car with James Wu over the usual death-defying rural roads.

After entering the community, which was primitive to say the least, we proceeded to the foundry where we were met by the owner and five of his managers. Apparently this foundry is the major employer for the villagers. We then toured the operation, which was in the process of melting and pouring. As we entered the pouring area I was taken aback with the smoky and dusty condition in this building. I could see perhaps only ten feet ahead of myself, and I could barely breathe. I thought: *people must die young here!* The castings and control processes, however, were satisfactory for our needs.

The owner insisted that we stay and have lunch with him and his managers in their office, explaining that food would be brought in from elsewhere on the premises. We were all seated at a table in the office while various dishes were brought out and set on the table. One particular aroma, though, caused my stomach to leap up into my throat – it was a shrimp dish that stunk to high heaven. I thought: *these shrimp must have died many moons ago!* My other immediate thought was that if I were to eat those shrimp I would be a very ill man. I partook sparingly of the other dishes, and took an antidote pill just in case, since the ride back would take three hours – and food poisoning usually occurs within two hours. The pill worked, as I suffered no illness. During that same lunch I had another unique experience when I was served hot Coca-Cola. It was their custom to heat the Coke to tea temperature. All I can say is: *ugh, ugh!!!*

Kunming, Yunan Province

In November 2003, Cherie and I visited Kunming, in southwest China. The city is very close to the Vietnam border. The vegetation in the area is semi-tropical and we observed many different and strange fruits and vegetables growing. The flowering plants were particularly beautiful to see. We stayed in a state-owned hotel, the King World, which was actually a sister to the Shanxi Grand. It was rated at three stars and not up to the standard of the Grand, although the lobby was larger and grander. The room we had at the hotel was comfortable and fairly clean, but in the bathroom, after flushing the toilet or draining the bath, water would spout from the drain in the floor. After a few failed attempts to explain the problem to the staff we finally found a maintenance person who understood the problem. The solution: change rooms!

After checking into the hotel, we visited a local museum that was featuring a showing of the history of the Catholic Church in China. The show consisted of a series of black-and-white photos of churches and church life from around 1920 to the present. It was interesting to note that most of the history pictured was from Kunming, Shanghai, and Taiyuan.

Yunan Province is the home to a large number of different ethnic minorities, all with their own traditional cultures. It was an experience to see some of the different types of clothing and the cultural diversity of these people. Yunan is famous for the Stone Forest, which consists of karst topography of limestone columns. This natural phenomenon is enclosed in a large park, and much walking and climbing is involved to experience its wonders.

When we visited, the park was a three-hour drive along the now-familiar primitive and congested roads. We were two months too early to be able to take the almost-completed expressway, which would have made the trip much safer, and would have dropped the time to one hour. During the ride we actually saw the narrow gauge train that runs between China and Vietnam.

We hired one of the ethnic minority people, a delightful and beautiful girl dressed in her culture's costume, to be our guide for the Stone Forest. It was November but the temperature in this part of the country was 27°C. This area, approximately 2,670 square km with formations believed to be over 270 million years old, was another must-see site in China!

Figure 22 Stone Forest near Kunming

The people in south China are generally smaller and more lightly built than those from the north. The culture and food habits are also different. We accordingly visited around the city to experience the markets and the different foods. The variety of foods being exhibited by the street vendors was incredible: fish of all kinds (fresh and dried), squid, snakes, and many, many unidentifiable meats. There was also an incredible variety of vegetables and fruits being sold – but their names are totally (at least for me) untranslatable into English. All the food, however interesting, was left completely out in the open in the hot weather. The streets of Kunming were generally narrow and cluttered with street venders. While we were walking about, we were caught in a tropical downpour, and nipped into a roofed market and purchased a large umbrella (cost: 15 Yuan) to protect us on the short walk back to the hotel. When we got to the hotel and sat in the lobby the rain was so heavy one could hear it while inside. This was a three-day vacation trip for Cherie and I and we thoroughly enjoyed the experience.

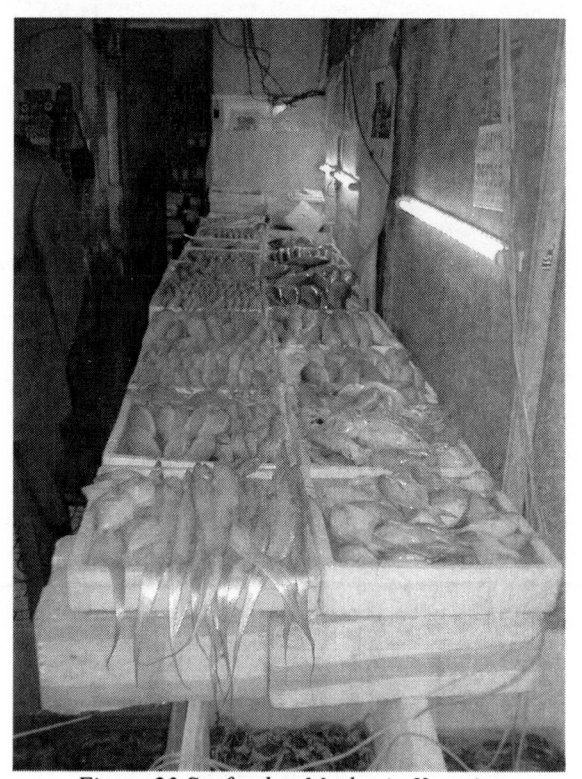

Figure 23 Seafood at Market in Kunming

Harbin, Capital of Heilongjiang Province

Late in February 2004 I had the opportunity to visit one of SCW's customers in Harbin, a city of six million people located in northeast China close to Russia and North Korea. The area historically has had a strong Russian influence. Harbin is famous for its heavy industries as well as its annual ice sculptures. Not only do they build a complete ice city that if real would accommodate 10,000 inhabitants, but the airport expressway and other major streets are lined with large ice sculptures.

On this trip I flew with Wei Yu and Camry Yang (a salesman for SCW). The flight from Taiyuan was about two and a half hours long. During the last hour the ground below us was completely covered with snow. When we arrived at the Harbin airport around 5 p.m. we were met by our customer and driven to our hotel in the city some half an hour away. This was our first exposure to the incredible ice structures along the roadway. The outside temperature was a brisk -35°C.

We were hosted by the customer to a state dinner that evening. Wei Yu and I nominated Camry to be our toaster for the Mao Tai drinks. The hosts were told that I preferred beer, and they immediately brought in some Harbin beer and informed me that Harbin is also famous for the brew. This beer is made using water from special wells and the volume is restricted by regulation. This is very good beer and I told the hosts so!

The next morning we were picked up and taken to their plant for in-depth meetings. The meetings were very successful and both companies came away satisfied with the outcome. For lunch the customer took us to a very large restaurant with a tropical theme. Inside the approximately two-football-field-sized structure was a large open area with many exotic flora and some birds, and round tables both large and small were dispersed throughout. Along both sides and one end of the building were numerous private rooms varying in size for 6–8 people to seating for perhaps 50 people. Harbin Valve Co., our host, had 11 of their top managers present, and with the three of us from SCW we totaled 14. They had reserved a private room for the occasion. There was no Fen Jiu – only Harbin beer and tea were to be served. Lunch was an epicurean's delight. After a long meal we returned to our hotel. Since lunch had consisted of many dishes and we had overeaten (and not finished eating until 3:30 p.m.), we three respectfully declined a dinner invitation.

It was dark by 5 p.m., and Wei Yu, Camry, and I decided to visit the ice sculpture city. It was again very cold at -35°C. Wei Yu and Camry, in spite of wearing many layers of clothing, were very cold. I found that with fewer layers, a good coat and something to cover my ears, I was quite comfortable. The ice sculpture city, lit up at night, was a spectacular sight to behold and is another must-see in China.

Figure 24 Harbin Ice City

The next morning we were due to return to Taiyuan. Wei Yu insisted since I liked Harbin beer that we should take some back with us. I informed her we would not be able to take it as carry-on baggage. "No problem," she said, "we will check it in our bags." But there was a problem, as their bags would not hold all the bottles – and she insisted that I put the extra two bottles in the bag with my computer and check it in. I complied! However when the luggage arrived on the conveyor in Taiyuan I was dismayed to see liquid dripping out of my computer bag. Only one bottle had broken, but that three Yuan beer had destroyed my $3,000.00 hard drive. Wei Yu was leaving for meetings in Portland in four days' time and I asked her to take the laptop with her and deliver it to the IT department there to replace the drive. When she delivered the unit in Portland she told the people that "John got a little water inside his computer." I was lucky again, as I did not lose any of the data from the hard drive. But since, the word has spread around China that "John likes Harbin beer" and so customers and suppliers now routinely bring or have sent to me cases of Harbin beer, which I have been happy to share with my many friends.

Tonglin, Anhui Province

SCW had developed a new customer in the small city of Tonglin, and as was customary Wei Yu wanted me to accompany her and others to meet with the appropriate people at the operations. So in June 2004, Wei Yu, Liu Yu Feng, Camry, and I flew from Taiyuan to Hefei, the capital city of Anhui Province in the southeast of China. This area is subtropical, and therefore hot and humid at that time of the year. Once we landed at Hefei we were picked up and driven to Tonglin, one and a half hours away. The drive was along well-laid-out roads, however, and the scenery was interesting, with a different flora compared to Shanxi and other parts of China that I had visited. The customer in question operated a copper mine and indeed "Tonglin" means copper in Chinese. After check-in at the recommended hotel (three stars) we were driven to the mine office. After introductions and card-changing all around, business discussions proceeded, and were followed by a tour of the mine operations. The meetings were extremely successful and we came away with many new orders.

Since the customary state dinner was not to begin until 8:30 p.m. and we were finished the tour at 4 p.m., we decided to walk in a large nearby park. It was hot and humid, and rife with innumerable mosquitoes – especially around dusk. I was fortunate that these mosquitoes preferred Chinese "meat" to Western "meat"! Wei Yu and the others suffered many bites while I did not get bitten even once.

The dinner banquet was another unique experience. It was the customary spread with many dishes (although different foods than I typically saw), and of course, it came with the usual rounds of toasting. The customer was apprised that I did not favor the Chinese liquor and preferred beer, which was provided. As always, I appreciated their thoughtfulness. We nominated Camry again to be our toaster. Our host was also notified that I liked beef, and they obliged with two beef dishes that, unfortunately, were the toughest cuts of meat I had ever experienced. I think I am still picking bits of it out of my teeth today! As the dinner progressed, I partook of all the different foods. One particular dish came around the lazy Susan and I nonchalantly took some in my chopsticks, thinking it was eggplant, and put the item into my mouth. Much discussion was occurring around me and I realized I was eating small frog legs. Suddenly my system rebelled – it hit me that this was a *whole* small frog and I was going to be eating it – guts and all. No one saw me take the item from my mouth and place it on the scrap plate. I carefully watched to ensure that that dish passed me by for the balance of the meal. The next morning I felt fine, and we were driven back to Hefei to catch our plane back to Taiyuan.

Perhaps this is the place to mention some of the many foods I have experienced while in China. The list is long and filled with unique "delicacies": frog legs; pig stomach lining; fish maw; jellyfish; fish skin; sea cucumber; tofu; river eel; several unidentified (to me) fish species; duck and chicken heads; chicken, duck, and goose feet; 1,000-year-old eggs; dog; and donkey meat. In addition to foods that are translatable into English, I have eaten so many delicious but unidentifiable vegetables and fruits. Fortunately I have not suffered the opportunity to have snake or snake blood, water beetles, scorpions, or other bizarre foods that I have heard are eaten in China. I must say that almost everything I have eaten in China, however strange it may seem, tastes good!

I have eaten in fine restaurants in the developed cities as well as some less desirable places in some of the villages I have visited. Amazingly, I have never suffered food poisoning, but in a few instances have had minor loose bowels. (Nothing like when poor Fred, back in the early days at SCW, ate the spoiled turtle!) In cases where I felt the food may have been bad or if cold food was washed in unsafe water, I would take an antidote (a prescription pill), to head off any potential suffering. In one instance Liu Min hosted Cherie and I to a "hot pot" dinner at a restaurant specializing in 16 different kinds of mushrooms, which were to be fed into the pot. As we were eating Liu Min announced "this is a purgative you know." His word was spot on, and when Cherie and I arrived back at the hotel she and I reenacted the Archie Bunker and Meathead scene from *All in the Family*, seeing who could get through the bathroom door first. Both of us took the antidote, however, and were quickly seized up!

The Three Gorges, Shenzen, & Sanya

In November and December of 2005 Cherie and I decided to take a long vacation during our time together in China. We began the trip with plans to take a river tour through the Three Gorges area. The excursion began with a flight from Taiyuan to Chongqing, in the eastern part of Sichuan Province. We arrived in this heavily populated city (an estimated 30 million people live there) in the evening, before our ship's departure the next afternoon. After checking into our hotel we did the usual and toured the city, which was very hilly with mostly narrow and winding streets. As usual there was heavy traffic, consisting of many different modes of transportation. Sichuan is the province where very spicy food is the norm. Accordingly, we partook of this new cuisine and found it very tasty to say the least. The next morning we visited the large modern museum which provided a thorough history of the province. Unfortunately it was school tour day at the museum, with myriad elementary and middle school classes in attendance. All were curious of "the foreigners." Cherie and I managed to keep a step ahead of the crowds but the noise when the classes moved from exhibit to exhibit was deafening!

At 4 p.m. we departed by taxi to meet our ship on the Yangtze River. We arrived at a muddy parking area high above the river. Before we could get out of the taxi the car was surrounded by indigenous "river" people. Five of them surrounded us; two of them grabbed our luggage, hoisted it on their shoulders, and proceeded down the steep incline towards the ship. We had no say in the matter! It was a precipitous trip down the muddy and steep incline, so it was nice, after all, not to have to carry luggage.

Once at the bottom, the rest of the distance to the moored ship – around 200 meters away – was across wonky floats. As soon as we made it to the ship, our "porters" demanded payment: 500 Yuan for all five pieces of luggage. I may have been on vacation, but being at home in China, I was no typical tourist: I handed the two who had done the work 100 Yuan each and told the others to get lost!

We boarded the ship, which had a capacity of 200 people. It was complete with cabins and dining areas to make the long journey comfortable: it was a three-day trip from Chongqing to the dam; from there we would go through the gates and then finally disembark in YiChang, a city below the dam. There is an enormous amount of traffic on the Yangtze River, mainly commercial carriers, tourist boats, and fishing boats. Some of the commercial carriers are huge, and the locks at the dam have been sized to accommodate their passing. The tourist boats range in size and are rated from one star to five stars. (Our ship was rated four stars and was intermediate in size.)

Upon boarding our ship, all 200 passengers were assembled in a common area and assigned our rooms. On this trip there were only 10 foreign guests: Cherie and I, two young couples from New Zealand, an American family of four, an American from Minnesota and his Chinese "squeeze," and a single Frenchman. The rest of the guests were Chinese. All we foreigners were shown that for lunches and suppers we would be seated at our own table.

I must comment on the American family. The father and mother were from Washington, D.C. The eldest daughter (a Caucasian) was a university graduate teaching English in Guangdong (she was fluent in Chinese), while the younger 10-year-old daughter was an adopted Chinese child who had never been back to China since the adoption. She spoke no Chinese! The family told us the following story: When they traveled to Guangdong to meet the older daughter and while entering their hotel, a policeman grabbed the younger daughter, thinking she was a beggar clutching onto the foreigners. The child was terror-struck! She could not explain, as she knew no Chinese. After a few moments the older daughter was able to clarify and diffuse the situation. I wondered, though, what the policeman thought with a Caucasian speaking Chinese, and a Chinese speaking only English!

Our cabin was fairly small, relatively clean, and comfortable with an outside view. The ship, a four decker, set sail about 6 p.m. downriver. At 7 p.m. we assembled in the dining room and were seated at our assigned table with the other foreigners. Apparently except for the desserts, our food was slightly different than that served to the Chinese guests, but the food at this meal and subsequent meals were nothing to write home about.

After breakfast the next morning (again nothing special), we foreigners all were on the top outside deck looking at the wonders of the river: the variety of boat traffic and the vastness of the three gorges of water, which were slowly being backed up by the new and huge dam. Unfortunately the pollution conditions masked the beauty of the moment. Around 10 a.m. we pulled over to a dock and disembarked to visit an ancient city called the Ghost City. This city was situated high up on the cliffs and would not be inundated with the rising waters. There were numerous stairs to climb and many hawkers pressing us to buy their wares. After passing through the throng and climbing for about 15 minutes we arrived at the city. We toured the city for a couple of hours, then returned through the hawker gauntlet to the boat and set sail again down the river. There were many wonders to view during the trip. It is significant that while all the foreigners were up and watching the scenery, the majority of Chinese passengers stayed below either playing cards or watching TV.

In the afternoon the ship put on a presentation showing the planning and construction of the Three Gorges Dam project, including an update of the situation at the time. We were sailing in a 600-km lake created by the damming of the river. The water had already risen some 75 meters and was expected to rise a further 45 meters when it was complete. Of course this resulted in the country having to move millions of residents to new locations. I was amazed to learn that most of the villages to be drowned were not dismantled, nor the years of garbage accumulation removed – they were left as is. Most of the historic sites were preserved, however, by walling them or moving them up the hills. We learned during the trip that people were paid to collect garbage as it rose to the surface.

The next day we entered the gorge, and again the significance and magnitude of the dam project was obscured by the polluted air. At noon we were transferred to a smaller boat and cruised up a feeding inlet with towering cliffs on both sides. We were amazed to see high above, ancient wooden coffins stuck in caves and on ledges. I noticed the rocks were limestone, and wondered if the Chinese were aware that the acidity of the water was going to eat the limestone over time.

Two hours later we were docked, and after passing through the usual throng of hawkers, were transferred to small dugouts (canoes) with outriggers and a crew of polers. We then were poled up a small shallow river to its end. This was the clearest water I had seen in China and the air was surprisingly clear, allowing us to view the foliage and birds on the surrounding hillside. It was stunning! Immediately after arriving at this beautiful area, however, we turned around and proceeded rapidly downriver, avoiding the many exposed and hidden rocks. Upon arrival at the dock we again ran "the gauntlet" and boarded our boat for the return to our larger ship, where the crew, prior to dinner, held a demonstration of traditional Chinese dumpling making.

During the night and the next day we continued downriver, and again the magnitude of the project and the mountain scenery was awesome – although by now it was raining. At about 10 p.m., on this last day, and in the dark, we proceeded into one of the massive locks to bypass the dam. This was one of many locks, and it contained several larger and smaller ships. Over the course of several hours the ships were lowered some 75 meters, and by early morning we were docked below the massive dam. We disembarked for the final time and toured the dam site, including the information center which was complete with a scale model of the dam and whole project. It was impressive!

Cherie and I had an early evening flight from YiChang, near where the dam was located, to Shenzhen in the south of China. We avoided the harassment of the porters this time and hailed a taxi to take us to the city. After arriving, we were so unimpressed (it was hard to top all of that gorgeous gorge scenery), that we decided to head directly to the airport, which at that time of day was virtually deserted, so we had a quiet time together and – finally – some decent food.

Shenzhen, Guangdong Province

The flight to Shenzhen was about two hours. Cherie and I arrived in the early evening and were met by an old friend, Dominic Song. I had previously visited Dominic with Wei Yu on two other occasions. He is the owner of a manufacturing and sales company serving the crushing industry, and a customer of SCW. (He has hinted he wants to hire me, but Wei Yu told him she would kill him if he so dared!) He drove us to a fine hotel in the city and told us that he was going to shepherd us to all the sites of the city during the six days we were there. Shepherd us he did!

Shenzhen is the city that Deng Xiao Peng built from scratch, and in a very short time. In the early 1980s, the area had around 2,000 residents, and now it is one of the most modern cities in the world with about six million inhabitants. On a clear day one can see Hong Kong across the bay. Our hotel was located near two major theme parks that are connected by a bridge. We had a nice dinner in the hotel dining room – a Western style buffet! The hotel was very nice, except we had a continuing problem with excessive heat in the room. It was warm outside and opening the windows did not help! This was southern China, and even in November the temperature was quite warm.

The next day after breakfast Dominic dutifully picked us up for a tour of the city. The roadways are magnificent in Shenzhen, with wide streets and avenues laid out on rectangular grids. Even more significantly, the drivers seem to obey rules that we Westerners are more accustomed to! The city is surrounded by mountains and has many spectacular parks with beautiful flora and man-made lakes. It is a well-planned city! On the surrounding mountains, we noted many large mansions owned by the more prosperous residents. Perhaps the only shortfall with the city is the major roadway that crosses it, connecting heavy truck traffic between Hong Kong and Guangdong. Shenzhen's harbor is one of the busiest in China with numerous container ships loading and unloading. We observed thousands of containers waiting on the docks.

One of the many parks we visited was a petrified forest that covered several acres. What was astounding was that this forest was "planted" in the park: the trees and logs had been imported from remote regions! The setting was so natural that one couldn't detect that the forest wasn't indigenous to this specific area. Over the next six days we able to visit nearly all the parks in the city, and they all exhibited unique features of landscaping and flora.

Figure 25 Petrified Forest

The evening of our second day in Shenzhen was Thanksgiving Day, and we told Dominic that we would prefer to have dinner by ourselves. We feasted on a real turkey dinner complete with all the trimmings in the hotel restaurant. A great treat!

On the third day we had more tours of the city. After lunch Cherie and I decided to go to one of the theme parks across the bridge from the hotel. This proved to be a good decision. The park exhibited large-scale models of many Chinese historical sites: the Forbidden City, Tibet, the Great Wall, and others. The exhibits covered several acres, and it took us two hours to complete the tour. The park also featured a large lake with classic bridges spanning its arms. But one of the more awesome sights we were fortunate to attend that day was the Mongolian horsemanship exhibition held in a large field with grandstand seating. This show was a reenactment of the battles from the time of Genghis Khan. This was a superb performance consisting of at least 100 riders in battle dress dashing back and forth, flashing their weapons.

We found out that each evening in Shenzhen, at 8 p.m., a spectacular play entitled "The Phoenix and the Dragon," a reenactment of the history of China, was performed. Around 6 p.m. Cherie and I found an arena with grandstand seating. Thinking this was where the performance would be held, and noting the early time and good front row seating available, we decided to sit and wait there for the two hours before play time. While waiting, we were entertained by two competing bands practicing for their performances. About 7:15 p.m., however, we realized that there were very few people in the grandstand – but we observed streams of people passing by on their way to somewhere else. By 7:45 p.m. we figured it out – we were in the wrong place! We exited, followed the crowd, and came to a large amphitheater with a partial roof. Here was where the crowd waited for the show! Luckily we were able to squeeze into some seats near the front row. The theater reportedly was built at a cost of $15 million USD. The stage area was huge, with numerous hydraulics used to swing platforms and move them up and down, accommodating the various sets and acts. The play was spectacular – replete with actors, acrobatics, horses and chariots, and beautifully costumed ladies. Live fireworks (this being China, of course) were set off throughout the two-hour performance.

Dominic picked us up at the hotel on the morning of the fourth day and told us that we would be going to a nearby mountain park, where one could see Hong Kong across the bay. He also informed us that he had given his employees the day off in order that they join us and get some good exercise climbing to the top. What a thoughtful boss! The drive up the mountain road wound through a lovely setting of different trees and flowering shrubs, finally ending in a parking lot at the base of a long set of stairs that led to the top of the mountain. Off went Dominic and his people in a competition to see who could attain the top first. Opposite the steep stairway and a mere 45 meters above us (also via stairs) Cherie and I noticed an observation post. We elected to do this less-arduous exercise and climbed to the post. We were then able to observe our friends in their climb and noted that their progress had slowed down considerably. While at our position we examined the variety of beautiful flowering shrubs covering the surrounding hillsides.

Figure 26 Dominic and his workers climbing

After about an hour and a half Dominic and his people returned to ground zero. We were then transported to the ocean near the port to experience a seafood lunch. This was again a chance to sample a different Chinese cuisine. The group numbered 15 and we were seated with view of the ocean and harbor. So many different dishes were ordered, that there was an excess of food, including fish, shrimp, prawns, shellfish, crabs, and many other delights. One delicacy that both Cherie and I did *not* like was served in abundance – some kind of crustacean that looked like a giant wood or sow bug about 5 inches long. It again had what I imagined to be the taste of Croc Dundee's grubs.

That evening Cherie and I were invited for dinner with Dominic, his wife, young son, and his wife's parents. The dinner would be held at Dominic's club. The gated complex where he and his family lived covered a large area with very modern-looking housing, lighted outdoor tennis and soccer facilities, along with and beautiful landscaping. (Very different from many of our earlier experiences with Chinese habitations.) The club was part of the complex and the facilities included private dining rooms, a spa, and workout areas with sophisticated exercise equipment. We would be having dinner in one of the club rooms. Our host exhibited a certain amount of largesse in ordering various dishes. Large amounts of lobster, which is very expensive in China, were served as well as other expensive fish and meat dishes. Very little alcohol was served – so we truly enjoyed the food and all in all it was an excellent meal and good company.

We spent the morning of day number five with Dominic visiting the "Western" food area near the ocean, and indulging in some Starbucks coffee. While in this area we noticed that an international food fair was taking place that evening and Cherie and I invited Dominic and his wife to join us there later. He said he would be delighted. We also told him that we wanted to invite Bai Ling Mei (Stella), who he had met at dinner with me and Wei Yu on a previous visit. We had arranged to visit with Stella early that afternoon and Dominic drove us to the office of the exporting business she works for, then left until food fair time. We toured Stella's display area which included many different items manufactured at the company's factories, things such as electronic foot baths, electric shavers, and other familiar consumer items that were shipped to the rest of the world.

Figure 27 Stella at her place of work

After all of the anticipation, the food fair was a disappointment – most of the offerings were somewhat tasteless; however the company was good and we all enjoyed talking to each other.

So ended our visit to the modern city of Shenzhen, where we had a wonderful time experiencing the culture, visiting the sites, and having a good time with friends. Taiyuan, where I spend much of my work time, is rather far from Shenzhen, and thus I didn't travel there often. However, the trip had been a good opportunity to reestablish my friendships with Stella and Dominic. With us all together in Shenzhen it truly made me feel that China was not so large a country, and that it is a small world!

Sanya, Hainan Province

Our last morning in Shenzhen we elected to take it easy and stay around the hotel, as we had a flight to Sanya scheduled to leave at 2 p.m. Sanya is located on the South China Sea and the Gulf of Tonkin in Hainan Province, the southernmost part of China. The climate is tropical there, and temperatures at that time of year (early December) were around 30°C. Until recently Sanya was quite rural and as yet undeveloped as a tourist area. In the past few years, however, major Western hotel chains have sprung up along the area's fine beaches. We were booked into the Marriott, which at the time was two-plus years old.

The Marriott complex, which is on the ocean, is huge. We entered the grounds via a wide roadway to the hotel's main entrance. The grounds were spectacularly landscaped. Upon check-in we were informed that this was our lucky week – the Miss World contest was being held next door at the Hyatt Resort. Not our cup of tea! Since it was mid-afternoon and hot, instead we donned our bathing suits and headed to the beach area for a swim. To reach the beach we had to walk about 300 meters along paths through the finely landscaped property, passing the oversized swimming pool and its bars/cafes. I can only describe the area as very similar to Cancun, Mexico – sandy beaches stretching for miles, low tidal conditions, clear, blue-green water with nice surf conditions. The water temperature compares with that of Cancun, too. The first evening for supper we partook in a lavish BBQ/buffet dinner in one of the many dining facilities in the hotel. We felt spoiled!

The Marriott facility is lush and vast with extensive beautifully groomed grounds – more a resort than a hotel! There is a club and special swimming pool for children, a spa and massage building, and a main swimming pool that is vast – the largest I have ever seen. Its maximum depth is only 4 feet, but it is about 30 feet wide and it winds and twists for over 300 meters. It is lined by numerous walls with cascading waterfalls that dot the pool, and several bridges cross it at strategic points. In the areas enclosed by the winding pool are several bar/restaurants. In between swimming in the ocean and other activities, we used this pool a lot.

We were scheduled to stay at the resort for two weeks, so we had much time to plan, see, and do! The resort features parasailing, sailing, motor boating, scuba diving, and snorkeling. The daytime temperatures were generally around a pleasant 28°C, with clear blue skies all around. Cherie and I went swimming in the warm ocean water two or three times a day for about an hour each time. We especially enjoyed the water when the waves were up and we could body surf. Interestingly, on most days the hotel raised a red flag because of the surf conditions. Most Chinese are not accomplished swimmers and these conditions were deemed unsafe for them. Cherie and I had permission from the hotel to disregard the flags and we had a great time in the water. The Chinese also tend to avoid the sun, preferring to walk the beaches in early morning or at dusk. In the daytime they tend to stay covered up in the many cabanas that dot the shoreline.

People also fish from the shoreline casting their bait far out – but the catch I observed was invariably small fish. I am an avid ocean fisherman, and accordingly, I arranged with the head bellman and his friend to rent a boat and go reef fishing. The fishing was great, and the catch included many fish of different species. I caught significantly more fish than the other two, and even caught a rather large puffer fish that puffed up to the size of a basketball when I brought it to the surface! I was about to release it when the bellman said they wanted to keep it. After fishing I gave my catch to them, and as they lived in a dormitory they said they would have a big cook-out for their friends.

The hotel also features many different dining cuisines, from Chinese to Western style foods. Breakfasts were a lavish buffet spread of fruits, Chinese dishes, juices, meats, bacon and eggs, waffles, pancakes, and cereals. One Friday the hotel set up a large BBQ spread on the grass near the ocean. Decorated tables were set up in front of a large stage readied for entertainment. The entertainment was sort of a Chinese Don Ho, emceed by an Australian-accented Chinese lady; an interesting mix of cultures.

After 10 days at the hotel we were well known as the longest-term residents there except for one Chinese gentleman who had stayed for one month. Interestingly, the average stay for the Chinese visitor was reported to be only one night. After our first week, the head chef, a Chinese Malaysian, introduced himself to us and said he would like to cook us special dinners for the remainder of our stay. Apparently he was bored with routine! We did experience some excellent meals that were prepared only for us.

There were many interesting things to do in the Sanya area. There is an island called Monkey Island that tourists go to see monkeys romping around in the wild. Tigers and other fearsome beasts roam around in another a safari-type tourist area. There were many other advertised attractions in the area, but with so many facilities and activities at the resort we elected to forego these. Cherie and I did spend a few hours at the local pearl market, which was a real tourist trap. We also visited the small city of Sanya, about an hour's taxi ride from the resort area: here we saw again a number of different foods being sold in the street markets. We decided to try a local restaurant, and we hosted our taxi driver for lunch. We selected our seafood from several aquariums there, and also ordered some veggies and noodles. For the seafood we picked a large geoduck-type clam and some prawns. The prawns were delicious but the clam was as tough as shoe leather and tasteless – and it cost 600 Yuan ($80 USD)! Such is the luck of the experimental traveler. Beyond the fields of pineapples, watermelons, and orchards we saw on the road to Sanya, we saw much evidence of the use of water buffalo for plowing as we passed by the farming areas.

Cherie and I thoroughly enjoyed our vacation time while in Sanya and we extolled its virtues to our daughter Mary and her family (while they were in China on a family vacation) as an alternative to a planned side visit to Bali. They took our advice, changed their plans, and off to Sanya they went in March of 2006. The family reported it was a good decision and everyone enjoyed the time spent there.

Cherie's recollections of Mary's family's visit to China:

The year after John and I went to Sanya our daughter Mary and her family (John, 17; Christine, 13; Geneva, 10; and husband Joe) came for a visit. Grandson John was most nervous about what he would eat. He wanted to forgo bringing clothes and instead just bring chunky soup and crackers. But in Beijing he soon forgot his food phobia and chowed down. He found pizza, Big Macs, German food, Brazilian food, Belgian food, Western food and fabulous Chinese food. He did not suffer. The rest of us fared well, but as we had learned, one has to remember to follow local traditions and listen to advice. We of course all went to the obligatory Peking Duck place, and Joe ordered a duck for each of us. One duck goes a long way as it is large and greasy and a food that has been known to stress one's system.

The waiter tried to reduce the number of ducks coming to our table, but to no avail. We had duck, lots of duck, and when we left, completely satiated with duck there was lots and lots of duck leftover!

After Beijing they came to Taiyuan and then I went to Xi'an with them. Later, they went on to Sanya by themselves.

The kids enjoyed all the sights of seeing a new country and culture, but it was a wonderful experience for them. It was not without its perils, however. We planned to take the family to Pin Yao, the World Heritage Site near Taiyuan. We were in the parking lot of the Wang family mansion, another site on the way and were disembarking from the van, and Geneva was momentarily standing alone. All of a sudden we heard a caffuffle. Fortunately Mark Wong, Wei Yu's husband, is a very large man and was quick. A scruffy, very small man had grabbed and picked Geneva up. She was so stunned she did not scream. We were all shocked! Mark was very nonplussed and said the man was a peasant and has never seen someone so beautiful before and wanted to greet her. Some greeting! The peasant moved off and disappeared into the crowd but we certainly kept a better eye on each other from then on. Geneva did not say much about the experience, other than the man did not smell good.

We had a lovely time in Xi'an, seeing the Terra Cotta Warriors. It is so much fun to revisit places through the eyes of children and see what impresses them. This time we also stopped at a famous bath, near the site. I had not been there before and it was beautiful and interesting, not only because of the history of the baths, but as an important point of war history, as Generalissimo Chiang Kai-shek was captured there by the Communists. The visible bullet holes got the kids attention!

In Xi'an we also visited the Muslim market. That was fascinating, and we made some purchases. I was delighted to see that the taxis from our first trip to Xi'an had been replaced with much more modern (and safer) vehicles. Mary's family travels very intelligently; they really research cities they visit, then they move fast and see many sites. The research pays off as translations are written down, directions confirmed, and they learn a great deal. Xi'an is one of China's four walled cities, and once again we rode bicycles in the polluted air enveloping the wall.

I left Mary and family in Xi'an and returned to stay with John in Taiyuan. They continued on to Sanya and fell in love with the beaches the pools and the sites of nearby Hainan Island. They relaxed, made friends with people from Australia and Shanghai and all got too much sun!

Back to John

Finishing our stay at Sanya, Cherie and I headed to Shanghai for two days. We had been to this city previously and had visited the main sightseeing attractions – the Bundt (the famous European buildings from the imperialist days in Shanghai), a river cruise, Sun Yat Sen's house, and the museum scene. This time, we arrived at Shanghai in the early evening, and after waiting for an hour in line for a taxi, we went to our hotel some forty minutes away. It was a clear evening and the skyline of the city was spectacular. We checked in and were met by Liu Min, who hosted us to a fine Chinese meal at a crowded, small restaurant. Shanghai is a very modern city, but unlike Beijing the streets are fairly narrow, taxis are difficult to hail, and sidewalks are clogged with throngs of people. Cherie and I spent the next day walking around the city visiting stores and malls. It was just two weeks before Christmas and we were surprised to see how much the Chinese were into the "festive mood." All the major streets were decked out with elaborate decorations and every mall and department store was blaring Christmas songs. The Chinese had captured the "consumerism" essence of the season! In the evening we were hosted by Percy Chang and Tian Jian at the Pauliner, a popular German restaurant. Our two-night stay in Shanghai went by very quickly and the next day we were off to Beijing, where we would overnight before our return home to Canada late in the afternoon the next day.

Beijing is a very modern city as well – but it has wide streets and sidewalks and unlike Shanghai, taxis are relatively easy to hail. As I mentioned earlier, Beijing has moved all heavy industry away from the city, and most of the *hutongs* (small villages) have been removed except for a few saved for tourism purposes. Most people now live in high-rises. I prefer Beijing over Shanghai mainly because it has more open space and does not appear to be as crowded.

Of the many cities I have visited in China, some are now highly modernized, while many others are in the process of modernizing. Beijing, Shanghai, and Shenzhen are arguably among the most modern cities in the world! However to experience the "real" China, which is fast changing, one has to visit the villages – these are as they were for centuries, as many places still were when I first began my journeys to this captivating country only a decade ago. I am extremely lucky that I have experienced much of China as it *was* and have witnessed massive changes to a burgeoning center of business and a modern nation.

As I continue to write, it is now February 2008; the Beijing Olympics are only a few months away; China continues with its spectacular economic growth; the Chinese Communist party has recently completed its 17th 5-year planning session; China's Chang'e I is in successful orbit around the moon; Taiyuan city has again undergone major changes; and the "kids" are now on their respective paths. Such is the nature of the rapid changes in China that I need to add updates even though I sat down to begin this manuscript only a year ago. So, here's the latest dispatch.

2008 Beijing Olympics – Most of the physical facilities have been completed or are on target to be completed, and they meet or exceed expectations. There continues to be massive tree and shrub plantings along all major routes in Beijing and the rapid transit system joining the international airport to downtown is almost complete. Another terminal is set to open soon to alleviate the severe overcrowding at the present airport. The plan is to ban all state-owned company and government vehicles from the city roads during the Olympics. It remains to be seen if the air quality in and around Beijing will be to expected standards by the time the Olympics arrive, as currently conditions are far from ideal. There is concern that if conditions are not improved, the endurance events may have to be relocated.

Economic growth – Despite government efforts to slow the growth rate, the economy was still expected to grow by over 11.5 percent for 2007. China will surpass Germany as the world's third-largest economy in 2007. Petro China has become the world's largest corporation. Over 480 million tons of steel will be produced in 2007, and China has now become the world's second-largest user of energy, behind the U.S. China, along with a rapidly growing India, has put an extreme demand on the world's oil reserves. This, with other critical factors such as terrorism fears and world weather conditions, has driven oil prices to unprecedented highs. High world oil prices combined with the current poor condition of the housing market in the U.S. has caused the U.S. dollar to drop to historic lows against most major currencies. This has affected many people including yours truly – I am paid in U.S. dollars. Until 2006, the exchange rate was 830 Yuan per $100 USD, and currently it is at only 715 Yuan. In addition, the Canadian dollar has risen from 0.65 to the U.S. dollar to a current value of parity.

With the tremendous economic growth largely at the expense of environmental considerations, more and more people are asking "at what cost?" The central government is increasingly targeting environmental conditions for dramatic improvements. Water shortages, especially safe potable water, continue as a major concern for government action. Numerous rivers and lakes are severely polluted and are slated for clean up. Massive tree and greenery plantings continue in northwest China to help retard desertification and aid in cleaner air. All the foregoing requires expensive, extensive, and long-term solutions. In my opinion, with extreme effort the environmental remediation for water, air, and land to acceptable standards will take at least a generation to achieve. Remember: China is a big onion!

17th Chinese Communist party meeting – during this meeting, a new 5-year plan was presented and agreed to by the delegates. The two current leaders, President Hu Jintao and Premier Wen Jiabao were "re-elected" as the country's top governing officials. However, two other "old hands" were not reelected and were replaced by two up-and-comers. The party now has a much more diverse representation. Numerous new initiatives, as well as amendments to current issues, were put into play for the next five years. Increased emphasis is to be directed towards significantly improved environmental conditions. Many new regulations have been enacted to improve air pollution, increase water conservation, and solid waste stream control and recycling, but time will tell how rapidly these initiatives can take place and significant environmental improvements occur. Disappointingly, corruption and bribery continue to be rampant, especially within government and state-owned enterprises.

Chang'e I – The launch of this lunar orbiter has shown the world how far and fast China has come since the end of the Cultural Revolution. This latest success illustrates the country's rapid and spectacular technological growth in science and technology. Is there another space race coming?

Taiyuan City – Big changes continue in this city. On awakening one day last June, I was awed by the massive upheaval everywhere in the main core of the city. Major roads, especially the main drag, Yingze St., were completely torn up; the majority of lanes on the bridges crossing the canal were closed while reconstruction was carried out; several buildings (some fairly new) were demolished; and new facings were installed on some of the major buildings. *What was happening?* I wondered. Apparently, Taiyuan was hosting a world symposium on coal technology and expected thousands of visitors from all parts of the world. This event was to occur in mid-September 2007 and the city was determined to put on a good face. Total disruption of traffic and business along the many roads under reconstruction (due to widening) was to be the norm until completion by mid-September. Trees and shrubs were planted along the sides of the major roadways.

Unbelievably the massive work was completed in time, and traffic now flows somewhat better, especially with the constant police presence at all major intersections (still the lady officers). A good portion of Yingze Street is now six lanes wide each way. Extraordinary efforts were expended to put on a good show during the event, even to the extent of curtailing operations at all major polluting industries three days prior to and during all days of the symposium. (thankfully SCW – likely because we were so small or under their "radar" – was not required to do so.) Wow! The result was extremely clean air for six days. However, immediately after departure of the foreign guests, the pollution began to build once again.

I must say that environmental conditions, although not ideal, are improving gradually with time in Taiyuan. A new expressway from the airport twenty-seven kilometers away was to be completed for the symposium but was not finished until late October. This expressway completely eliminates the drive through city streets with the many crossings and stoplights, and it cuts ten minutes off the previous trip. I would expect that the foreign visitors there for the symposium were not encouraged to visit the parts of the city that had not seen major improvements. Since 2006, several new parks have been created throughout the city – the most significant one about five times larger than Yingze Park. This park is located at the northern part of the city adjacent to the golf course and is totally man-made, with lakes and a canal gouged into the ground, trees and shrubs, and miles of pathways. It was a pretty impressive undertaking.

Many things are changing in China, but many vestiges of the old remain. Mr. Luo, the "political animal" and former human resource manager who left SCW in 2005, returned to TZ. Recently he has been promoted to a very senior management position in the SOE. Some things in the SOE environment take time to change! At the Shanxi Grand, the two Chinese gentlemen (the one who stated emphatically to Cherie that he was Chinese and the other with the irritating throat problem) still frequent the hotel lobby.

The kids – Wang Guochen, (Simon), Han Ting Ting, (Jane), Li Xin, (Gaylene) and Wang Zi Wei have all moved along in life. Simon is attending the top school in Taiyuan and is in senior 1 (10th grade) and is near or at the top of his class. Ting is in senior 3 (12th grade) and is near the top of her class; she is majoring in science and plans on becoming a doctor using both Western and traditional Chinese medicine practices. Xin is also in senior 3 at a different school and plans on studying journalism. All three continue with extra classes on both Saturdays and Sundays. Zi Wei (the singer that Cherie and I sponsored) wrote further exams and qualified to attend a university in northwest China. Cherie and I plan to again attempt to get the Canadian Embassy to grant a visa for Zi Wei to visit us at Quadra during the summer of 2008. Both Cherie and I have thoroughly enjoyed our ongoing relationship with these fine young people and their very supportive families.

Just about the time when one believes he/she has grown and experienced the full array of surprises during China's march to modernization, another giant surprise pops up. While it has not been unusual for SCW to experience gas shortages for its high-temperature heat treating during the winter months, the complete curtailment of all gas supplies for 16 days in December 2007 and the announced cutoffs for a further 16 days in January 2008 was a total surprise to all industries. The cutoffs to industries are due to a government policy of first supplying the needs of the citizens, and then allotting what is left over to industry. The extreme current shortages result from a poorly thought out government regulation recently put into effect to shut down a significant number of coal mines in Shanxi Province, due to poor safety performance. While these were indeed dangerous operations, this action has resulted in severe coal shortages to generate both heating gas and electrical power. Rumor has it that both power and gas restrictions will occur in remote areas during the Olympic Games, since the government has mandated all resources be directed to Beijing during that period to ensure the tourists see China's best side!

In late January 2008 I attended the SCW annual employees' dinner, which is held just before the Chinese Lunar New Year's holiday. Prior to dinner being served, the daughters and sons of many employees were conscripted to hold a variety show. The "kids," most of them university students, were a talented bunch. I was greatly impressed that our employees had so many accomplished kids and that a great majority of them were able to attend universities. This was a change of great magnitude from when I first started coming to China 10 years ago. Indeed, average wages for SCW employees have increased from 12,000 Yuan in 1999 to 38,000 Yuan in 2007.

Several SCW employees recently told me of a very highly placed manager in an allied facility that is rumored to have demanded that all his subordinates and lesser supervisors resign their positions and then apply to be rehired. This would supposedly cost them money to get their positions back and would make the manager a very rich man! It was a rumor, but it probably held some truth! Our employees are very happy they work for an honorable, trustworthy company that espouses a Western work ethic. With these new surprises, and those that I continue to experience, I am now convinced that there is no such thing as an "old hand" in China.

The book has been on furlough for about one year now and an epilog is deemed necessary to bring things up to date. Much has happened in the interim! I retired on January 31.

The Beijing Olympics have come and gone with China having exhibited a world class spectacular performance that exceeded all expectations. China had resorted to extraordinary efforts to improve the traditionally bad air quality for the Olympics but the world was apprehensive regarding the potential air quality especially for the health and well being of athletes participating in endurance events. Indeed up to the week prior to the start of the games, pollution conditions rated on world standards was below standards. Miraculously, a few days before the games, the air improved dramatically. I watched the awe inspiring opening ceremonies on NBC while out of China. I noticed the looks on the faces and the expressions of wonderment of the NBC reporting crew: Incredulous!

2008 was a record year for SCW in both total sales and profitability although the looming world recession was beginning to be felt with decreased booking rates for future sales. During September, SCW celebrated its 10th anniversary with formal ceremonies involving Chinese dignitaries, some Esco Corporation senior managers, TZ senior managers, SWC management team, and SCW employees.

Growth in China remained 9+% although the world economy slowdown was beginning to affect future growth rate. Thousands of factories in the Pearl River area closed down as export demand for their commercial products plummeted. This caused hundreds of thousands of migrant workers to be dismissed – in many cases without their due wages! However, the central government stepped in quickly to honor such wages. By late November in 2008, China recognized that the world recession was going to severely affect the country's growth and decided a 500 billion dollar stimulus was required to keep the country growing. This stimulus was to be directed solely to infrastructure construction in immediate projects and not to line the pockets of bankers and interest groups. This process is in direct contrast to the bailouts in the USA where the first 350 billion has essentially disappeared! The winter of 2008 was the worst and most prolonged on record for the southern portion of the country. There was snow and ice in areas of the country that had never experienced such conditions. During this time China was suffering power shortages due to lack of coal supplies for power generation (in their wisdom the central government had shut down several thousand mines below a certain size, deeming them unsafe operations). In addition the severe weather of cold, snow, and ice led to massive accumulation of ice on the power giant transmission poles carrying power form the Three Gorges dam to other parts of the country. The combined coal shortage and loss of transmission from the dam resulted in massive and long term power outages in the southern most populated part of the country. Time wise, these outages could not have happened at a worse time – right at the beginning of the Chinese New Year when travel in China is at a maximum especially with the millions of migrant workers attempting to get back to their villages for the traditional family holidays. Since most of the trains (the main mode of travel) were electric, nothing moved and people were trapped in railway stations or factory buildings for up to two weeks. At one time it was reported that between 500,000 and 1,000,000 people were trapped in the Guangzhou railway station alone. During 2008, Eastern China experienced a major earthquake (magnitude >7.7) centered near Chendu in the eastern part of Szechwan Province. This quake flattened many villages including schools (built rather recently) and resulted in thousands of deaths. It was reported that every communist party member was required to contribute a specified amount depending on rank (up to one month's salary) to disaster relief. Despite rapid and often heroic individual and government actions to rescue, tending to the injured, and provide clothing and shelter to the survivors, there were many questions in the aftermath put to the 'officials' regarding the poor standards of construction throughout the area. As usual some individuals and officials have been found wanting and either removed from their posts or criminally charged. In China, blame must be placed! China businesses continue to flaunt laws and sound safety procedures as evidenced by the tainted milk scandal wherein a non organic chemical was added to dairy products on a large scale to increase the apparent protein rating of liquid and powdered milk, and egg products to increase the yield of the products. Many infants died and many thousands were hospitalized for significant periods of time. As usual after much protests and government investigations, several heads of companies and health inspectors either received the death sentence or severe punishments.

Taiyuan City continued its rapid modernization program with many new roads constructed, bridges and existing roads widened and improved. However, traffic conditions continue to worsen with ever increasing number of cars on the roads since there is a continued and rapid increase in the number of people achieving a new middle class. Contributing a great deal to the massive reconstruction of the city was another international coal show in September. As in the previous year, beginning in April vast areas of the city's roads were torn up and closed for reconstruction, and two of the river bridges were closed for widening. Until completion in mid September, the traffic in the city was in total chaos.

Figure 28 Simon older now, with his parents

Where are the kids? Simon has moved to Dalian a city on the ocean north of Beijing to finish his high school senior year in one of the top schools in China. Both he and his parents are determined that he will attend university in either Canada or the

USA. Ting is in her freshman year at a top university in Nangjing while Xin is attending the same university in Beijing that her mother graduated from. During the latter part of the year my contact with these three was limited to phone calls and text messages although the parents would visit me at the hotel occasionally. Cherie and I did see Xin (Gaylene) in Beijing in November.

Cherie and I visited Wang Zi Wei at her university in Yinchuan capital city of Ningxia Autonomous Region (near Inner Mongolia) in April. We arrived in Yinchuan after a 70 minute flight from Taiyuan. Zi Wei met us at the airport and we took a 30 minute taxi ride to our five-star hotel in the city. The region is almost all a desert very similar to South Arizona but has, astoundingly, plentiful water everywhere due to the proximity of the Yellow river basin and numerous aquifers. Yinchuan is a modern city developed in the last 6 years from a minor agricultural village. All roads are wide and well paved with new vegetation planted everywhere. New modern building structures were in evidence in all parts of this city of some 500,000 inhabitants. The whole region is being built as a tourist mecca because of the surrounding lakes, sand hills and proximity of forests and mountains. We visited Zi Wei's university which is a beautiful campus entered through as wide tree lined 500 meter long boulevard. Some of the university buildings all circa 2002 were located around a nice lake while the rest of the new campus was located in park like settings. We also met some of her roommates (8) and her lead professor who agreed to write a letter to the Canadian Embassy in Beijing extolling her virtues and recommending her acceptance for a visa to visit Canada later in the summer. She now 20 years old subsequently was granted a visa to visit Canada in July. While visiting we did many interesting things especially the day we decided to visit a resort called Sand Lake some 60 km outside Yinchuan. Sand Lake covers a large surface area but only averages 1.5 meters deep and has an enormous number of clumps of reeds growing throughout the lake. A large sand mountain lies immediately across the lake. Upon arrival at the entrance to the resort we were stunned to see the hordes of people congregating at the ever present merchant stalls. We bypassed this area and proceeded to get tickets for the boat ride to the island. There were 3 alternatives to get there: quickest was by 17 foot speed boat, next was a forty-foot water taxi, and the third was a 3 deck ferry boat. We elected the water taxi which held approximately 50 passengers and took about twenty minutes to get to the island. For most Chinese, this was a first and unique experience. During the twenty minute trip, we saw parasailing, ultra lights, jet skis, hot air ballooning and many different resort type things. When we disembarked there were many choices for recreation. We chose to take a chair lift to the top of the hill and take the zip line down. For the naïve Zi Wei this would prove a frightening but exhilarating thrill. When we arrived at the top and looked around, Zi Wei asked "how do we get down?" Cherie answered "we go down by zip line." Zi Wei was aghast! Accordingly we agreed that I would go first followed by Cherie, and then Zi Wei. The run was long and steep and stopping at the bottom was essentially done with a set of springs with some handlers to assist. In the event of failure there was a padded wall about 3 meters beyond. I set off and sailed down the incline accelerating quickly until about 40 meters from the springs. As my weight (85 Kg.) is significantly more than the average Chinese, I consequently built up more momentum, I sailed right through the springs, and the handlers and into the wall luckily with no damage. Zi Wei saw this and in addition observed Cherie sail through the springs but caught by the handlers. Zi Wei let out a scream of terror or delight but managed to get stopped by the springs. After some walking around we returned to the boat to take us back across the lake. As luck would have it, we arrived at a different embarking place and had to take the 3 decker ferry back to the park exit. This was somewhat perturbing – before embarking more and more people kept boarding until there were wall to wall people on all three decks. I felt like we could be in the situation that we read about in the news wherein a highly overloaded ferry goes down. Luckily, for us in this hot weather, the Chinese people in general do not carry body odors and in addition no ferry accident occurred.

After landing we decided to visit two adjacent historic forts that had been turned into fascinating movie lots. In addition to the historic value there were camels to ride. Cherie convinced the timid Zi Wei to accompany her on a camel ride. Both of them reeked somewhat after the ride in the hot sun. Whew!

Subsequently, Zi Wei was successful in obtaining a Visa for a visit during July–August. I had returned home some 2 weeks earlier and she made the trip by herself testing her fortitude since she had rarely traveled by air and had never flown internationally. During her visit, she performed at several cafes and knocked the socks off all audiences. Before she sang Ave Maria at our local Church, she was downstairs practicing and providentially a woman from California (a summer visitor) who was a professional voice teacher was attending the church that day and agreed to be Zi Wei's accompanist. As they practiced, Zi Wei hit a high note perfectly. The look on the woman's face was astonishment! She, a voice teacher repeated the line also hitting the note correctly, Zi Wei's face lit up – they both instantly bonded and were in awe of each other's abilities. The congregation was also later astounded by her performance. Zi Wei is now in her sophomore year at the university, has won scholarships, and even makes pin money singing at local night spots. We continue to keep in touch via e-mail on a regular basis.

The following is portions of Zi Wei's e-mails and recollections of her trip (in her own spelling). When we first met her at 13 she did not speak English.

After a visa rejection:

...thank you for your letter and thank you for your encouragement. Please don't worried about me, everything will be OK. Though I can't visit your home, a little bit disappointment has happened in my mind, I will say I will never give up. I will keep on my dream and my goal and try to achieve them.

After visa acceptance:

I think I'm so luck this time, because I have got the visa today, I feel a little bit excited...what should I take, such as the shampoo and toothpaste, should I bring them there? What about the cloth? At this time will the weather there become hot or cool? What other things should I bring? When I arrive there, how can I get touch with you.

Day before her trip:

The day after tomorrow I'll take the air fly to you. I'm looking forward that time and hoping to see you as soon as possible. I believe I'll have the most wonderful time of my life there. It must be unforgettable.

Zi Wei back in China:

The trip to Canada is very helpful to me my school leader said that. I also think so. I told my friends the view, food, house, building and the culture and show them the pictures, they all felt it was unbelievable. It does the significant trip to me, I really tahnksful to you and John.

I think I really achieve a lot in Canada, now I no longer afraid of cold and I often feel so hot and don't afraid the dog so much as before. I just don't look at them when I meet them. I don't afraid the bee when they fly around me and sometimes tell myself they are lovely animals.

Some of my friends admire meso much, even they can't believe I can go to Canada, they always said I am really luckily enough, I miss you and your house, your beach, your sea and your sky, It should be say I miss everything.

Later that year:

I feel very excited now, because I have good news to tell you. I have passed the National English Four Levels examination. It is really unbelievable this time, even I can't believe my eyes. I really should say thank you. You improved my English so much and let me to learn it as an interest, I am so happy now!!!

Love Ziwei

Finally, my son recognizing that the October-December trip would be my last visit to China, decided that it would be a valuable experience for his family to visit China and meet some of my many friends and visit some of the sites in China. The family lives in South Carolina. Both daughters (aged 12+ and 15+) are tops in their schools and engaged in various extracurricular activities. For this reason, the only appropriate time for the family to visit was during the Thanksgiving holiday period. Accordingly, we planned to meet at the Holiday Inn LiDo in Beijing on November 19: I would come from Beijing; Cherie from Vancouver; Brock from a business trip in Korea; and Jacquie, Lauren, and Madeline from Charlotte. In the previous two weeks, I had organized and ambitious agenda for the 9 days we would be together. I flew from Taiyuan to Beijing on the 19th, met Cherie upon her 3:00 p.m. arrival at the airport and we proceeded to the LiDo. Brock came in around 7:00 p.m. and the balance of the family arrived at 10:00 p.m. The next morning with the weather clear but cool at 10 degrees Celsius, we visited the Forbidden City and after a quick lunch we visited the Great Wall where we rode a chair lift up to the wall. After dropping off the lift we proceeded to tour the wall. The weather was unseasonably warm and clear at 17 degrees C. To descend back to ground level, we had two options: either returns by the chair lift or ride a bobsled like stainless steel slide down on single sleds. We elected the chute! When I was about to slide myself onto the sled, the attendant asked "how old are you?" I replied "*lu ba.*" She said "68, maybe you should take the chair down." I replied "*mao wente* (no problem)," and proceeded to take the sled. After returning to the LiDo, We were met by Li Xin (Gaylene) and the whole group enjoyed dinner at the Pauliner a German restaurant in the Lufthansa Center. Xin left us after dinner citing homework and the family all attended a performance of the famous Chinese acrobatic group at a theater.

We were up early the next morning for our flight to Taiyuan and after check in at the Shanxi Grand, we visited the ancient city of Ping Yao. After a cold windy 5 hour visit to Ping Yao, we all returned to Taiyuan at 2:30 p.m. and then Brock and family visited the Taiyuan museum for the balance of the afternoon. Beginning at 6:00 p.m., Wang Zi Wei performed for some of our many friends in the lobby bar. At 7:00 p.m. my guests (21 including family) proceeded upstairs to the Chinese restaurant to an upscale, delicious, and many course meal – the menu was set out by Jane of the hotel.

Early the next morning we all set out to the Taiyuan airport for a one hour flight to Xi'An (home of the Terra Cotta Warriors) in the next province. After checking in at the Hyatt, our prearranged tour to the site began at 1:00 p.m. It was an unforgettable experience for the Brock family and although both Cherie and I had visited this historic site on two other occasions, it was again a rewarding experience for us. The next morning dawned clear and cool at 12 degrees C and we all decided to rent bicycles and ride around the top of the ancient wall around the old part of the city before our plane back to Taiyuan. This was a fun event but slightly frustrating since normally the complete circuit takes about one hour but due to bicycle malfunctions, the trip took almost two hours. We returned to Taiyuan by mid afternoon and before dinner, Brock took the girls to a local electronics market to compare goods and prices to home. Dinner was a family affair at the previously mentioned spectacular restaurant (two football fields in size) where we elected to eat amongst the flora and streams. We had a spectacular variety of dishes including flash fried scorpions which all but Madeline ate. Once one got over the scorpion thing, we found they were quite delicious and we actually ordered seconds.

Figure 29 The Hemmingsen's

Next morning, after a 6:00 a.m. breakfast, Brock and I were met by the SCW driver and taken to the plant where Brock had some business meetings scheduled. Cherie, Jacquie, and the girls were picked up from the hotel at 9:00 a.m. for a plant tour. SCW hosted a lunch at one of the Brazil BBQ's. Immediately after lunch Cherie, Brock, and family proceeded to Number 12 Middle School where Cherie, Jacquie, and Madeline hosted the more junior students while Brock and Lauren talked to the seniors. This session was such a hit that they were invited back for a repeat performance at 4:30 p.m. for a makeup class for volunteer students who were normally on a free time period. This session was attended by over 200 students. After the class, Brock left for the airport to fly to Shanghai while the rest of us had dinner at the Dumpling House near the Shanxi Grand. The next morning, the rest of us flew to Shanghai to meet up with Brock. One of the days was spent attending Bauma (an international equipment exhibition) where both Esco and Brock's company were represented. I must say that the girls (Lauren and Madeline) aroused curiosity during the whole trip – wherever they went!

After two days in Shanghai, Brock and family left for home and we had all experienced an excellent rewarding time together. After another day in Shanghai Cherie and I visited the Esco Corporation Plant at Xuzhou. For the next two days I presented 8 hours of seminars to the technical people after which I asked them what they thought of the material and presentation. They all said it was comprehensive and while they were technical graduates and had studied this material at college, my presentation was the first time they totally understood the material. I felt pretty good! After Xuzhou, we flew to Beijing for an overnight stay before Cherie left for Vancouver. I returned to Taiyuan to finish off my last tour. During my final two weeks, my many friends, SCW managers and employees, expat friends, and the Shanxi Grand insisted on several farewell parties. Almost every evening, I was hosted.

I finished my long term association with China upon my retirement on January 31, 2009. I had spent some 2000 days between mid-1998 and the end of 2008 in China. I believe that these 10 years were the best times for anybody to experience the changes in China. Conditions in areas other than the main coastal cities were still rather primitive in 1998 but by 2008 the outlying areas had achieved a large degree of modernization. I believe that this period had the most significant and rapid rate of change of any other 10 year period! Over these 10 years, China has seen the rise of a middleclass of ~100 M outside of bureaucrats and government officials.

I have enjoyed my relationships with almost all the Chinese people I have met over the past years. In particular I will be in contact with many of the closest colleagues and families I have met over the years although I will surely miss the intimacy of personal contact with them.

What I will not miss will be the corruption both on a more minor day to day scene and with the higher levels of business and government dealings. I definitely will not miss the frustrations of dealing with some of the ridiculous red tape issues I experienced during my tenure. China has a great future but to attain the utmost it has many and significant issues to address along the way. These include maintaining a growth rate consistent with bringing the balance of 850 million people to a decent living standards and providing them with potable water, improving environmental standards in air, land, and water, eliminating corruption, and continuing to improve human rights. One final note – as the anniversary of the Tibet unrest and the 20 year of the Tianemen Square uprising approached, China predictably has placed severe restrictions on the internet usage for its citizens. This restriction has continued into late June of 2009.

In closing, I feel privileged to have served in China during a very dynamic period in China's history. I was also privileged to have many relatives visit while I was in China. These included my scientist brother, my daughter and family, my son and family, and my cousin's two boys. Especially I enjoyed the many visits that Cherie was able to come while I was in China.

These books are my favorites – the ones that I found most entertaining and informative. I hope they help fuel your interest in China, too.

Deng Xiaoping and the Cultural Revolution: A Daughter Recalls the Critical Years, by Rong Deng, Foreign Languages Press, 2002

We Signed Away Our Lives: How One Family Gave Everything for the Gospel, by Kari Torjesen Malcolm, published by William Carey Library, 2004

1421: The Year China Discovered the World, by Gavin Menzies, Bantam Press, 2002

Chasing the Dragon: A Veteran Journalist's Firsthand Account of the 1949 Chinese Revolution, by Roy Rowan, The Lyons Press, 2004

"The New China," by Roy Rowan, *Fortune Magazine*, October 11, 1999, pages 251–262

The New Emperors: China in the Era of Mao and Deng, by Harrison E. Salisbury, Avon Books, 1992

Riding the Iron Rooster: By Train Through China, by Paul Theroux, G. P. Putnam's Sons, 1988

The River at the Center of the World: A Journey Up the Yangtze, and Back in Chinese Time, by Simon Winchester, Henry Holt and Co., 1996

Jan Wong's China: Reports from a Not-So-Foreign Correspondent, by Jan Wong, Doubleday Canada, 1999

Red China Blues, by Jan Wong, Doubleday and Anchor Books, 1996

The Man who loved China, by Simon Winchester, Harper Collins, 2008

Newspaper article Translation by Kara

Since 2002, Canadian lady, Cherie, helped the Taiyaun girl, Wang Zi Wei, then Wang Zi Wei starts to help her classmate who is in serious illness situation.

Span the ocean, the spirit of helping each other is transferring.

March 12 it I the 11th trip for Canadian Lady Cherie. It is 12 years after her first visit. "It is amazing to see the development so fast" said Cherie.

John, Cherie's husband came to Taiyuan for a joint-venture project in 1994. Since 1998, he volunteered to teach three teenagers English once a week till now. Cherie was influenced by her husband: she donated money through an organization to help local poor children buy books for their s studying.

Cherie came to Taiyuan in March of 2002 again. She felt big changes of the city and she had the first thought of visiting local school. "Education is the hope of city development" said Cherie. She met her husband's friend's wife who was teaching at Taiyuan #12 middle school. Cherie then had a chance to see Chinese children in school. She had a deep impression of the Chinese girl Wang Zi Wei. "She is talented, I recommend her to continue studying singing." but Wang Zi Wei's parents had divorced many years ago, she never thought that she could have the chance to continue her studying. Cherie decided to help her ever since then. Every time she comes to Taiyuan, Cherie volunteers to teach English at school.

When Wang Zi Wei knew her classmate who had blood cancer, she donated all the money she saved. "I help other, then others help others who need more help; this will build our world more beautiful."

Cherie decided to invite Wang Zi Wei to visit Canada after her provincial exam in 2007. John, her husband who is 66, also decided to postpone his retirement in order to take her to Canada.

Wang Zi Wei's mom asked Cherie with tears: "What can I do to repay what you did for us?" Cherie said: "You don't have to say this, if one day somebody asks you for help, you do your best to help them like how I had helped you.

Zhemin Gui, Wang Zi Wei's teacher said: This is transferring of spirit. The more people receive help, the more people will help others. Cherie always says that she did a little, not worth letting other people know."

John's Newspaper Interview
Translation of Newspaper article -- translator Chen Wei 2003/11/25

John Hemmingsen, technical expert from the United States, is well known in SCW that is because he has lived and worked in Taiyuan for more than 5 years. He has become sort of Taiyuaneese. In recent years the improvement of Taiyuan and the improvement in SCW makes him feel happy at the same time unsolved problems in SCW and the problems in Taiyuan also makes him worried. He told people Taiyuan is my home away from home. I have kind of an attachment to it. We come to visit John Hemmingsen in SCW in a winter morning among many work shops in the Taiyuan Heavy Machinery Group we founded SCW. When we entered into the office, we were impressed the clean environment and also can feel the strong atmosphere of their own enterprise culture. John met us in the meeting room,. After shaking hands he also greeted us in Chinese. How are you or "Ni Hao"! He gave us a strong impression that he is so kind and so sincere. John Hemmingsen looks strong and has a pair of sharp eyes. We can feel his smartness and agility from his eye contact. In Order to help us to have a better communication, the General Manager of SCW, Mrs. Wei Yu took the role of interpreter. John told us he was born in 1940 in Canada, and after his graduation from university in 19063 he became a metallurgist. He joined ESCO Corporation in 1976 and in 1980 he became Vice President of ESCO Corporation and in charge of production and technology. In 1994 He let a group of people from ESCO to TZ to discuss the project of setting up a joint venture. During the interview were attacked by his wit, his quick thinking and wit narration and almost had no chance to plug in our questions. When we talked about how ESCO choose TZ to be a partner John said, "we have had the contact and mutual understanding with TZ since 1985 and signed a contract for a licensee by then. ESCO also helped TZ to Educate two groups of technicians so when we were going to find a partner in China, TZ is the first to be considered. This is because we have two parties had already had co-operations and understanding at a certain level plus the Human Resources training by Esco, of course this only the first step of a successful cooperation. During 4 years negotiation there are ups and downs and almost failed. With the establishment of market economy in china and China's entering the world trade organization all these favourable conditions helped to reach the final result in 1998 SCW joint venture between two sides is established. Due to the culture difference between the east and the west there must be a lot of conflicting happened in this joint venture. When we were talking about this topic, John told us, as one of the directors of this joint venture and also the person who in charge of the technical management of it during initial stage, he had seen and experienced many conflicts. But in order to achieve the success of the cooperation, management from both sides all took efforts to create harmonious human based and working environment. We had gone through a developing stage full of difficulties and finally the win win. During this 5 years what impressed him most is that employee here were gradually learning the importance of standard production. Take the example of high manganese products, the reason ESCO Corp is one of the best high manganese casting producers lies in the perfect chemical control but when I was here at first I noticed during melting there was no proper control on the alloy elements so there if no base to achieve quality. Under my instruction and suggestion people here learned to work by specification and instruction and the quality level here improved to an acceptable level. So SCW spent 5 years time to develop in the promising direction. John lives and works in Taiyuan for almost 5 years. He has a lot of his own feelings actually he had already treated Taiyuan as a second home. China is a country with a long civilized history this is something that many other countries cannot emulate. With admiration to ancient Chinese Culture he will be glad to herald to promote the communication of two parts. During this 5 years he live in Shanxi Grand Hotel he has read a lot of China Daily in English Version to understand china's open door policy and also paid a close attention the big changes in Taiyuan in recent years. He expressed his concerns on some social issues such as environment, pollution, traffic to municipal government. In order to raise the attention of relevant government departments and to establish a more beautiful Taiyuan jointly. With the openness degree intensified in China people Chinese people will gradually realize the importance of learning English well. During his stay in Taiyuan some three children who want to learn English make friends with him. One of them whose name is Wang Guo Chen (Simon) happened to get to know him in the Grand Hotel He brought two other students who are also eager to learn to John. This is the beginning of their learning process and the friendship. Sometimes they go to the English Corner in the square giving those Chinese who are eager to learn English a chance for communication. Now these three children are all grown up and they all can speak pretty good English. Weeks ago john's wife Cherie also came to Taiyuan she went to a middle school in Taiyuan to give them English lessons. She really made major contributions to improve the communication of two different cultures. During our discussion John pointed to a grey sky and said to us the city i ever lived in Chicago once had a polluted river that could be burned in the 60's last century. You can imagine how bad it was how bad the environment during that period of time but within a couple of decades improvement the river turned clean and the water could be drunk directly. Taiyuan is also a heavily polluted city with in years efforts the quality of air is improved dramatically but there is still a long way to go. I believe Taiyuan will become cleaner and more beautiful within the near future.

Reporters Zhang Shi Pan and Lei Ming

Lilies mean Good Sex for Gray Haired People

Cherie came to Taiyuan to visit in late fall of 2002. The hotel had warmly welcomed her and had provided the hotel room with a large bouquet of lilies which provided a rich aroma that helped to alleviate the stale air in the room. After the flowers lost their freshness, we decided to go out into the maze of alleys and purchase another bouquet. Accordingly, Cherie and I bundled up (it was cold and slippery outside) and started along one of the narrow vendor streets where I knew there was a florist shop. We were walking along the clogged sidewalks holding hands for security. We noticed many Chinese covering their mouths and 'tee-heeing' as we passed. We arrived at the florist shop, purchased a nice bunch of fragrant lilies, and walked back to the hotel some one kilometer away. Again many people, both old and young, were covering their mouths and tee-heeing. When we entered the hotel lobby, many of the staff broke into audible laughter. We asked the lobby manager what was so funny and she replied, "Oh you don't know. You are both older and are carrying lilies and in Chinese tradition lilies mean good sex for gray haired people."

Acknowledgements

Thanks to Karalyn Ott and Michele Whitehead, (Seattle), for your able assistance pre-editing the manuscript.

With gratitude to Author Jocelyn Reekie, (British Columbia) your mentorship program gave me much valuable advice and encouragement. Thanks for telling me that **"it is a Barn burner and must be published"** now the competition is on, will my book sell?

Thanks to the Bold Point book club for reading my manuscript and making valuable suggestions.

Lastly, thanks to my many friends and co-workers, without your participation there would be no "2000 Days". I hope my book meets your approval. Thanks for a fabulous 13 years.

Figure 30 Photo of Great Wall by Cherie